" YOU LIE! "

ALSO BY JACK CASHILL

"If I Had a Son": Race, Guns, and the
Railroading of George Zimmerman

Deconstructing Obama: The Life, Loves, and
Letters of America's First Postmodern President

Popes and Bankers: A Cultural History of Credit and Debt,
from Aristotle to AIG

Hoodwinked: How Intellectual Hucksters
Have Hijacked American Culture

What's the Matter with California? Cultural Rumbles from the
Golden State and Why the Rest of Us Should Be Shaking

Sucker Punch: The Hard Left Hook
That Dazed Ali and Killed King's Dream

Ron Brown's Body: How One Man's Death Saved
the Clinton Presidency and Hillary's Future

First Strike: TWA Flight 800 and the Attack on America
(with James Sanders)

Snake Handling in Mid-America: An Incite-ful Look
at American Life and Work in the '90s

"YOU LIE!"

THE EVASIONS, OMISSIONS, FABRICATIONS, FRAUDS, AND OUTRIGHT FALSEHOODS OF BARACK OBAMA

JACK CASHILL

BROADSIDE BOOKS
An Imprint of HarperCollins*Publishers*

HarperCollins books may be purchased for educational, business, or sales promotional use. For information, please e-mail the Special Markets Department at SPsales@harpercollins.com.

FIRST EDITION

Library of Congress Cataloging-in-Publication Data has been applied for.

ISBN 978-0-06-234750-3

14 15 16 17 18   OV/RRD   10 9 8 7 6 5 4 3 2 1

In a world of lies, kudos to those who have helped show me the truth: James Sanders, Elizabeth Sanders, Kathleen Janoski, Nolanda Butler Hill, Terry Lakin, Sundance, Peter, and Debra.

ACKNOWLEDGMENTS

I would like to thank executive editor Adam Bellow for developing the idea; Eric Meyers and the editors at HarperCollins for striking the right balance; publicist Joanna Pinsker for getting the story right; attorney Chris Goff for not overly acting like an attorney; my agent, Alex Hoyt, for taking good care of me; and my wife, Joan, for bearing my unorthodoxy.

CONTENTS

"YOU LIE!"

THE POSTMODERNIST

On the night of September 9, 2009, a still highly popular President Barack Obama spoke spiritedly to a joint session of Congress. He had summoned the members of both parties to introduce his plan to transform American health care. The promises he made that night were many and, to most in the television audience at least, sounded fresh. "Nothing in this plan will require you or your employer to change the coverage or the doctor you have," said the president. "Let me repeat this: Nothing in our plan requires you to change what you have."

If the assembled Democrats found reason to applaud, the Republicans did not. There was little about the proposals that appealed to any of them. Nor could they have liked being scolded by Obama for the "scare tactics" they had presumably used to block reform and the "partisan spectacle" they had presumably created. "Well, the time for bickering is over," Obama warned the presumed bickerers sternly. "The time for games has passed."

Simmering throughout this public spanking was an obscure five-term South Carolina congressman named Joe Wilson. He had taken abuse long enough. When Obama denounced as false the claim that this proposed health care system "would insure illegal immigrants," Wilson could hold his tongue no longer. "You lie," he said, but widespread Republican grumbling drowned him out.

Obama elaborated, saying, "The reforms—the reforms I'm proposing would not apply to those who are here illegally." Now Wilson burst out even louder, "You lie!" and this time there was no crowd noise to cover him. A distracted Obama turned his head to the source of the outburst, and as he did, the Democrats erupted in the kind of indignant gasp one hears in a playground before the cry of "I'm telling."

For his part, Wilson promptly apologized. "While I disagree with the president's statement," said Wilson soon after the speech, "my comments were inappropriate and regrettable. I extend sincere apologies to the president for this lack of civility." Apology or not, respectable Republicans rushed to the microphones to denounce Wilson's remarks, and Democrats rushed to their direct mail vendors to exploit them.

Forgetting for the moment that Senate Majority Leader Harry Reid had admittedly called President George W. Bush a "liar" on multiple occasions and a "loser" at least once, the Beltway punditry convinced itself that Wilson had done something unprecedented, had led his party across a rubicon of coarseness into a brash new world. Unaware perhaps that a Democratic congressman from his home state had once clubbed a Republican senator nearly to death, House Majority Whip James Clyburn from South Carolina called Wilson's behavior "embarrassing" and "a new low" for the state's congressional delegation.

Missed in the hubbub over Wilson's remark, however, was the particular nature of his locution, "You lie." He might have said, "That's a lie" or, "You're lying," but, in fact, Obama's health care reforms did not apply to illegal aliens. No one really expected that promise to hold, but technically Obama was not lying. As history records, Wilson could have safely shouted out "That's a lie" on at least five other occasions during that same speech. He did not. Instead he made the existential declaration "You lie." So saying, Wilson spoke to what he saw as the very essence of the man: Sinatra sings, Astaire dances, Obama lies.

Five years later, almost all Republicans and more than a few Democrats would agree with Wilson's assessment. Obama has subjected America to what Marc Thiessen described in the *Washington Post* as "a fundamentally dishonest presidency." This was not easily accomplished. It took a near perfect alignment of environmental factors to elevate to the White House a man who, in the words of the veteran civil libertarian Nat Hentoff, "doesn't give a damn, because he can get away with whatever he wants."

Get away Obama does. Before his second term was halfway through, Obama would be caught in major lies on any number of critical issues, such as the terrorist assault on the Benghazi consulate, the IRS's targeting of the Tea Party, the Fast and Furious gunrunning operation, and Obamacare, among others. Yet it has almost always been Fox News or the conservative blogosphere that has done the catching. The major media, excluding Fox News, have done their best not to notice. The Obama faithful have done their best not to know. And Obama has kept on fabulating.

Obama's distinctive upbringing had much to do with making him the serial fabulist he has become. Many who have studied the president have been led astray by trusting Obama's own accounts of that upbringing. Like Obama himself, they have focused on his father and Obama's "dreams" thereof and slighted the parent who really shaped him, his mother, Stanley Ann Dunham. Although she indulged the young Obama in many ways, Dunham failed to give him a genuine sense of who he was. The parent of a mixed-race child in a world with monolithic expectations, she could have infused him with the most powerful and compelling of all identities—that of an "American." She did the opposite.

In one of the more believable passages in his 1995 memoir,

Dreams from My Father, Obama told one revealing story about his mother's allegiances. During their years together in Indonesia, Dunham's then-husband, Lolo Soetoro, asked Dunham to meet some of "her own people" at the American oil company where he worked. She shouted at him, "They are not my people." Obama absorbed the attitude. Even as a boy, he saw his fellow citizens abroad as "caricatures of the ugly American," and they would not grow prettier over time.

Obama and Dunham—"a lonely witness for secular humanism," according to her son—were hardly unique among liberals in their shared disdain. Condescension, in fact, may be the most enduring of liberal traits. Sinclair Lewis had his Babbitts. H. L. Mencken had his booboisie. Obama would have those benighted souls in backwater Pennsylvania who "cling to guns or religion or antipathy to people who aren't like them or anti-immigrant sentiment or anti-trade sentiment as a way to explain their frustrations."

When he returned to Hawaii as a ten-year-old, Obama struggled to define who he was. Given what he knew about Americans, he could hardly have wanted to be one. As to being an African American, all he knew was what he saw on TV. And so he told his new schoolmates that his father was a prince and his grandfather a chief of a great African tribe. The story worked on his classmates and almost on himself. "But another part of me knew that what I was telling them was a lie," he writes, "something I'd constructed from the scraps of information I'd picked up from my mother." For the next forty years, Obama would continue constructing identities for himself: high school stoner, college Marxist, New York intellectual, Chicago Alinskyite, Harvard cosmopolitan, African American ward heeler, all-American presidential candidate. He would continue constructing identities for himself into his presidency, and it is around these identities that this book is structured.

By the time *Dreams from My Father* was written, Obama had picked up enough postmodern patois to rationalize these identity shifts and the lies needed to ease the transitions among them. Like pornography, postmodernism is hard to define but easy to spot. In *Dreams*, Obama showed all the symptoms. He acknowledged spending much of his life "plugging up holes in the narrative"— one of the many references to "narratives," "fictions," "poses," and "grooves" that constitute the "stitched-together" nature of his life. The result is a biography that cannot be trusted.

Even a supportive Obama biographer like David Remnick called *Dreams* a "mixture of verifiable fact, recollection, re-creation, invention, and artful shaping." An equally friendly biographer, David Maraniss, agreed. "The character creations and rearrangements of the book are not merely a matter of style, devices of compression, but are also substantive," wrote Maraniss, four years after his protective 2008 biographical piece in the *Washington Post* helped Obama get elected. "We didn't understand why his politically calculating chameleon nature was never discussed," an aide to Hillary Clinton told Remnick. "We were said to be the chameleons, but he changed his *life* depending on who he was talking to."

Obama's early influences—such as his communist mentor in Hawaii, Frank Marshall Davis; and his Marxist professors and friends at Occidental College—did not encourage truth telling. Although leftists are not uniquely guilty of lying, they are uniquely guilty of lying as a conscious strategy. As Vladimir Lenin once reportedly said, "A lie told often enough becomes the truth." Although Obama did not drink deeply at this well, he drank deeply enough to be intoxicated with its spirit.

Obama's appearance mattered at least as much as his influences. He had the good fortune of growing up thinking and acting much as white liberals do but in the body of a black man. He believed what they believed and spoke as they spoke. They noticed, they approved, they marveled. "I mean, you got the first mainstream African-American presidential candidate who is articulate and bright and clean and a nice-looking guy," said Joe Biden of Obama in early 2007. In still another unwittingly honest revelation, Senate Majority Leader Harry Reid found comfort in Obama's having "no Negro dialect."

By the time Obama emerged as a national candidate, every major newsroom in America—save one—was chockablock with people who thought like Biden and Reid or Maraniss and Remnick. All serious surveys of journalists' political preferences have shown a leftward skew, one that has been only getting sharper over time. It is harder to calculate newsroom attitudes toward race, but the collective media indulgence of well-spoken black liberals—black conservatives get no such pass—is impossible to deny. As the beau ideal of the progressive wish-dream, Obama would enjoy an unprecedented immunity from major media criticism. This did not encourage truth telling, either by him or by the media.

Obama's first public controversy is worth revisiting, as it shows just how early in his political career he adopted lying as strategy. At the time, late 1999, Obama found himself challenging two black candidates for Congress, each of whom favored gun control as conspicuously as he did. One was the former Black Panther Bobby Rush, whose seat in the US House of Representatives Obama coveted; the other a fellow state senator, Donne Trotter.

His opponents sensed the same vulnerability that Jesse Jackson would exploit years later, namely Obama's felt lack of authenticity as a black man. "He went to Harvard and became an educated fool," said Rush during the campaign. "Barack is a person who read about the civil-rights protests and thinks he knows all about it." Trotter was rougher still. "Barack is viewed in part to be the white man in blackface in our community," he said. "You have only to look at his supporters. Who pushed him to get where he is so fast? It's these individuals in Hyde Park, who don't always have the best interest of the community in mind."

Shortly after Christmas in 1999, Obama missed a critical vote on the Safe Neighborhoods Act, a gun control measure in the Illinois state senate. Rush and Trotter promptly let the voting public know that Obama had abandoned Chicago in its hour of need. The front-page headline of the January 5, 2000, edition of the *Hyde Park Herald*, a community newspaper, captured the spirit of the brouhaha: "Obama Misses Gun Law Vote, Draws Criticism from Rivals." What made the missed vote so awkward for Obama was that when Governor George Ryan desperately tried to find him, he was doing some *holoholo* time in the Aloha State. His opponents seized the opportunity to show how very unblack such a sojourn was. Trotter, for one, described Obama's absence as "irresponsible" and a "dereliction." Rush's campaign spokeswoman meanwhile pointed out that while some public officials were trying to get guns off the streets of Chicago, "other public officials are on a beach in Hawaii."

When contacted by the *Herald*, Obama swore that he intended to be in Springfield for the special session, but his "18-month old daughter had a bad cold," and he "determined it was too difficult to make a nine-hour flight." Said the *Herald* in something of an understatement, "Rush didn't buy Obama's explanation." Apparently, not many others did either. A week later, Obama felt the need to employ his monthly *Herald* column in his own defense.

Obama titled the column "Family Duties Took Precedence." It was so maudlin and misleading that he might as well have titled it "How Checkers Ate My Homework." To undo the narrative laid down by his opponents, Obama had to create a counternarrative that positioned him not as the self-serving outsider Rush and Trotter imagined but as the very incarnation of responsible fatherhood. To make this plotline work, Obama would ground his excuse in a foundation of half-truths and flat-out lies.

As to the first issue, why he went to Hawaii on this "extremely short trip," Obama claimed, "Our visit is the only means to assure my grandmother does not spend the holidays alone." He traced the solitude of his grandmother, Madelyn Dunham, to the deaths of her daughter and husband. Obama neglected to say, of course, that the daughter—his mother—spent little time in Hawaii and had died four years prior, and that the husband—his grandfather—had died four years before that. To account for his grandmother's not coming to Chicago, Obama endowed her with a "variety of ailments."

As to the second issue, why he stayed once the vote was scheduled, Obama sensed correctly that ten-footers on the North Shore would not impress his South Side constituency. So he cited once again the illness of baby Malia, now elevating her "cold" to a "flu." This was a necessary adjustment to explain why Michelle could not have stayed with the baby. "We hear a lot to [sic] talk from politicians about the importance of family values," Obama pontificated at the saga's end. "Hopefully, you will try to understand when your state senator tries to live up to those values as best he can." If no one else did, the individuals in Hyde Park bought the story. Obama got the editorial support of the *Hyde Park Herald* and the majority of white votes, but even with that support, he secured only 30 percent of the votes district-wide. "I was completely mortified and humiliated," Obama would later tell Remnick.

In the future, Obama would improve his storytelling. To sell himself to America, black and white, he would have to. He would further refine his pitchman's talents to sell a center-right nation a variety of unwanted left-of-center nostrums. As Obama sensed, his line of goods would have forever remained on the political shelf had he honored truth-in-labeling laws, but he did not feel the need. His allies on the left had been finessing labels for years: racial preferences to affirmative action to diversity; abortion rights to pro-choice to reproductive rights; global warming to climate change; gay marriage to marriage equality; liberal to progressive.

Obama has been able to advance this ignoble tradition for two reasons. One is obvious: the media let him. The second needs explanation. Like any gifted sleight-of-hand artist, Obama has had his audience focus on the wrong object. The pundits debated his ideology—Marxist, socialist, progressive, pragmatist—and even his religion—Christian, Muslim, atheist—but they rarely questioned his commitment. Yes, those ten-footers in Hawaii likely did mean more to Obama than gun control laws in Illinois. Although immersed in leftism since childhood, he never left the shallow end of the pool. He proved so adept at breaking promises because he did not care deeply enough to keep them. What mattered more was that he be seen striking the right pose, finding the right groove, spinning the right narrative.

For a quick example, one need look no further than the first major promise he broke as a national candidate. Back in September 2007, when his candidacy was still a long shot, Obama vowed, "If I am the Democratic nominee, I will aggressively pursue an agreement with the Republican nominee to preserve a publicly financed general election." This promise appeared virtuous and cost him nothing. It was classic Obama.

By June 2008, Obama had renounced the pledge. Like everyone else with eyes, the *Washington Post* attributed the renunciation to his "groundbreaking success in raising money." Still, in spite of the evidence, Obama hoped to maintain the reformer's pose. This meant, as it often did, creating a complex fiction. So he told the *Post* that, of course, he still supported the *idea* of public financing. Unfortunately, though, the current system was "broken" and favored Republicans who had "become masters at gaming" it. Given these circumstances, he would carry the banner of reform into the breach as virtuously as the rules of war allowed. In this instance, even before his party nominated him for president, Obama had set the pattern: make a promise, break it if need be, find a high-minded excuse, blame the Republicans. The media would move on quickly. They almost always did.

READ MY LIPS: NO NEW TAXES

All presidents exaggerate their accomplishments. All presidents finesse the truth on national security issues. Many presidents, perhaps most, lie about their personal life. But few presidents get really and truly nailed on a lie. In the modern era, President Dwight Eisenhower may have been the first. He lied about the mission of a U-2 spy plane over the Soviet Union, and he publicly owned up to it only after the Russians produced the plane and the captured pilot. At the time, the lie itself was a major news story, in no small part because Eisenhower did not have a reputation as a liar.

The first president since Eisenhower to draw intense fire for a specific "lie" was George H. W. Bush. To fend off his conservative primary challengers during his 1988 campaign, Bush promised not to raise taxes or introduce new ones. He solidified the promise at the Republican National Convention when he said memorably and defiantly, "The Congress will push me to raise taxes and I'll say no. And they'll push, and I'll say no, and they'll push again, and I'll say, to them, 'Read my lips: no new taxes.'" Bush was not intentionally lying, but like Obama, he lacked the conviction to honor his own pledge. When the tax-hikers pushed, he yielded much too readily.

Richard Nixon was a special case. In 1950, his opponent in the California race for the US Senate, Helen Gahagan Douglas, gave him the nickname "Tricky Dick." The name stuck in no small part because Nixon-haters in the media made it stick. They were still smarting from Nixon's lead role in outing one of the most formidable liars in American history, the establishment golden boy and Soviet agent Alger Hiss. Tricky or not, Nixon never got tagged with a memorable lie. His enemies would accuse him of countless things—dirty tricks, war crimes, break-ins, cover-ups—but lying was just one out of many misdeeds, real and imagined.

Still, had it not been for the doggedness of the *Washington Post*, history might well remember Richard Nixon as the president who won forty-nine states in his reelection bid and brought peace to Vietnam. Nixon did try to call attention to the shenanigans of his two Democratic predecessors, Kennedy and Johnson, each of whom had stretched the laws of God and man as far as Nixon did. But by the early 1970s the media had little interest in sharing Republicans' laments. Liberals had reached a critical mass in America's newsrooms, and the information flow was being filtered accordingly.

In the 1990s two phenomena tested the effectiveness of the late-century media filters. One was the Internet. The other was the Clintons. On January 26, 1992, America writ large first met Hillary Clinton. Earlier that month, an Arkansas state employee, Gennifer—with a "G"—Flowers, confessed to a tabloid that Bill Clinton had been dallying with her for some twelve years. In a desperate attempt to save Bill's candidacy for president, the Clintons agreed to be interviewed by Steve Kroft on CBS's *60 Minutes*. To his credit, Kroft forcefully stuck it to the Clintons. In the not-so-distant past, journalists expected the truth from public officials, even Democratic front-runners for the presidency. Starting with this interview, the Clintons would dramatically lower that expectation.

When Kroft asked Bill if he had had an affair with Flowers, he answered, "That allegation is false." Hillary, her hands lovingly intertwined with Bill's, nodded in affirmation. Later in the *60*

Minutes interview, Bill swore, "I have absolutely leveled with the American people." He had done no such thing.

The Clinton era was a turning point in the history of journalism. Although liberals had been on a long march through America's newsrooms for years, it was not until after the Republican sweep of Congress in 1994 that they largely abandoned their role as watchdogs. America has always had scoundrels, but never before had the media collectively championed one, let alone two.

Throughout Clinton's presidency, Bill and Hillary lied as necessary to protect the Clinton brand. Appalled by Hillary's performance in particular, the usually restrained columnist William Safire notably designated her "a congenital liar" in a 1996 *New York Times* op-ed titled "Blizzard of Lies." In the piece, Safire made no reference to Clinton's sexual misadventures. He referred instead to Hillary's commodity trading scandal, her obstruction of justice in the aftermath of the death of White House counsel Vince Foster, her role in the Whitewater affair, and her machinations in a grubby in-house scandal known as "Travelgate." In each case, wrote Safire, "She lied for good reason." Lying preserved Bill Clinton's shot at reelection and possibly even spared Hillary a pantsuit of prison orange.

Six years and a day after she lied on *60 Minutes* to protect Bill's candidacy, Hillary finessed the truth on the *Today* show to protect his presidency. "There isn't any fire," she told Matt Lauer about the "smoke" surrounding her husband's involvement with an intern, Monica Lewinsky. Unlike Steve Kroft in 1992, Lauer did not challenge her. He shifted his inquiry from the charges facing the president—perjury and obstruction of justice—to the fairness of independent counsel Ken Starr's "thirty-million-dollar" investigation. This was all the license Hillary needed to introduce a new and memorable subplot. "The great story here," she said ominously, "is this vast right-wing conspiracy that has been conspiring against my husband since the day he announced for president."

The late Christopher Hitchens easily saw through the subterfuge. Said he of the Clintons in his indispensable book *No One Left to Lie To*, "Like him, she is not just a liar but a lie; a phony construct of shreds and patches and hysterical, self-pitying demagogic improvisations." The proudly left-of-center Hitchens took his title from a quote by David Schippers, a Democrat and the chief investigative counsel for the House Judiciary Committee. Said Schippers for the ages: "The president, then, has lied under oath in a civil deposition, lied under oath in a criminal grand jury. He lied to the people. He lied to his Cabinet. He lied to his top aides. And now he's lied under oath to the Congress of the United States. There's no one left to lie to."

THE WHITE HOUSE HAS BEEN CAUGHT IN A LIE

It was not easy being a Democratic pundit while memories of the Clintons' skullduggery were still fresh. Some future historian may want to trace the genesis of the left's strategy to restore the reputation of two chronic liars, one of them a serial sexual predator, but the operational tactic quickly became clear: its apparatchiks would debase the word "lie."

An article by Jerry White from September 28, 2001, on the *World Socialist* website—one of a thousand comparable articles— showed how the strategy played out. White, a future Socialist Equality Party presidential candidate, began his article with the words "The White House has been caught in a lie." The lie, White reported, was that a terrorist threat against Air Force One had forced George Bush to avoid Washington until late on September 11. Although White did not suggest any real rationale for the lie beyond Bush's presumed cowardice, he strung together enough half-truths to convince the willing. "If Bush lied about his activities on the day of the attacks," he argued, "why should anyone assume he has not lied about the government's investigation, the identity of the perpetrators, the motives and aims of US war preparations, and the intent and scope of expanded police powers demanded by his administration to wiretap, search and seize, and detain suspects?" Why indeed?

The strategy quickly migrated from the fringe to the center. The summer of 2004 witnessed the publication of three mainstream books that reinforced the "lie" motif. Each had the word "lies" in the title, applied not to the Clintons, but to Bush and others on the right: Joe Conason's *Big Lies*, Al Franken's *Lies and the Lying Liars Who Tell Them*, and the most serious of the three, David Corn's *The Lies of George W. Bush: Mastering the Politics of Deception*. Although the release of the books does not appear to have been coordinated, the strategizing that inspired them had to occupy more than a few man-hours at Ebenezer's on Capitol Hill.

On the plus side, Corn created a durable framework for evaluating presidential honesty. Starting with the basics, he quoted the ethicist Sissela Bok's standard definition that a lie "is an intentionally deceptive message in the form of a statement." Because intention is hard to discern, Corn elaborated, writing that "if a president issues a statement, he or she has an obligation to ensure the remark is truthful." If the statement proves to be untrue, Corn continued, the president "has a duty to acknowledge and correct any significant misstatement he or she utters—especially if that slip somehow worked to his advantage." Appropriately, Corn extended this obligation to the president's spokespeople. It may be useful to summarize Corn's theorizing mnemonically as the FIG factor. A politician "lies" when he or she says something *false*, either *intentionally* or fully *indifferent* to the truth, with the hope of securing some advantage or *gain*. "False" is a more precise word here than Bok's "deceptive."

For reasons only partly strategic, the George W. Bush presidency drove legions of the left-leaning into an irrational and un-precedented media madness that sought its rationale in Bush's presumed dishonesty. The *SFGate* columnist Mark Morford per-fectly captured the movement's thinking, such as it was, in a 2008 article headlined, without irony, "The 935 Lies of George W. Bush: Yes, you already knew. But now they're actually quantifiable. Like, say, stab wounds."

The fashionably cynical Morford began with the understand-ing that presidential lying was something of a "national pastime," sort of like baseball. The game Morford chose to play, however, was a semantic one. Although he conceded Bill Clinton lied, he insisted he did so "in a harmless civil lawsuit." The House of Rep-resentatives obviously had a different understanding of the word "harmless." Its members impeached Clinton, only the second president to be so honored. The Supreme Court had a different take too. In 2001, the justices disbarred Clinton from ever prac-ticing law before the high court. The Arkansas supreme court did not think perjury harmless either. That court suspended Clinton's law license for five years and ordered him to pay a $25,000 fine.

BUSH LIED, PEOPLE DIED

In *The Lies of George W. Bush*, Corn subverted his own fundamen-tals by declaring in the book's opening sentence, "George Bush is a liar." Although an imperfect president, Bush was not a liar, and Corn could not make the case that he was. For the six years including his first term and the campaign that preceded it, the major media did all within their power to make Corn's research easier. The same folks who ignored Clinton's sordid sex-and-drug romp through Arkansas spent reportorial man-years trying to document Bush's alleged cocaine use, turned a twenty-five-year-old DUI into a national scandal on election eve, and twisted themselves into knots—CBS's Dan Rather most spectacularly—trying to prove that Bush did not dot every "i" and cross every "t" in fulfilling his National Guard duty.

Despite all the media help, Corn was hard-pressed to establish one lie of consequence that Bush told as president or even as candidate. The lack of evidence did not deter him, however, from libeling Bush as a president "who soils the Oval Office with lies." Corn wrote this, by the way, just three years into the Bush presidency. The only explanation other than strategic agitprop for such stunning bile is BDS, Bush Derangement Syndrome: what the pundit and psychiatrist Charles Krauthammer diagnosed as "the acute onset of paranoia in otherwise normal people in reaction to the policies, the presidency—nay—the very existence of George W. Bush."

Corn, for instance, took Bush to task for the harmless claim "I'm a uniter, not a divider." In fact, Bush had reason to say that when he first campaigned for president. In 1998, he was reelected governor of Texas with 69 percent of the vote, including 49 percent of the Hispanic vote. If that were not proof enough of his bipartisan appeal, he had the endorsement of every major Democratic politician in the state.

Three days after being sworn in as president, the "polarizing" George Bush proposed his signature piece of legislation, an education bill known as No Child Left Behind (NCLB) cosponsored by the liberal lion Senator Ted Kennedy. Politics does not get more bipartisan than that except perhaps in 2006, when, as President Obama phrased it, "the unlikely trio of John McCain, Ted Kennedy, and President Bush came together to champion [immigration] reform." If these efforts by Bush polarized anyone, it was his conservative base. And yet Corn's indictment of Bush on this count is no stronger than any of the others made in his contorted book.

To be fair to Corn, though, he was not as deranged as the "Bush lied, people died" crowd on the question of weapons of mass destruction. Still, Corn accused Bush of being "crafty and disingenuous" in the way he represented the findings of past UN inspections. Among the experts Corn cited in opposition to Bush's position on WMDs was the former chief UN arms inspector Richard Butler. Corn did not mention, however, that in the year 2000, before politics clouded the picture, the Australian Butler published a book whose very title affirmed Bush's anxiety, *The Greatest Threat: Iraq, Weapons of Mass Destruction, and the Growing Crisis of Global Security.*

After being booted from Iraq in late 1998, Butler considered Iraq's ongoing plea of innocence "the blackest lie," and no one knew Saddam's capabilities better than Butler. Corn made a fuss about the four-year gap in information from 1998 to 2002, but others exposed to the same evidence came to the same conclusion. Said Senator Hillary Clinton in October 2002, "In the four years since the inspectors left, intelligence reports show that Saddam Hussein has worked to rebuild his chemical and biological weapons stock, his missile delivery capability, and his nuclear program. He has also given aid, comfort, and sanctuary to terrorists, including al Qaeda members."

A corollary to the "Bush lied" trope was "Bush knew." As Ben Smith reported in *Politico*, Ohio University and Scripps Howard did an extensive poll in 2006 that asked, "How likely is it that people in the federal government either assisted in the 9/11 attacks or took no action to stop the attacks because they wanted the United States to go to war in the Middle East?" More than half of all Democrats answered "very likely" or "somewhat likely."

As to why Bush wanted to go to war in the Middle East, the opposition could never quite agree on what Bush stood to gain, the essential "G" in the FIG factor. Suggestions included avenging an assassination attempt on his father, exploiting Iraq for oil, harvesting votes for future elections, enriching Halliburton, and/ or providing "the Israeli government with greater wherewithal to impose its terms and conditions on the Palestinian people"—this last possibility suggested by the other Joe Wilson, the so-called whistle-blower spouse of the utterly fabulous CIA agent Valerie Plame. There was no political gain, however, in claiming that Saddam had large caches of WMDs and then not finding them—no logic either. Most famously, the Clinton-appointed CIA director George Tenet assured Bush that the case for WMDs was a "slam dunk." It obviously was not.

In the run-up to war in late 2002, the great majority of those prominent politicos who would later denounce Bush as a liar agreed with Butler, including the two Democrats who ran against Bush for president. Said the former vice-president Al Gore in September 2002 of Saddam, "We know that he has stored secret supplies of biological and chemical weapons throughout his country." Two years later, Gore, now a borderline 9/11 truther, was saying of Bush, "He betrayed this country! He played on our fears. He took America on an ill-conceived foreign adventure dangerous to our troops, an adventure preordained and planned before 9/11 ever took place."

As a member of the Senate Select Committee on Intelligence, Senator John Kerry, Bush's opponent in 2004, had access to all the intelligence that Bush did. Said Kerry in October 2002: "I will be voting to give the President of the United States the authority to use force if necessary to disarm Saddam Hussein because I believe that a deadly arsenal of weapons of mass destruction in his hands is a real and grave threat to our security."

In September 2013, as secretary of state, John Kerry said publicly that as a US senator he "opposed the president's decision to go into Iraq." In fact, Kerry voted to authorize the war. As the *Washington Post* noted, "This is at least the second time since becoming secretary that Kerry has asserted that he opposed the

2003 invasion of Iraq while serving as a Democratic senator from Massachusetts."

In truth, Democrats had a near monopoly on real, FIG-factor Iraq lies. When Vermont governor Howard Dean burst out of the Democratic primary chute in 2003 howling against the war, his opponents began to fudge their prior support. They did so to secure an advantage, namely to keep pace with Dean. In 2008, Barack Obama forced Hillary Clinton to do much the same. In 2004, the media largely obliged the fudgers and focused their wrath on a Republican president who, despite great temptation, faced the facts of a difficult war at least as honestly as had his predecessors, if not more so. In the final analysis, the one statement that met Corn's definition of a lie was that bumper-sticker favorite, "Bush lied, people died."

CHAPTER 2

THE AFRICAN AMERICAN

I n February 2001, as part of an oral history of black America, Julieanna Richardson interviewed then–state senator Barack Obama. Richardson seemed to capture the thirty-nine-year-old politician as he was—cautious, ambitious, and more than a little vain. Although the social philosophy on display in the interview did not vary much from that expressed in *Dreams from My Father*, at least not in content, the tone was much softer.

Obama told Richardson that his childhood in Hawaii was "idyllic" and that "the image that [he] had of being a black American was almost exclusively positive." He added, "All the children around me were of some mixture, and so I was not unusual or untypical in Hawaii." He mentioned not a single racial affront.

Obama was either deceiving Richardson or deceiving the readers of *Dreams*. The evidence suggests the latter. David Remnick, the author of *The Bridge: The Life and Rise of Barack Obama*, conceded that Obama "darkens the canvas" in *Dreams* and that many of the grievances cited were "novelistic contrivances." The biographer David Maraniss, the author of *Barack Obama: The Story*, said much the same thing, claiming Obama portrayed himself as "blacker and more disaffected" than he really was. As to motive, the much too generous Remnick insisted that Obama "heightens whatever opportunity arises" to score a racial point, "obviously" because he was going "after an emotional truth."

It was never about "truth," emotional or otherwise. Obama cataloged his racial slights, real or imagined, to redefine himself as an African American and to forge a political bond with the black community. *Dreams* was published in 1995, the same year that Obama launched his political career. Although seriously calculated, *Dreams* was too revealing in too many troubling ways—drugs, the Reverend Jeremiah Wright, the communist Frank Marshall Davis—to boost an aspiring presidential candidate. Almost assuredly, the manuscript was fine-tuned to launch a future mayor of Chicago, a career path actually aided by the allusions to Wright and Davis.

"I met [Obama] sometime in the mid-1990s," Obama's mentor Bill Ayers would later tell *Salon*. "For the first two years, I thought, his ambition is so huge that he wants to be mayor of Chicago." A friend of Obama's, Cassandra Butts, traced that ambition back at least to Harvard. "He wanted to be mayor of Chicago and that was all he ever talked about as far as holding office," she would tell the Chicago reporter David Mendell, author of the valuable 2007 biography *Obama: From Promise to Power*. The young Obama modeled his career's trajectory on that of his political hero, the late Chicago mayor Harold Washington. Washington had moved from the Illinois state senate to Congress to the mayoralty. Obama took that first step and tried for the second. *Dreams* rooted Obama in the Chicago experience and in the progressive tradition thereof. As such, it was finely calibrated to attract the black–lakefront liberal coalition needed for a Democrat not named Daley to achieve high office in Illinois.

NOT AS LONG AS YOU SAY "BARACK" RIGHT

In reviewing Maraniss's biography of Obama, Ben Smith of *Buzz-feed* "counted 38 instances in which [Maraniss] convincingly disputes significant elements of Obama's own story of his life and his family history." Many of these, perhaps most, were contrived or exaggerated racial slights. To have others accept him as an African American, Obama had a lot of exaggerating to do.

Long before Obama met his future wife, Michelle, he met "Regina," a coed from Chicago's South Side who somehow found her way to Southern California's pricey Occidental College. In *Dreams*, Obama described her as "a big, dark woman who wore stockings and dresses that looked homemade." And although Obama had no romantic interest in Regina, Remnick rightly labeled her a "harbinger" of Michelle, more literary device than flesh-and-blood woman. It was she who set him on his journey to find his inner African American, and rather forcefully at that. "Her voice," Obama wrote, "evoked a vision of black life in all its possibility, a vision that filled me with longing—a longing for place, and a fixed and definite history."

Bizarrely, as Maraniss noted, Obama pulled the name of this character and some of her life's details from the Swiss grandmother of a white friend at Occidental College named Caroline Boss. An aspiring young Marxist like Obama, Boss tried to convince him that the enduring struggle should be based on class, not race, and thus her washerwoman grandma—all young Marxists have a washerwoman in the woodpile—made a useful model for all the world's oppressed.

Although the character was largely fictional, Obama assigned Regina a tangible real-life task. It was she who convinced Obama to abandon the name "Barry," a name that presumably sounded much too white and middle class. "Do you mind if I call you Barack?" she asked. "Not as long as you say it right," he answered. Coming straight from the motherland, Barack Senior pronounced his name BEAR-ick, not buh-ROCK. Barack Senior himself was known as "Barry" when he was in Hawaii. When Obama visited Africa, well after he became "Barack," all of his kin called him "Barry." It was Obama who would contrive the new pronunciation, perhaps because the new pronunciation sounded more forceful, more revolutionary, more black.

I HAD MY OWN OFFICE, MY OWN SECRETARY, MONEY IN THE BANK

In the 1991 promotional brochure put out by Obama's literary agency Acton and Dystel—the same brochure that listed Obama's birthplace as "Kenya"—Obama was said to have "worked as a financial journalist and editor for Business International Corporation." In *Dreams*, Obama inflated his stint at Business International to even grander proportions. In the retelling, he had his own office, his own secretary. He wore a suit and tie. He had in-person interviews with Japanese financiers and German bond traders. "I would imagine myself as a captain of industry, barking out orders, closing the deal, before I remembered who it was that I had told myself I wanted to be and felt pangs of guilt for my lack of resolve," Obama wrote.

Obama told the story not to boast of his own seeming success but to show how inaccessible this career path was to his oppressed brethren. "As far as I could tell I was the only black man in the company," he claimed. This was not at all a source of pride for Obama. Rather, in full grievance mode, he considered it "a source of shame." As early as July 2005, however, a former coworker and Obama fan, Dan Armstrong, revealed Obama's whole account to be a "serious exaggeration." Obama did not work at a multinational corporation; he worked at a "small company that published newsletters." He did not have his own office, wear a jacket and tie, interview international businessmen, or write articles. He mostly just copyedited business items and slipped them into a three-ring binder for the company's customers.

The author Shelby Steele, who is biracial himself and came of age in a segregated world, knows how tempting it is to manufacture grievances. In his underappreciated 2008 book, *The Bound Man: Why We Are Excited About Obama and Why He Can't Win*, Steele argued that in his eagerness to seem an "authentic" black man, Obama all too often fictionalized the state of black victimization and cast himself among the victims. He would continue to do this even during his presidency.

I WAS HAUNTED BY THE LOOK ON CORETTA'S FACE

In response to the *Washington Post*'s breathless revelation during the 2012 campaign that Mitt Romney had hazed a classmate while in high school, John Nolte of *Big Hollywood* fired back, "Does WaPo Know Obama Shoved a Little Girl?" But did he really? The story that Nolte cited from *Dreams* was no more believable than the other racial melodramas in that fanciful tome. In this particular reminiscence, Obama reflected on his own first days as a ten-year-old at his Hawaiian prep school, a transition complicated by the presence of "Coretta," the only other black student in the class.

When the other students accused Obama of having a girl-friend, Obama shoved Coretta and insisted she leave him alone. Although "his act of betrayal" bought him a reprieve from the other students, Obama understood that he "had been tested and found wanting." Like virtually all the racial contretemps in *Dreams*, this one smacked of willful contrivance. Obama's biographer David Remnick identified a woman named Joella Edwards as the "Coretta" of the story. The difference, Remnick admitted, was that "Barry never rejected Joella." *Au contraire*, as Joella gushed, "He was my knight in shining armor."

THERE ARE SEVERAL BLACK LADIES OUT THERE WHO'VE BROKEN MY HEART JUST AS GOOD

As with so much in his life—his choice of a church, for instance—Obama's selection of Michelle as bride seemed fragrant with calculation, on both an emotional and a political level. A black campaign worker in South Carolina told David Remnick that Obama's selection of a black wife, particularly a dark-skinned one, "matters to people here." The Princeton political scientist Melissa Harris-Perry elaborated, "I don't think Obama could have been elected President if he had married a white woman." She added, "Had he married a white woman, he would have signaled that he had chosen whiteness."

Yet, as David Maraniss pointed out, Obama chose whiteness in every documented relationship pre-Michelle. In his 2012 biography of Obama, Maraniss profiled two former girlfriends. Obama apparently drew from each of them to create a white "composite" girlfriend in *Dreams*. One of them, the Australian Genevieve Cook, provided most of the grist for Obama's "mystery woman," the only girlfriend mentioned in *Dreams*. "Like many characters in the memoir," said Maraniss of Cook, "[Obama] introduced her to advance a theme, another thread of thought in his musings about race." When lesser memoirists do the same—James Frey of *A Million Little Pieces* fame comes quickly to mind—Oprah trashes them on national TV.

In the case of the composite girl, for instance, Obama told of how their relationship came to a bitter end over her failure to understand black angst. "We had a big fight, right in front of the theater," wrote Obama. "When we got back to the car she started crying. She couldn't be black, she said." Cook denied that this ever happened. As Obama later explained to Maraniss, "I thought that [the anecdote] was a useful theme to make about sort of the interactions that I had in the relationships with white girlfriends." Frey felt much the same way. "A memoir literally means my story. A memoir is a subjective retelling of events," he protested, adding, "I never expected the book to come under the type of scrutiny that it has." When Obama used the theater story in *Dreams*, he never expected this kind of scrutiny, either. At the time, no one beyond his neighborhood knew who Obama was.

Dreams, though, was pure calculation. Mindful of the way many black women—more precisely, many black female voters—feel about black men who ignore black women, Obama added a caveat about his relationships. Immediately after telling his half sister, Auma, about this ruptured relationship with a white woman, he added, "There are several black ladies out there who've broken my heart just as good." There are? Not a single sentence about any of these ladies appeared in *Dreams*. Nor in the years of Obama's rise has a single black girlfriend come forward to tell her story. Maraniss certainly did not identify any. The astute reader wonders whether these black ladies exist. The cynical reader wonders whether the white ones do.

Dreams culminates in Obama's wedding to Michelle. At his most romantic, Obama said of Michelle, "In her eminent practicality and Midwestern attitudes, she reminds me not a little of [his grandmother] Toot." He might have said the same about the fictional "Regina" from Occidental. In *The Audacity of Hope*, Obama got the date of his first meeting with his future wife wrong. "I met Michelle in the summer of 1988," he wrote, "while we were both working at Sidley & Austin." In fact, Obama interned at Sidley and Austin after his first year at Harvard Law School. It was 1989. But did he and Michelle really meet at Sidley and Austin? In 2009, speaking to university students in Russia, Obama wondered out loud, "I don't know if anyone will meet their future wife or husband in class like I did." With the Obama "narrative" it is hard to tell where the errors end and the lies begin. There is an ash heap of falsehood and fabrication to sort through.

SO DON'T TELL ME I DON'T HAVE A CLAIM ON SELMA, ALABAMA

On many an occasion, Obama has told the story of his origins with a distinctive twist to establish a particular advantage. When speaking to a black audience, as he confessed to David Remnick, he did so "[in] a slightly different dialect." On the campaign trail in March 2007, he gave a critical speech in Selma, Alabama, the Concord Bridge of black history. There, Obama used his best black preacher's voice to tell his audience a story so comically unanchored to reality that had a black Republican told it, his candidacy would have died before the evening news aired.

"My very existence might not have been possible had it not been for some of the folks here today," Obama told the civil rights veterans gathered to mark the events of "Bloody Sunday" forty-two years prior. "Something happened back here in Selma, Alabama," Obama continued. This something "sent a shout across the ocean," which inspired Obama Senior, still "herding goats" back in Kenya, to "set his sights a little higher." This same something also "worried folks in the White House" to the point that the "the Kennedys decided we're going to do an airlift."

As the saga continued, Obama Senior got a ticket on the airlift and met Obama's mother, a descendant of slave owners. "There was something stirring across the country because of what happened in Selma, Alabama, because some folks are willing to march across a bridge," preached Obama. "So they got together and Barack Obama Junior. was born. So don't tell me I don't have a claim on Selma, Alabama. Don't tell me I'm not coming home to Selma, Alabama."

He didn't, and he wasn't. Something about Selma inspired Obama to aggrandize his history to Homeric levels. For starters, herding goats in his father's town was like mowing lawns in an American one. Everyone did it as a kid, even the son of the village's most affluent guy. As a boy, Obama Senior dressed in western clothes and attended English-speaking Christian schools. He was working as a clerk in Nairobi, not a goatherd in East Bejesus, when he applied for the first airlift. For the young or those of short memory, Dwight Eisenhower, a Republican, was the president in 1959 when Obama Senior came to the United States.

Although born in Kansas, Stanley Ann Dunham was not exactly Dorothy. Dunham spent her formative years in the state of Washington, where she earned the nickname "Anarchist Annie" under the tutelage of some hipster teachers. By the time of the Selma march, Dunham had long since been seduced and abandoned by the roguish Obama Senior. In fact, her son was conceived four years before anyone outside Alabama had ever heard of Selma.

What amazes in retrospect is how Obama found the nerve to tell so flagrantly dishonest a story. Having dependably obliging media surely fortified his spine. It was more than a year later that the *Washington Post*'s Michael Dobbs got around to checking the facts, and only then because he was prodded. Wrote Dobbs, "A reader, Gregory Gelembiuk of the University of Wisconsin, thought there was something strange about the story told by Barack Obama in his Selma speech last year, and asked me to look into it."

THERE'S NOT A BLACK AMERICA AND WHITE AMERICA AND LATINO AMERICA AND ASIAN AMERICA; THERE'S THE UNITED STATES OF AMERICA

To be fair, early in the 2008 campaign Obama did attempt to share some harsh truths with the black community. In a particularly bold move, during a Father's Day sermon at a Chicago church he scolded a large black congregation for allowing the black family to collapse. Obama leaned particularly hard on the absentee fathers, too many of whom "have abandoned their responsibilities, acting like boys instead of men." No sooner did Obama lay into these baby daddies than one of them, the nothing if not authentic Jesse Jackson, threatened on a live microphone "to cut [Obama's] nuts off." Chastised, Obama quickly retreated to his fictions, finding it much easier to fix blame on white America than to fix problems within the black community.

This retreat was never more evident than after George Zimmerman was acquitted in the 2012 shooting death of the seventeen-year-old African American Trayvon Martin. If the president had called attention to the all too typical collapse of Martin's family, his suppressed criminal record, his descent into drugs and violence, and especially his reckless "knockout" attack on a man several inches smaller than he, Obama might have persuaded his followers to let go of the lies that keep them emotionally shackled. But he did not. Instead, he tacitly encouraged them to protect their myths and project their anxiety onto the racial scapegoat Zimmerman.

The president who promised in his breakout 2004 Democratic National Convention speech that there was "not a black America and white America and Latino America and Asian America" fully identified himself with Martin for the sole reason that Martin looked more like his "son" than did the "white Hispanic" Zimmerman, a civil rights activist and Obama supporter. As Shelby Steele anticipated, this strategy has not made for good governance. Instead, said Steele, it "commits [Obama] to a manipulation of the very society he seeks to lead."

By way of clarification, the "win" in the title of Steele's book— *The Bound Man: Why We Are Excited about Obama and Why He Can't Win*—refers not to the outcome of the election, but rather to the fate of the black community under an Obama presidency. That fate has not been a happy one. In the month of his inauguration, 63 percent of African Americans held a favorable view of race relations in America. By July 2013, that figure had fallen to 38 percent. Among whites, the proportion had declined from 79 percent to 52 percent. Obama, alas, has failed in the one area in which even the opposition hoped he would succeed: bridging the racial divide.

CHAPTER 3

THE ALL-AMERICAN

To move from an obscure Chicago pol to a prominent national figure, Barack Obama needed the uncritical support of the soft Democratic center. Being African American was not enough. With the help of what even his biographer David Remnick conceded was "generally adoring press coverage," Obama was able to bury his un-American past and his radical roots and re-create himself as a red-blooded, all-American middle-of-the-roader. Even more impressively, Obama pulled this off almost totally in one glorious, God-fearing, flag-waving speech at the 2004 Democratic National Convention.

MY PARENTS SHARED NOT ONLY AN IMPROBABLE LOVE. THEY SHARED AN ABIDING FAITH IN THE POSSIBILITIES OF THIS NATION.

As Barack Obama elaborated in his famed speech at the 2004 Democratic National Convention in Boston, his father, Barack Obama Senior, had grown up in Kenya "herding goats." His mother, Stanley Ann Dunham, he traced to Kansas, as he always did. "My parents shared not only an improbable love," Obama continued, "they shared an abiding faith in the possibilities of this nation."

Following the convention, Obama and his media acolytes invested enormous political capital in what Remnick called Obama's "signature appeal: the use of the details of his own life as a reflection of a kind of multicultural ideal." In the years that followed, the media told the story of Obama's birth more often than that of anyone's since Jesus. Unfortunately for America, the story they were telling was demonstrably false.

Obama lied when he spoke at both the 2004 and the 2008 Democratic conventions about his parents' "improbable love" and "abiding faith in the possibilities of this nation." Obama's parents never lived together. They had no affection for America, and the father likely never even saw the baby. All of this Maraniss confirmed in *Barack Obama: The Story*. "In the college life of Barack Obama [Senior] in 1961 and 1962," wrote Maraniss, "as recounted by his friends and acquaintances in Honolulu, there was no Ann; there was no baby." One friend, a Cambodian named Kiri Tith, knew the senior Obama "very well." He had also met Dunham through a different channel. "But he had no idea," wrote Maraniss, "that Ann knew Obama, let alone got *hapai* (pregnant) by him, married him, and had a son with him."

Having established the facts, Maraniss refused to explore the implications of his own reporting. The most salient of these was that Obama had grounded his 2008 campaign—his very persona for that matter—on a family story that was pure fraud. The casual reader of Maraniss's book is left with the impression that Dunham and Obama had a one-night stand that they both regretted, but that they consented to marriage because that is what people did back in 1961.

As to the wedding in February 1961, the usually thorough Maraniss offered no detail at all. His endnotes said only this:

"Marriage facts recorded in divorce records." The immigration authorities certainly wondered about the wedding as well. An April 1961 INS memo notes, "If his USC [United States Citizen] wife tries to petition for [Obama Senior] make sure an investigation is conducted as to the bona-fide of the marriage."

In *Dreams* Obama wrote, "In fact, how and when the marriage occurred remains a bit murky, a bill of particulars that I've never quite had the courage to explore." To be sure, Dunham and Obama claimed a wedding. It suited both their purposes, Obama's to extend his visa and Dunham's to legitimize her baby. As to the divorce, Dunham at the time was desperately trying to keep her future husband Lolo Soetoro in Hawaii. The INS believed her to be married to Obama. Even if she was not married, a divorce would have been useful to clear the way for a marriage to Soetoro. Maraniss explained none of this.

Like all other mainstream biographers of the Obama family, Maraniss shared not a single word about Dunham's whereabouts in the six months between the alleged wedding in February and Obama's birth in August 1961. Given the controversy surrounding Obama's place of birth, Maraniss should have commented on a void of this duration, and he knew it. Later, when discussing Obama's murky New York years, he opined, "Nothing is so tempting for conspiracy theorists as what appears to be a hole in a life." Although Maraniss attempted to flesh out Obama's sojourn in New York, he made no effort to fill the critical prebirth hole in Ann's life.

MY FATHER LEFT MY FAMILY WHEN I WAS TWO YEARS OLD

In September 2009, President Obama delivered a prescribed address to the nation's assembled schoolchildren. "I get it," he told the kiddies about the various challenges in their family lives. "I know what that's like. My father left my family when I was two years old, and I was raised by a single mother." He had made the same claim in *Dreams* and elsewhere.

Those two years made a huge difference in the narrative Obama was at pains to construct. Maraniss hinted at where home was not, namely the residence Dunham's parents shared with the Pratt family at 6085 Kalanianole Highway, the address listed on Obama's birth certificate. Said Maraniss, "[Ann] and Obama and the infant never lived [at 6085 Kalanianole]." Indeed, the young family never lived together, and this Maraniss conceded. "Within a month of the day Barry came home from the hospital," he wrote, "he and his mother were long gone from Honolulu." They had, in fact, decamped for Seattle, where they would live for the next year.

In their respective biographies of Obama and his family, each published in 2010 or later, the *New Yorker*'s David Remnick, the *Boston Globe*'s Sally Jacobs, and the *New York Times*' Janny Scott and Jodi Kantor all failed to address the six-month lacuna in Obama's prenatal life. Worse, each contorted the time line of Dunham's Seattle hegira to sustain the illusion of a functioning Obama family even if for a short period. For his part, Maraniss debunked this fraudulent birth narrative much too quietly. Perhaps he felt guilty about contributing to it himself. In a ten-thousand-word biography of Obama for the *Washington Post* in August 2008, he made a total botch out of the birth narrative. Had he gotten the story straight then, he might not have had a presidential biography to write four years later.

THERE IS NOT A LIBERAL AMERICA AND
A CONSERVATIVE AMERICA

"Now even as we speak, there are those who are preparing to divide us," Obama told the freshly enthralled throngs at the Boston Convention Center in August 2004. "Well, I say to them tonight, there is not a liberal America and a conservative America—there is the United States of America." Although this sounds like innocent-enough campaign folderol, Obama knew there was a liberal America, indeed a leftist America, because he had spent his life wandering its byways. For Obama and his handlers the speech represented a conscious strategy to deceive the American people and to sell Obama as something he was not, never was, and never intended to be—namely, a centrist. At almost every step of the way, the major media encouraged this deception.

Dr. John Drew saw the unedited Obama up close. He was the one friend of Obama's from Occidental College with useful information whom Maraniss did not interview. Drew had founded a Marxist-Socialist student group on the Occidental campus two years before Obama arrived. He met the future president during Obama's sophomore year through his girlfriend Caroline Boss, a.k.a. "Regina." Everything Obama told Drew during a nightlong bull session, Drew remembers, "was consistent with Marxist philosophy, including the ideas that class struggle was leading to an inevitable revolution and that an elite group of revolutionaries was needed to lead the effort."

Said Drew, "I distinctly remember Obama surprising me by bringing up Frantz Fanon and colonialism. He impressed me with his knowledge of these two topics." In *Dreams*, written before he entertained national ambitions, Obama confirmed Drew's

memory. "I chose my friends carefully," he wrote. "The more politically active black students. The foreign students. The Chicanos.
The Marxist professors and structural feminists and punk-rock
performance poets." With his new friends, Obama discussed
"neocolonialism, Franz [*sic*] Fanon, Eurocentrism, and patriarchy" and flaunted his alienation. The literary influences Obama
cited include radical anti-imperialists like Fanon and Malcolm
X, communists like Langston Hughes and Richard Wright, and
fellow travelers like W. E. B. DuBois.

In *Dreams*, Obama never suggested this reading was something
of a youthful indiscretion. He found no new heroes, adopted no
new worldview. In *Audacity*, he acknowledged John Adams and
Thomas Jefferson largely to disparage them. Twice he mentions
Adams in reference to the the Alien and Sedition Acts, which he
linked with the internment of Japanese Americans and a "hundred years of lynching" as historic American evils.

From Occidental, Obama headed to Columbia University in
New York City. As Stanley Kurtz observed in his deeply researched
2011 book, *Radical-in-Chief: Barack Obama and the Untold Story
of American Socialism*, Obama had a "transformational moment"
while attending the Socialist Scholars Conference in 1983. Kurtz
documented that this was one of the two or three such conferences Obama attended in New York. In *Dreams*, Obama himself
talked about "the socialist conferences I sometimes attended at
Cooper Union." In Maraniss's book, there was no mention of
Cooper Union, and the word "socialist" was used only in reference to people like Caroline Boss and Obama's Pakistani friend
Hasan Chandoo, both of whom, Maraniss assured the reader,
were "to the left of Obama."

IT SOUNDS IN SPIRIT THAT IT'S TALKING A LITTLE BIT ABOUT MY GRANDFATHER

Although his mother and grandfather both leaned strongly to the left, the first capital-C Communist to influence Obama was his Hawaiian mentor, Frank Marshall Davis. "Here are the facts and they are indisputable," wrote the historian Paul Kengor in his insightful book *The Communist—Frank Marshall Davis: The Untold Story of Barack Obama's Mentor,* "Frank Marshall Davis was a pro-Soviet, pro-Red China, card-carrying member of [the] Communist Party (CPUSA). His Communist Party card number was 47544."

As Kengor observed, Obama dedicated 2,500 words in *Dreams* to Davis, who "surfaces repeatedly from start to finish, from Hawaii to Los Angeles to Chicago to Germany to Kenya . . . from the 1970s to the 1980s to the 1990s." Davis, in fact, played such an essential role in Obama's formation that, as David Maraniss admitted, he became "a subject of some of [Obama's] teenage poetry." Obama has had at least two poems about Davis published. "An Old Man" appeared in his prep school's literary magazine. "Pop" appeared in Occidental College's. When *Vanity Fair's* Todd Purdum showed Obama "An Old Man" in 2008, Obama responded, "That's not bad. I wrote that in high school?" He recovered quickly, adding, "It sounds in spirit that it's talking a little bit about my grandfather." No, the poem in question, the "it," was not talking about Gramps. The poet was talking about Davis. The two were that close.

Yet as crucial as Davis was to the formation of this fatherless teen, Maraniss managed to write a ten-thousand-word piece for the *Washington Post* on Obama's early years without, said Kengor, "a single mention of Davis." Davis, as they say, had some "issues."

He was not only a Communist, but also a bisexual pornographer and nude photographer. David Remnick dismissed the charges of "communist" and "pornographer" against Davis as mere noise from the "right-wing blogosphere." He preferred to introduce Davis as an "aging poet and journalist" whose relationship with Obama was of "no great ideological importance." In one of those unguarded asides that expose the progressive mind, Remnick described Stanley Dunham's introduction of his grandson to a communist pornographer with at least a fictional taste for sex with minors as "one of the more thoughtful and consequential things Stanley did in his role as surrogate grandfather."

IF I HAD SET THE SAME POLICIES THAT I HAD BACK IN THE 1980S, I WOULD BE CONSIDERED A MODERATE REPUBLICAN

In an interview with Noticias Univision 23, the network's Miami affiliate newscast, in December 2012, Obama pushed back against the accusation made in some corners of south Florida's Hispanic communities that he had socialist ambitions for America. "The truth of the matter is that my policies are so mainstream that if I had set the same policies that I had back in the 1980s, I would be considered a moderate Republican." This, of course, was a continuation of the con he had first laid on America at the 2004 convention, a con that *Newsweek*, among others, bought into when the magazine made Obama its cover boy a few months later under the headline "Seeing Purple"—meaning a blend of red state and blue.

In his 2006 book, *The Audacity of Hope*, Obama encoded the con in more than 450 pages of strategic dithering that gave new meaning to the phrase "purple prose." Although an Obama acolyte, Joel Klein of *Time* magazine admitted to having counted no fewer than fifty instances of "excruciatingly judicious on-the-one-hand-on-the-other-handedness." Klein called the pattern "so pronounced that it almost seems an obsessive-compulsive tic."

Throughout this ascent, however, there was another Obama hiding in the shadows. That Obama emerged in all its pinkish glory on an October 2008 afternoon in Holland, Ohio. There a plumber named Joe Wurzelbacher (soon to be known as Joe the Plumber) approached Obama, then on a walking tour of Wurzelbacher's neighborhood, and asked about the effects of Obama's tax policies on a small businessman. "It's not that I want to punish your success. I just want to make sure that everybody who is behind you, that they've got a chance at success, too," said Obama before adding the unwittingly honest kicker, "I think when you spread the wealth around, it's good for everybody." As Obama knew, this was not a comment a moderate Republican would have made in 1880, let alone 1980.

SUTTON'S SPOKESMAN RETRACTED THE STORY

In August 2012, a video interview surfaced that had the potential to subvert Obama's carefully crafted all-American image. Obama did not himself say word one on the subject for the simple reason that reporters chose not to ask. One or two did ask his aides, and the aides lied in response. By Corn's standards, if the president fails to correct a relevant lie, he is as guilty as the liar himself. In this case, Obama stands accused.

The story might best begin with a November 1979 syndicated column written by Vernon Jarrett, a powerful voice in the black community and the father-in-law of Obama's closest adviser, Valerie Jarrett. Vernon Jarrett began the column by asking an African

American attorney named Khalid al-Mansour about the "rumored billions of dollars" that oil-rich Arab nations were said to bestow on African American institutions. "It's not just a rumor," al-Mansour assured him. According to Jarrett, al-Mansour had been urging the rich Arab kingdoms to provide "financial help to disadvantaged students."

The fact that al-Mansour singled out Jarrett to promote a program designed to spend "$20 million per year for 10 years to aid 10,000 minority students" suggests a prior relationship. Obama also had a connection to Vernon Jarrett, who died twenty years after Obama first came to Chicago. Obama's Hawaiian mentor Frank Davis, once a prominent Chicago journalist, had taken the then–young reporter Vernon Jarrett under his wing. According to Paul Kengor, Davis and Jarrett worked together on a number of projects, most notably the communist-controlled Citizens' Committee to Aid Packinghouse Workers. It so happens, too, that Obama began his studies at Occidental College in September 1979, two months before Jarrett's column was written. In *Dreams*, Obama tells how he visited "Frank" before departing for the mainland, and Davis gave him the cynical lowdown on college life.

These seemed to be just so many loose threads until a former Manhattan borough president, Percy Sutton, tied them together in late March 2008 on a local New York City show called *Inside City Hall*. When asked about Obama by the show's host, Dominic Carter, the octogenarian Sutton casually explained that he had been "introduced to [Obama] by a friend." The friend was Dr. Khalid al-Mansour, and the introduction had taken place about twenty years prior. According to Sutton, al-Mansour was "raising money" for Obama's education and had asked him to "please write a letter in support of [Obama] . . . a young man that has applied to Harvard." Although Sutton did not specify a date, this would likely have been in 1988, when the twenty-six-year-old Obama was applying to Harvard Law School. Sutton gladly obliged.

Sutton described al-Mansour as "the principal adviser to one of the world's richest men," the Saudi prince Al-Waleed bin Talal. This was the same bin-Talal whose $10 million offer to help New York rebuild after 9/11 Mayor Rudy Giuliani rebuffed. In September 2001, Giuliani was in no mood to hear out "Israel knew" theories even from a benefactor. Like his patron, Khalid al-Mansour was no friend of Israel. In one of his typical videotaped rants, "A Little on History of Jews," he scolded the world's Ashkenazi Jews: "God gave you nothing. The children from Poland and Russia were promised nothing. But they are stealing the land the same as the Christians stole the lands from the Indians in America."

If Obama had been a Republican, someone at the station would have rushed the tape of Sutton on *Inside City Hall* to the networks before you could say "47 percent." After all, a respected black political figure had just announced that a borderline anti-Semite, backed by an ambitious Saudi billionaire, had been guiding and possibly financing Obama's career for perhaps the last twenty years. If this wasn't news, what was? No matter, the video interview stayed on the shelf for nearly six more months.

When the Sutton interview finally did surface in the conservative media, Ben Smith, then with *Politico*, reported, "Barack Obama's campaign is flatly denying a story told by former Manhattan Borough President Percy Sutton." The Obama camp denied that Obama even knew al-Mansour. After some hemming and hawing, al-Mansour rejected Sutton's account as well. "The scenario as it related to me did not happen," he reportedly told Smith.

Still, there was no denying what Sutton had said or how unambiguously he had said it. To make sure the story did not bleed from the right into the mainstream, an obscure character named Kevin Wardally, an alleged spokesman for Sutton's family, intervened. In an e-mail Wardally gave Smith all the permission he needed to *move on.* "The information Mr. Percy Sutton imparted on March 25 in a NY1 News interview regarding his connection to Barack Obama is inaccurate," wrote Wardally. "As best as our family and the Chairman's closest friends can tell, Mr. Sutton, now 86 years of age, misspoke in describing certain details and events in that television interview." Smith seemed eager to make the story go away. He was satisfied that Wardally's statement seemed "to put the story to rest for good."

Not quite. Ken Timmerman, a veteran reporter writing for the conservative web journal *NewsMax*, kept digging. The Obama camp offered no help. Obama's spokesman Ben LaBolt told Timmerman that Sutton's tale was pure "fabrication." When asked which part was fabricated, LaBolt said "all of it." Bolt elaborated, "Al Mansour doesn't know Obama. And Sutton's spokesman retracted the story. The letter, the 'payments for loans'—all of it, not true."

Timmerman contacted Sutton's personal assistant Karen Malone and questioned her about Wardally. Malone had never heard of him. After consulting Sutton's son and daughter, she "confirmed that no one knew Kevin Wardally or had authorized him to speak on behalf of the family." Timmerman then questioned Wardally himself, who now claimed a nephew of Sutton's had retained him. Given his background, Wardally made an unlikely family spokesman. In 2006, he had been mentioned in a *New York Magazine* profile as one of New York's "New New Guard" challenging the old "lions" like Sutton and Charles Rangel.

With Hillary out of the race, no newsroom in America felt compelled to follow up on Timmerman's research. At the time this story was gelling, in early September 2008, the media were doing most of their digging in Alaskan Dumpsters. Through a series of denials, lies, and slanders about Sutton's mental health, the Obama camp and its allies in the media did all within their power to make the story disappear. They were remarkably successful. When Sutton died in December 2009—"an enormous loss" said Obama—the story was buried with him.

THE PERSON I SAW YESTERDAY WAS NOT THE PERSON THAT I MET TWENTY YEARS AGO

In March 2008, Obama had to pull out the origins saga once again, this time to neutralize the fallout from the recently surfaced sermons delivered by his wild-eyed pastor, Jeremiah Wright. In his thoroughly finessed Philadelphia speech, immodestly titled "A More Perfect Union," Obama reminded those few registered voters who might somehow have forgotten, "I am the son of a black man from Kenya and a white woman from Kansas." This story of his own upbringing seared into Obama's "genetic makeup" the idea that "this nation is more than the sum of its parts—that out of many, we are truly one." The bottom line, said Obama: "I can no more disown Wright than I can disown the black community."

The speech wowed Obama's white supporters and silenced his critics. The *Philadelphia Inquirer* summed up the speech in a one-word headline: "Brilliant." The *New York Times*' Janny Scott called it "hopeful, patriotic, quintessentially American." MSNBC's Chris Matthews, his legs a-tingle, celebrated it as "worthy of Lincoln" and "the best speech on race ever given in this country." That was Obama's gift in 2008: to make a disingenuous speech defending a crazed racist pastor seem patriotic, even Lincolnesque. Of course, having an uncritical audience of media groupies did not hurt.

Obama's promise not to disown his pastor lasted just forty days and forty nights. Unfortunately for Obama, Wright kept saying what he always had been saying. After a speech at the National Press Club in late April 2008, a reporter asked Wright whether he truly believed that the government lied about inventing the HIV virus as a means of genocide against people of color. Said Wright, "I believe our government is capable of doing anything."

Obama had been attending Wright's church with some regularity for twenty years. Wright officiated at Obama's marriage to Michelle. He baptized Obama's children. Yet when faced with the fallout of the HIV quote, Obama claimed that he had never seen this side of Wright before. "The person I saw yesterday was not the person that I met twenty years ago," he said indignantly and dishonestly. Oh, no? In fact, just twenty years earlier an equally deranged sermon of Wright's moved Obama to become Christian, or something like it. That sermon, "The Audacity to Hope," featured classic Wright gems like "White folks' greed runs a world in need," a line that Obama approvingly quoted in *Dreams*. Ten years later, Obama would name his second book, more or less, after the sermon.

For the Philadelphia speech to be the best ever given on race it would have helped a good deal if it were honest. It obviously wasn't. Obama swore he never before heard the kind of "profoundly distorted" remarks that got Wright into trouble, added the usual claptrap about his Kansas roots and his racist grandma, and, of course, vowed not to "disown" his pastor. The *Los Angeles Times* headlined this new twist in the controversy with a neat little dollop of irony, "Obama Angrily Disowns Pastor."

THIS IS A GUY WHO LIVES IN MY NEIGHBORHOOD

In an April 2008 presidential debate broadcast live on ABC, the moderator, a former Clinton adviser, George Stephanopoulos, blindsided candidate Obama with a question he was not expecting from a fellow Democrat. On the "general theme of patriotism" Stephanopoulos asked Obama about his ties to Bill Ayers. "He was part of the Weather Underground in the 1970s," Stephanopoulos reminded the younger members of his audience. "They bombed the Pentagon, the Capitol, and other buildings. He's never apologized for that." He then asked Obama, "Can you explain that relationship for the voters and explain to Democrats why it won't be a problem?"

Upon gathering himself, Obama answered Stephanopoulos, "This is a guy who lives in my neighborhood. He's not somebody who I exchange ideas from [sic] on a regular basis." Obama then proceeded to hector Stephanopoulos for asking a question about a man who "engaged in detestable acts forty years ago, when I was eight years old." To suggest that this relationship somehow reflected on him and his values, huffed Obama, "doesn't make much sense."

A visibly peeved Obama thought this issue had been settled months earlier. In February of that year, an Obama adviser, David Axelrod, told the ubiquitous Ben Smith, then with *Politico*, that Obama knew Ayers because their children "attend the same school." Initially, this satisfied the incurious Smith. Later, upon learning Obama's oldest child was born eighteen years after Ayers's youngest, Smith did not retract the story. Instead, he added a circuitous "update." That was the way the media rolled in 2008.

No one in the major media made a serious inquiry into whether Obama was telling the truth about his relationship with Ayers. He was not. On the most superficial level, Obama turned eight in 1969. Ayers launched his bombing career in 1970 and did not surface from the underground until December 1980, when Obama was nineteen. At the time, according to fellow Occidental student John Drew, Obama was "a garden variety Marxist-Leninist." The surrender of Ayers and his wife, Bernardine Dohrn, was big news in 1980. Given his own sympathies, it is hard to imagine that Obama ever found Ayers's actions "detestable."

Ayers, in his 2013 book, *Public Enemy: Confessions of an Amer-*

ican Dissident, spoke about his relationship with Obama, but not honestly. "We lived a few blocks apart, and he and I had sat on a couple of nonprofit boards together. So?" So, instead of talking at length about their shared time on the board of the small-potato Woods Fund, Ayers should have talked about Bill and Barry's excellent adventure, the Chicago Annenberg Challenge (CAC), an organization Ayers cofounded with a fellow small-c commie, Mike Klonsky. The Annenberg Foundation had breathed the CAC to life with a $50 million grant, to be matched by $100 million from other sources. The money was to fund educational reform projects.

In 1995, Ayers plucked Obama from obscurity to chair this mega–slush fund. In 2008, the Obama camp felt the need to lie about this relationship. "Ayers had nothing to do with Obama's recruitment to the Board," said an Obama spokesman at the time. But *National Review*'s Stanley Kurtz shredded that lie, and even the Obama-friendly biographer David Remnick conceded, "Ayers helped bring Obama onto the Annenberg board." In his book *Public Enemy*, Ayers avoided lying about the CAC by not talking about it at all.

WHAT THAT BILL ALSO WAS DOING WAS TRYING TO UNDERMINE *ROE V. WADE*

Despite his consistent 100 percent ratings from NARAL Pro-Choice America, candidate Barack Obama portrayed himself as the "moderate" in the abortion debate. This ongoing deception required all manner of lies, omissions, and evasions to sustain. Particularly difficult to explain away was his solitary vote in the Illinois state senate against the Born-Alive Infants Protection Act, a vote that undermined any claim to moderation on the issue of abortion. Obama knew this. So he did what he invariably did when threatened with exposure. He abandoned the truth.

On the campaign trail in 2008, Obama swore repeatedly that he would have endorsed a federal version of the Born-Alive Infants Protection Act that had passed the US Senate unanimously in 2002. "That was not the bill that was presented at the state level," Obama protested during an interview on the Christian Broadcasting Network in 2008. "What that [state] bill also was doing was trying to undermine Roe vs. Wade." This was one wolf ticket that the *Washington Post*'s fact checker Josh Hicks wasn't about to buy. "From what we can tell, Obama misrepresented the facts during this interview," wrote Hicks. "The 2003 bill addressed his concerns about undermining *Roe v. Wade*, and it matched the federal legislation that he supported virtually word for word."

This was a political lie, routine for Obama. At the February 2014 prayer breakfast, he reached for the heavens and assuredly offended everyone who has safely made it there. "We believe that each of us is 'wonderfully made' in the image of God. We, therefore, believe in the inherent dignity of every human being— dignity that no earthly power can take away," said Obama with faux piety. "[F]or the killing of the innocent is never fulfilling God's will; in fact, it's the ultimate betrayal of God's will." Lest anyone suspect a change of heart, Obama was talking here about terrorism.

IT BEHOOVES A PRESIDENT—AND BENEFITS OUR DEMOCRACY—TO FIND MODERATE NOMINEES

Among the more appealing claims in *The Audacity of Hope* is Obama's professed affection for moderate nominees. Although Obama was referring specifically to judges, he implied that seeking moderate nominees who could muster bipartisan support was a good idea in general. In practice, however, Obama has filled a score or more of high-level positions with ideologues sufficiently radical they could not have been elected statewide anywhere east of Rhode Island.

Among the least moderate of Obama's prominent appointments was the attorney general–designee, Eric Holder, a Democratic perennial. When last seen around the White House, Holder was helping to stage-manage Bill Clinton's pardon of the fugitive billionaire Marc Rich. So deep was Holder in the muck of "Pardongate" that even the *New York Times* called it a "notable blemish" on his career. In one of its occasional nods to fairness, the *Times* allowed Representative Lamar Smith of Texas, then the ranking Republican on the House Judiciary Committee, to point out the obvious. "Marc Rich was a fugitive for nearly two decades, wanted by the federal government for fraud and tax evasion," said Smith. "If a Republican official had engaged in this kind of activity, he would never receive Senate confirmation."

The fact that Holder had serious baggage did not necessarily make him an ideologue. That distinction Holder would earn through his own initiative. This initiative was already on display in 1995, when as a US attorney sworn to defend the Constitution, he said, "We just have to . . . really brainwash people into thinking about guns in a vastly different way." As attorney general, starting with his suppression of the New Black Panther voter intimidation case—more on this later—and moving on through to the Department of Justice's intervention in the George Zimmerman case, Holder consistently made justice take a backseat to race.

This was never more evident than during Holder's appearance at Al Sharpton's National Action Network conference in New York in April 2014. That Holder appeared at the behest of Sharpton was troubling enough. This was the same Sharpton who mocked the work of "Socrates and them Greek homos"; the same Sharpton who instigated the lethal Crown Heights pogrom with the rallying cry, "If Jews want to get it on, tell them to pin their yarmulkes back and come over to my house"; the same unrepentant Sharpton who launched his public career with the racially divisive Tawana Brawley hoax. The day before his appearance, Holder had endured a tough but civil grilling at the hand of House Republicans. At Sharpton's conference, Holder dog-whistled his discontent with an ahistorical, race-baiting outburst, "What attorney general has ever had to deal with that kind of treatment? What president has ever had to deal with that kind of treatment?"

Holder was merely the most obvious of Obama's ideologues, and hardly the most hard-core. Compared with Obama's "green jobs" czar, Van Jones, Eric Holder was Ted Cruz. In September 2009, Jones's colorful past, which was actually quite recent, caught up with him and led to his forced resignation. As a young man, Jones had been active with Standing Together to Organize a Revolutionary Movement (STORM), a radical group with Marxist roots, and had advocated on behalf of the conspicuously guilty cop-killer Mumia Abu-Jamal. "I met all these young radical people of color—I mean really radical: communists and anarchists," Jones told the *East Bay Express* about his experiences while still a Yale law student. "And it was, like, 'This is what I need to be a part of.' I spent the next ten years of my life working with a lot of those people I met in jail, trying to be a revolutionary."

By his own calculation, Jones continued to play revolutionary until at least 2002. And it wasn't as though he changed course thereafter. As recently as 2004—just four years before the newly elected president tagged him—Jones had signed a "truther" petition demanding "immediate inquiry into evidence that suggests high-level government officials may have deliberately allowed the September 11th attacks to occur." Given the president's professed affection for "moderate" appointments, one would think that easily Googled words like "revolutionary," "jail," and "truther" would have set off some alarms at the White House staffing office—but that presumes that the staff took Obama's campaign promises more seriously than their boss did.

CHAPTER 4

THE GENIUS

n 2008, the people behind the Obama campaign machine likely believed what they were saying when they encouraged the faithful to "get out the vote and keep talking to others about the genius of Barack Obama." The Democrats had nominated smart people before—the professorial Woodrow Wilson, the "egghead" Adlai Stevenson, the Pulitzer Prize–winning author John Kennedy, the brilliant Bill Clinton, the wonkish Al Gore, but now, finally, they had a certified genius. As the historian Michael Beschloss put it, Obama was "probably the smartest guy ever to become president."

Everything seemed to point in that direction. After all, Obama was smart enough to graduate from Columbia University and to get into Harvard Law School. There, he awed the legal superstar Lawrence Tribe with his "stunning combination of analytical brilliance and personal charisma." At Harvard, Obama not only made the *Harvard Law Review* but was elected its president. The University of Chicago promptly recruited him to teach and write. In 1995, he published *Dreams from My Father*, a book Joe Klein of *Time* magazine called "the best-written memoir ever produced by an American politician." Even conservatives like Charles

Krauthammer called his 2004 convention speech "brilliant." That speech paved the way to an easy win in the Illinois race for the US Senate, but the US Senate could not hold Obama's attention. "The job was too small for him," wrote his biographer David Remnick.

The always observant Shelby Steele summed up the phenomenon, writing, "Blacks like Obama, who show merit where mediocrity is expected, enjoy a kind of reverse stigma, a slightly inflated reputation for 'freshness' and excellence because they defy expectations." Writing in 2007, however, Steele did not yet sense how hugely inflated was Obama's "merit."

HE'S JUST TOO TALENTED TO DO WHAT ORDINARY PEOPLE DO

"I think Barack knew that he had God-given talents that were extraordinary," Obama's most intimate adviser, Valerie Jarrett, told David Remnick. "He's been bored to death his whole life. He's just too talented to do what ordinary people do." As this quote suggests, Obama's insiders, with his tacit consent, have consciously created and sustained the myth of "the genius of Barack Obama." As the story has been told and retold, their man was not just bright but gifted beyond the reach of mere mortals. Not since the Piltdown Man, however, has so much been meaning been ascribed to one body on so little evidence.

"I heard he was a terrible student, terrible. How does a bad student go to Columbia and then to Harvard?" the inimitable Donald Trump told the Associated Press in April 2011. "Let him show his records." The Obama camp refused Trump's request. In fact, the Obama people have been declining to share Obama's records since their man first emerged on the national scene in 2004.

The sealing of Obama's grades, SAT scores, and LSAT scores fits a pattern. Among the many of Obama's records still not available are his baptism records, his Noelani Elementary School (Hawaii) records, his Punahou School financial aid or school records, his Occidental College financial aid records, his Harvard Law School records, his Columbia senior thesis, his Columbia College records, his record with the Illinois State Bar Association, his files from his terms as an Illinois state senator, his list of law clients, his medical records, and his passport records.

There is a nicely symbiotic explanation as to why these records remain sealed: Obama has not wanted to show them and the media have not wanted to see them. In late October 2007, when Obama was still very much an underdog, he shocked the friendly editors at the *New York Times* when "he declined repeated requests to talk about his New York years, release his Columbia transcript or identify even a single fellow student, co-worker, roommate or friend from those years." The *Times* never followed up. Neither did other major media organizations. Those who did question the absence of information were ridiculed. For other presidents, reporters and biographers filled those holes. For the transcendent Obama, the job was left to "conspiracy theorists."

There is little mystery about the academic performance of Obama's predecessors. George W. Bush, the man who inspired the bumper sticker "A Village in Texas Is Missing Its Idiot" released his transcripts. Although not stellar, his combined 1206 SAT score was at least above average. His undergraduate grades at Yale were equally unmemorable, but then again, no one campaigned on the "genius of George Bush."

David Maraniss put some effort into finding and reviewing the grades of Obama's mother in Washington (a 3.35 GPA in high school) and of his father in Kenya. He even discussed the grades and test scores of Obama's friend Hasan Chandoo in Pakistan, but as to Obama's records from Hawaii, Los Angeles, or New York, he shared only Obama's self-reported B+ average at Occidental.

The biographer David Remnick did some digging into Obama's academics, but not much. Obama apparently was an "unspectacular" student in his two years at Columbia and at every stop before that going back to grade school. A Northwestern University professor who wrote a letter of reference for Obama reinforced the point, telling Remnick, "I don't think [Obama] did too well in college." A Columbia graduation program from 1983 showed Obama graduating but without honors of any sort. As to his LSAT scores, they remain as tightly guarded as Iran's nuclear secrets.

Academically, in fact, Obama is the classic turtle on a fence post. The faithful may believe he climbed up that post, but Obama knows otherwise. In a rare honest moment at Harvard, he shared the secret that his followers refuse to acknowledge. Yes, as he explained in a letter to the *Harvard Law Record*, he was "someone who has undoubtedly benefited from affirmative action programs during my academic career, and as someone who may have benefited from the Law Review's affirmative action policy." Obama could not claim cultural deprivation as a reason for either his lackluster grades or his need for affirmative action. Unlike many young black men, he could tell port from starboard and knew how to pronounce "arugula."

I'VE WRITTEN TWO BOOKS. I ACTUALLY WROTE THEM MYSELF.

"Whatever else people expect from a politician," wrote Oona King in her *London Times* review of *Dreams from My Father*, "it's not usually a beautifully written personal memoir steeped in honesty." Two problems: one, *Dreams* was steeped in something, but it wasn't honesty; second, the beautifully written parts were not necessarily Obama's. Yet implicit in every review of the book has been the assumption that Obama, unlike other politicians, was able to write his memoir himself.

The hard evidence has always suggested otherwise. As a senior at Columbia, Obama wrote his first published article for a university publication called the *Sundial*. This article, "Breaking the War Mentality," was Obama's literary baseline. It captured all his stylistic tics: the random use of commas, the tortured sentence structure, the awkward participles, the inept word selection, and especially the misaligned nouns and verbs. Most of these flaws Obama repeated in a 1988 essay, "Why Organize," and in the previously cited 1990 letter on affirmative action that he wrote to the *Harvard Law Record*. These and his perfunctory columns in the *Hyde Park Herald* were the only prose pieces that bore his name before *Dreams*. Although David Maraniss dispelled many of Obama's myths, he failed to address the most potentially revealing evidence, namely that Obama did not write his books by himself.

More troubling still, Maraniss or someone in the editorial chain corrupted the evidence to preserve the illusion of Obama's literary genius. The one sentence from the clunky *Sundial* article quoted in Maraniss's book read as follows (italics added): "But the *states* of war—the sounds and chill, the dead bodies—*are* remote and far removed." That is not the original wording. The original read: "But the *taste* of war—the sounds and chill, the dead bodies—*are* remote and far removed." This was one of a jaw-dropping five sentences in Obama's eighteen-hundred-word essay in which the noun and verb did not agree.

Whether Maraniss intentionally covered for Obama remains unknown, but he certainly had the motive to do so. In the book and in postrelease interviews he defended Obama's literary reputation as earnestly as Hillary defended Bill's fidelity. When David Weigel of *Slate* raised the possibility that Obama had major help with his books, Maraniss responded contemptuously, "It is preposterous on its face, utterly made of whole cloth." With his fellow writers watching his back, Obama moved from tacitly accepting false praise into consciously lying about his own accomplishments. He did this most dramatically on the campaign trail in the summer of 2008 when he told an excited crowd of Virginia schoolteachers, "I've written two books. I actually wrote them myself." He added "actually" to distinguish himself from John McCain and other Republicans, presumably too dumb to write their own.

This author has made the case as early as September 2008 that Obama had considerable help crafting *Dreams*, almost assuredly from his friend and mentor Bill Ayers. This assertion rattled the Obama faithful for two reasons: the most salient being that Obama's myth of genius hinged on his unique authorship of *Dreams*; the second being that association with the tainted radical Ayers would have compromised Obama's 2008 campaign identity as some species of moderate. Rather than revisiting the Ayers issue, one may benefit from a review of Obama's involvement in the writing of his second book, *The Audacity of Hope*, which was published in October 2006, two years after Obama was elected to the Senate. Here, the evidence for outside help is even stronger than it is for *Dreams from My Father*, and if Obama had help writing either book, he lied shamelessly to the Virginia schoolteachers.

In his much-discussed January 2014 *New Yorker* article titled "Going the Distance," David Remnick raised the question of how much publishers might pay Obama for writing his postpresidential memoir. One agent suggested an advance somewhere between $17 million and $20 million. What Remnick did not ask was who would write this putative memoir. Remnick knows there was some controversy about Obama's writing skills. In his biography of Obama, *The Bridge*, Remnick scolded this author—and Rush Limbaugh by extension—for daring to suggest that Ayers helped Obama with *Dreams*. As a progressive feel-good activity, it should be noted, imputing racism to those who live west of Tenth Avenue ranks right up there with eating organic and watching *Law & Order.* True to type, Remnick called Limbaugh's entertainment of my thesis "racist" and insisted that our collective "libel about Obama's memoir—the denial of literacy, the denial of authorship—had a particularly ugly pedigree."

It was Remnick himself, however, who undercut Obama's claim to the unique authorship of *Audacity.* Obama had roughly an eighteen-month window to write what would prove to be a 431-page book, but, as Remnick noted in *The Bridge,* "He procrastinated for a long time." It is understandable why. Obama's workdays were packed, in his own retelling, with "committee markups, votes, caucus lunches, floor statements, speeches, photos with interns, evening fund-raisers, returning phone calls, writing correspondence, reviewing legislation, drafting op-eds, recording podcasts, receiving policy briefings, hosting constituent coffees, and attending an endless series of meetings." To complete the project, Remnick estimated that Obama had to write "nearly a chapter a week." The chapters are on average close to fifty pages long.

A talented pro with no conflicts would have a difficult time making this deadline. An amateur with an absurdly busy schedule and a Luddite approach to writing could not get close. "I would work off an outline—certain themes or stories that I wanted to tell—and get them down in longhand on a yellow pad," he would later tell Daphne Durham of Amazon. "Then I'd edit while typing in what I'd written." As to how he found the time, Obama told Dunham, "I usually wrote at night after my Senate day was over, and after my family was asleep—from 9:30 p.m. or so until 1 a.m." In *The Bridge,* Remnick confirmed this scenario. He quoted a person known only as an "aide" to explain that Obama "was punching the clock during the day and then coming alive at night to write the book."

In her review of *Audacity,* the *New York Times'* Michiko Kakutani described the book "as much more of a political document. Portions of the volume read like outtakes from a stump speech."

These passages sounded like "outtakes from a stump speech" precisely because they were outtakes from a stump speech. At least thirty-eight passages from speeches Obama delivered in 2005 or 2006 appear virtually word for word as ordinary text in *Audacity*. Here is one example from a speech Obama gave on October 25, 2005:

> *Those who work in the field know what reforms really work: a more challenging and rigorous curriculum with emphasis on math, science, and literacy skills. Longer hours and more days to give kids the time and attention they need to learn.*

Here is the parallel excerpt from *Audacity*:

> *And in fact we already have hard evidence of reforms that work: a more challenging and rigorous curriculum with emphasis on math, science, and literacy skills; longer hours and more days to give children the time and sustained attention they need to learn.*

The thirty-seven additional cribbed passages prove only that whoever wrote Obama's speeches wrote large sections of *Audacity*, perhaps all of it, and this was an issue only if someone other than Obama wrote his speeches. Someone did. The British author Jonathan Raban, who had called Obama "the best writer to occupy the White House since Lincoln," was "disconcerted" to learn that Obama worked with the twentysomething speechwriter Jon Favreau on his 2009 inaugural address. The Obama of Raban's imagination did not need speechwriters, but, in fact, Obama had been relying on Favreau since the convention in 2004.

Bill Ayers was not impressed with the results. In March 2011, he gave a talk at Montclair State University in New Jersey. When an audience member asked him to comment on *Dreams*, Ayers spoke first about *Audacity*. "The second one was more of a political hack book," he said. He then added, "But the first book's quite good. Did you know I wrote it?" On multiple occasions, Ayers has taken credit for *Dreams* with a playful bit of double irony. That was what got the audience's attention at Montclair. What was overlooked was his suggestion that *Audacity* had a different and lesser author. In this regard, he was right.

One Republican who voiced his suspicions about *Audacity* was a former adviser to President Bush, Karl Rove. He told of running into Obama soon after *Audacity* was published. "Hey, I understand you got me in your book," said Rove. "I don't think so," Obama replied. Rove continued, "I think you got me in your book saying, 'We're a Christian nation.'" Said Obama, "Where'd I say that?" Rove showed him.

I WAS A CONSTITUTIONAL LAW PROFESSOR

"I was a constitutional law professor," Obama told his supporters at a March 2007 fund-raiser, "which means unlike the current president I actually respect the Constitution." This one-sentence non sequitur contained three specific falsehoods. The one to be addressed here is the most superficial of the three: Obama's claim to be a law professor. As the evidence shows, he seriously—and knowingly—exaggerated his status at the University of Chicago Law School, and he did so to secure an advantage, namely to reinforce his status as an intellectual.

In fact, Obama was a senior instructor at the university. Although the law school administration has attempted to finesse the difference between instructor and professor, anyone who has spent time in a faculty lounge knows how wide the gap yawns. It is like pitching for the New York Yankees or pitching for their

Trenton farm team. The same executive may sign the paychecks, but no one puts the Trenton pitcher on a Wheaties box—and no one knows this better than the Trenton pitcher himself.

In an April 2009 op-ed in the *Washington Post*, Daryl Owen casually referred to Obama as a "constitutional scholar," and the designation passed unnoticed. Others had done the same, and the White House had failed to correct them. But a scholar Obama was not, at least not in any meaningful sense of the word. Jodi Kantor, who would later write a biography of Obama'a father, conceded as much in a July 2008 puff piece in the *New York Times*. "While most colleagues published by the pound," wrote Kantor, "[Obama] never completed a single work of legal scholarship." Kantor reported that the University of Chicago Law School gave Obama a fellowship based on "little more" than the editing suggestions he made on a particular article. Wittingly or not, she led the very next paragraph with a more credible explanation as to why the university recruited him: "The school had almost no black faculty members, a special embarrassment given its location on the South Side."

Despite his stunning failure to write a single journal article either at Harvard or in the ten years he taught at the University of Chicago Law School, Obama was given an offer by the law school's dean that was clearly an extension of the affirmative action largesse that eased Obama's ascent at almost every stage. According to Kantor, the offer included tenure upon hiring; a salary in excess of the sixty thousand dollars he was paid as an instructor; and a job for Michelle, then his fiancée, as the director of the legal clinic. The dean made this offer after Obama's humiliating congressional run against the former Black Panther Bobby Rush in 2000, when his political prospects were slight and his indebtedness was substantial, and still he turned it down. Had Obama accepted, he would have had to stop posing as a legal scholar and actually become one.

I FACE THIS CHALLENGE WITH PROFOUND HUMILITY

By the time he won the Minnesota primary in June 2008 and with it the Democratic nomination, Obama seemed so convinced of his own genius that he now saw himself as having X-Men-size powers. "I am absolutely certain that generations from now," said Obama to the enthusiastic masses, "we will be able to look back and tell our children that this was the moment when we began to provide care for the sick and good jobs to the jobless; this was the moment when the rise of the oceans began to slow and our planet began to heal; this was the moment when we ended a war and secured our nation and restored our image as the last, best hope on earth."

The fact that none of this happened does not make these promises lies per se. It had to be a head-turning experience to have even one major TV network ask, "Is Barack Obama the Messiah?" By this time Obama likely believed what he was saying, even the nonsense about the planet and the oceans. The lie had come a sentence earlier, when Obama introduced this passage with the phrase "I face this challenge with profound humility." Humility? Profound humility at that? One wonders what super feats Obama promised when feeling boastful.

Bottom line: The myth of Obama's genius, a myth based in large part on his imagined literary talent, got the man elected president. If there has ever been a greater hoax pulled in the history of American politics, one is hard-pressed to identify it. The only useful precedent for Obama's ascendancy is fictional. In his prescient 1971 satire, *Being There*, Jerzy Kosinski described how the amiable emptiness of a simpleton gardener confused his followers into thinking him brilliant, but even Kosinski could not imagine Chauncey Gardiner ascending any higher than the vice presidency.

THE GENIUS?

Although a political gaffe rarely qualifies as a lie, Barack Obama's propensity for gaffes of all sorts puts an even more definitive lie to the self-enhanced rumors of his genius. Granted, in the era of social media a president's words are subject to more scrutiny than in the past, but even if we control for added exposure, Obama has blundered enough to carve out a spot on the Rushmore of the presidentially tongue-tied.

The gaffes fall into a variety of categories. The routine gaffes are the kind anyone who speaks as much a president could make. It is just that when the president is a genius, a gaffe creates a cognitive dissonance that can shake the faith of the faithful. "Why have we not condemned Israel?" asked a generally supportive female student at a Tampa forum in January 2010. This was the kind of question that had the potential to divide his fan base, and the president was surprisingly unprepared to answer it. Off the teleprompter, he stuttered a little, took an awkward stab at humor, and then offered up an answer that left his audience confused and the "signer" for the deaf totally flummoxed. Said Obama, "The Middle East is obviously an issue that has plagued the region for centuries."

As is well understood even by his allies, Obama has no gift for impromptu speech. In May 2009, Vice President Joe Biden, who has been known to make a gaffe or two himself, quipped after his teleprompter fell down during a commencement speech at the US Air Force Academy, "What am I gonna tell the president? I'm gonna tell him his teleprompter is broken. What will he do then?" The remark reportedly got the day's loudest cheers.

What Obama did and said when the teleprompter broke could make even a friendly audience cringe. At a campaign event in Virginia in June 2008, Obama was making an impassioned speech about the wasteful use of ER services in the treatment of childhood asthma when, suddenly, he seemed to lose his place on the teleprompter. As he signaled his distress, he stuttered badly, talked about the use of a "breathalyzer," corrected himself to say "inhalator," laughed, stuttered some more, and blamed his performance on not having had much sleep in the last forty-eight hours. The right word, by the way, is "inhaler." In March 2014, Obama shifted from his left teleprompter to his right in reading a speech about Aretha Franklin's song "Respect" and in the process spelled the word "R-S-P-C-T." The audience laughed politely, if uncomfortably. His audiences usually did. The media would never forgive former vice president Dan Quayle his irrelevant misspelling of "potato." They would barely acknowledge Obama's misspelling of the iconic "respect."

Despite his reputation as an Ivy Leaguer and a man of the world, Obama has some major holes in his education. Although he makes few, if any, gaffes about his fields of deep study—basketball and African American culture, for instance—he has obvious trouble with more routine academic fare, including basic history, geography, math, and all things military. Obama has also had little exposure to the everyday life of the average American, and this manifests itself in a number of ways, including erratic manners and an ungainly sense of humor.

When, for instance, Obama told an audience in Beaverton, Oregon, on a 2008 campaign stop, "I've now been in fifty-seven states? I think one left to go. One left to go," he left his critics wondering what he could have been thinking—or drinking. Although Dan Quayle never did say, "I was recently on a tour of Latin America, and the only regret I have was that I didn't study Latin harder in school," Barack Obama actually did say, "I don't know what the term is in Austrian, wheeling and dealing." Austrians, of course, no more speak "Austrian" than Latin Americans speak Latin. Unfortunately for America's image in the world, Obama said this in an April 2009 press conference in Strasbourg, France. In a similar vein, Obama shocked his audience in Honolulu in November 2011 by saying, "When I meet with world leaders, what's striking—whether it's in Europe or here in Asia . . ."

Obama's grasp of history, especially military history, seems, at times, no firmer than his grasp of geography. He knew sufficiently little about things military, for instance, to pronounce "Navy corpsman" as "Navy corpse-man" at the 2010 National Prayer Breakfast. On another occasion, he betrayed his unfamiliarity with the idioms of military service when he talked about the nation's "fallen heroes" and then shockingly declared, "I see many of them in the audience here today." Although not a gaffe in the classic sense, the president's failure to intuit the military's response to the high-priced return of the accused deserter Bowe Bergdahl revealed just how little he understood about the military—or about America for that matter.

On other occasions, Obama showed an odd insensitivity to issues universally understood to be serious. In May 2009, for instance, he made his first appearance on the *Tonight Show* with Jay Leno. Obama told Leno how he had taken up bowling at the White House and bowled a 129. "That's very good, Mr. President," said Leno with more than a touch of irony. "It was like Special Olympics or something," joked Obama, a line that could have ended the career of a lesser politician. Obama showed himself even more insensitive when he took his smiling, much-publicized "selfies" at a memorial service for Nelson Mandela.

Obama has also occasionally stumbled over ordinary American clichés out of a failure to understand what those clichés mean. During tense talks over the debt limit in 2011, for instance, Obama said to House Majority Leader Eric Cantor, "Don't call my bluff." Obama made the "bluff" remark to sound unyielding, but instead he just sounded ignorant. In poker, a player who bluffs pretends to have a stronger hand that he actually does. A bluff works only when the other players are convinced that he is not bluffing. The last thing a bluffer would do is to do what Obama did—announce that he is bluffing.

Although many of these previous statements were false—America, at last count, had only fifty states—Obama had nothing to gain by saying them. A second category might include false statements that Obama made to secure an advantage, but that were so sufficiently and obviously false as to be considered gaffes. In these cases, Obama may or may not have been intentionally lying, but his indifference to the truth made this distinction irrelevant.

On Friday, May 4, 2007, an F-5 tornado roared through a friendly little Kansas town called Greensburg. Before the bodies had been pulled from the rubble, Kansas's Democratic governor and future secretary of the Department of Heath and Human Services, Kathleen Sebelius, was blaming the war in Iraq for the slow response to the disaster. Her rush to judgment would have played better save for one inconvenient truth: the state and federal response was conspicuously swift and purposeful. By Monday morning, May 7, Sebelius had backed down from her Democratic National Committee–bred accusations.

Then on the campaign trail, Obama either did not learn about Sebelius's about-face or, more likely, did not care. "In case you missed it, this week, there was a tragedy in Kansas," Obama told an excited crowd in Richmond, Virginia, on May 8, "Ten thousand people died—an entire town destroyed." Minor problem here: only fifteen hundred people lived in that town, and only three thousand lived in the whole county. The actual death toll in Greensburg was *twelve*. Here, Obama showed a truly epic misunderstanding of Midwestern geography and climatology. In America, tornadoes have killed fewer than ten thousand people in the last hundred years. Worse, Obama used these preposterous numbers to bolster an already discarded lie. "Turns out that the National Guard in Kansas only had 40 percent of its equipment," Obama dissembled, "and they are having to slow down the recovery process in Kansas."

To the degree that the major media covered Obama's seeming slip, it was to blow it off. The video of him speaking, however, does not show a tired candidate making a faux pas. It shows an aspiring demagogue making a dramatic accusation. The people onstage behind Obama didn't blink at the reference to ten thousand dead. The audience did not gasp. The antiwar folks had grown so used to lying to each other that they likely did not even notice.

Although Obama's lack of military experience or even of interest in it was not a liability during the veteran-free 2008 Democratic primary, in the general election it certainly could have been. To level the battlefield against the war hero John McCain, Obama turned to his relatives. One was his grandfather, Stanley Dunham. As Obama told the story in his famed 2002 Chicago antiwar speech, Gramps had fought in Patton's army and had "heard the stories of fellow troops who first entered Auschwitz and Treblinka." Another relative was his uncle, a great-uncle actually. Speaking in New Mexico on Memorial Day in 2008, Obama made the Holocaust connection more direct, claiming, "I had a uncle who was one of the . . . who was part of the first American troops to go into Auschwitz and liberate the concentration camps." So upset was this uncle by what he had seen that he "just went into the attic, and he didn't leave the house for six months." This was the setup for the strategic point Obama hoped to make: "Now, obviously something had affected him deeply, but at the time, there just weren't the kinds of facilities to help somebody work through that kind of pain."

When reminded that Obama's mother was an only child and his father a Kenyan, the Obama camp designated his "great-uncle" as the liberator of Auschwitz. This also proved problematic in that the Soviets liberated Auschwitz. As they typically did, the media rushed to Obama's defense. The website *PolitiFact* dug deep into the records to prove that Obama's *great*-uncle, Charlie Payne, was part of the 355th Infantry Regiment that overran Ohrdruf, a work camp near Buchenwald. For *PolitiFact*, this was close enough to merit a "Mostly True."

PolitiFact, however, did not dedicate a single word to any of the three related claims at the heart of the issue. Was Payne traumatized by what he saw at Ohrdruf? Did he spend six months in the attic? And did he stay in the attic for lack of mental health care? Although the *PolitiFact* researchers spoke to Payne's son, they give no sign of having asked him about his father's state of mind. They should have. At the time, an outraged blogger explained why. "What man could speak about the horrors of Auschwitz, and somehow make it not about the millions of Jews that suffered and died in the death camps," he wrote, "but instead about how terribly hard it was for his uncle to deal with it, and how it showed that we needed better mental health care."

Obama's great-uncle was alive at the time Obama began speaking about him. Although a lifelong Democrat and a supporter of his great-nephew, he was caught off guard by Obama's comments. "I was quite surprised when the whole thing came up and Barack talked about my war experiences in Nazi Germany," he told the German newsmagazine *Der Spiegel*. "We had never talked about that before."

Obama had a reason to fictionalize his family history. To counter John McCain's strength as a war hero, Obama was trying to position himself as a champion of veterans. On the issue of mental health, he had promised to increase the budget of the Department of Veterans Affairs (VA) "and recruit and retain more mental health professionals." To personalize his concern, he seems to have exaggerated his great-uncle's mental deterioration and overstated his link to the Holocaust. In the interview with

Der Spiegel, Payne did not hint at any trauma. "Until Barack mis-spoke," he said, "I hadn't thought about any of this for a very, very long time."

More curious still, in a speech just a month afterward, Obama refuted his earlier claim that America neglected its veterans' mental health, and to make his case he once again used his own family, this time his "father." Speaking to a group of Latino public officials, Obama said, "My father served in World War II. And when he came home, he got the services that he needed. And that includes, by the way, post-traumatic stress disorder."

Not surprisingly, most pundits on the right amused themselves with the claim that Obama's father served in World War II. In that Barack Obama Senior was born on June 18, 1934, either his son misspoke or the old man was the rare Kenyan preteen to fight the Nazis. This assertion by Obama would seem to fall into the pure "gaffe" category, at least the part about his father serving in the war. He surely meant his grandfather, Stanley Dunham. But with Obama nothing is quite that sure.

On this occasion, Obama had a new and different reason to lie: he was fueling the Latinos' sense of victimization, all the better to turn them against Republicans. He did this often. In October 2010, he urged the Latinos in his Univision radio audience to think of Republicans as "our enemies" and "to punish" them by voting. On a similarly discordant note, he told a 2008 campaign crowd in Philadelphia, "If they bring a knife to the fight, we bring a gun." This was the same Obama who was preaching the gospel of civility.

In his 2008 Texas speech, Obama reminded his audience of the lack of VA facilities in the Rio Grande Valley. He linked this idea to the claim that veterans in Puerto Rico "are not getting the same services as veterans in the fifty states"—or, by implication, the kind of services his grandfather and other "Anglo" veterans received more than sixty year prior. Said Obama piously, "We're betraying what I think is a solemn pact that we make with our veterans." As Americans would soon enough see, these words proved tragically prophetic on Obama's watch. Six years after bemoaning how badly veterans were being treated, the president claimed to be "madder than hell" upon "learning" that veterans were being treated badly.

Although veterans were suffering nationwide, there was no reason to believe that Hispanic veterans were suffering more than anyone else. In fact, the VA Caribbean Healthcare System features a state-of-the-art medical center located in San Juan, with satellite clinics in Ponce, Mayagüez, Saint Thomas, Saint Croix, Arecibo, and Guayama. There is also a modern VA health care center in Harlingen at the heavily populated end of the Rio Grande Valley, one of only six in Texas. In sum, Obama appears to have exploited a very real nationwide problem for no nobler purpose than to aggravate Latino grudges and to direct them against Republicans— and then he ignored the problem for the next six years. The savvy reader may also have taken note of Obama's seemingly gratuitous reference to "fifty states." Here, Obama may have been trying to reestablish his grasp of American geography.

The third category, a "Kinsley gaffe," derives its name from the journalist Michael Kinsley, who introduced the concept. It means that a speaker "accidentally reveals something truthful about what is going on in his or her head." Some of the more playful bloggers, for instance, argued that Obama's "fifty-seven states" reference was a Kinsley gaffe—Obama having confused American states with the fifty-seven member states of the Organization of the Islamic Conference (OIC).

A textbook Kinsley gaffe occurred when Obama answered a question at an April 2010 Nuclear Security Summit with the unwittingly revealing statement, "Whether we like it or not, we remain a dominant military superpower." This remark further fueled suspicions on the right that Obama, dismayed by America's alleged imperialism, hoped to render the United States something less than a world power.

On questions economic, Obama has made any number of Kinsley gaffes, the most notorious being his previously cited remark to Joe the Plumber, "I think when you spread the wealth around, it's good for everybody." The sheer number of these remarks suggests a major gap between what Obama thinks about economic policy and what he allows himself to say. Other classics along this line include, "If you've got a business—you didn't build that. Somebody else made that happen" and "I do think at a certain point you've made enough money."

Obama made the latter comment off the teleprompter during an April 2010 speech in Quincy, Illinois. In context it is even more revealing of his collectivist mentality. "We're not, we're not trying to push financial reform because we begrudge success that's fairly earned," said the president. "I mean, I do think at a certain point you've made enough money. But, you know, part of the American way is, you know, you can just keep on making it if you're providing a good product or providing good service. We don't want people to stop, ah, fulfilling the core responsibilities of the financial system to help grow our economy." As almost any entrepreneur could have told the president, his or her responsibility is not to grow the economy. The entrepreneur's responsibility is to grow the business and provide a decent return to stakeholders.

Nor was Obama in any position to preach. In 2008, the Obamas reported an adjusted gross income of more than $2.6 million. In 2009, the family income was roughly $5.5 million. The majority of that income derived from Obama's two books, neither of which would pass any reliable smell test for "good product."

On the issue of abortion, about which he has claimed to be a moderate, Obama said more than he likely intended when he claimed in an early 2008 debate, "I've got two daughters, nine years old and six years old. I am going to teach them first of all about values and morals. But if they make a mistake, I don't want them punished with a baby." Punished? That is not the kind of language professed moderates use to describe childbirth.

Obama fueled the debate on his religious inclinations with a gaffe, Kinsley or otherwise, when he said to George Stephanopoulos on ABC's *This Week*, "You are absolutely right that John McCain has not talked about my Muslim faith." The ever-protective Stephanopoulos corrected him with a sotto voce "Christian faith," and Obama went with the correction. Then again, in referring to his grandmother as a "typical white person," Obama did nothing to reassure white Americans that he has their interests at heart. In sum, it is hard to know whose interests Obama has at heart. Obama may not even know himself. This confusion helps account for a president who stumbles in places where Americans expect him to stride.

CHAPTER 5

THE ECONOMIST

n his flattering book on the Obama presidency *The Promise: President Obama, Year One*, Jonathan Alter described a White House awash in talent. As an alleged "product of the great American postwar meritocracy," Obama did not hesitate to surround himself, said Alter, with the nation's "best credentialed, most brilliant policy mandarins." Like their new boss, however, these big brains had one major shortcoming: as Alter conceded, "Almost none of them knew what it was like to work in small business, manufacturing, real estate, or other parts of the real economy."

Further weakening Obama's posture as an economic savant was his chronic inability to manage his own family's budget. Despite a combined income well into six figures, the Obamas were perpetually in debt until *Dreams* went gold in 2004. Of course, Obama was not the first transformative economic thinker to struggle with personal finances. Karl Marx himself was forever in debt and constantly hitting up others for cash. Marx, however, did not honeymoon in Napa. Nor did he jet off to Bali to write—or try to write—a book. In debt he may have been, but Marx lived as he preached, in a perpetual state of bohemian squalor.

The Obamas, by contrast, represent a stage of American liberalism that Marx could not have imagined. The author Fred Siegel traced its genesis back to the 1920s, quoting the socialist Norman Thomas on this emerging character type: "They have no illusions but one. And that is they can live like Babbitt and think like Mencken." In other words, as David Brooks conceptualized them seventy years later, the Obamas could consume like the bourgeoisie and condescend like bohemians. They were the quintessential "bobos in paradise."

Then too, if the Obamas lived their lives in this fashion—indulgent, irresponsible, maxed out on credit—why couldn't everyone? As he took over the machinery of government in late 2008, Obama would sell America on just such a notion. That notion took the real-life form of the $862 billion (or so) American Recovery and Reinvestment Act of 2009—a.k.a. "Porkulus." Obama employed some truly spectacular falsehoods to promote this massive "stimulus." In the years that followed, Obama would spew enough economic falsehoods and fabrications to fill an entire book. He did not necessarily know them to be false. Rather, given the importance of his mission and his immunity from rebuke, he felt little need to confirm that they were true.

WE'VE GOT SHOVEL-READY PROJECTS ALL ACROSS THE COUNTRY

In December 2008, when Obama was putting his economic team together and planning his first major action with Congress, he hit upon a theme that resonated: "We've got shovel-ready projects all across the country that governors and mayors are pleading to fund. And the minute we can get those investments to the state level, jobs are going to be created."

In the days that followed, Obama and his team repeated the phrase "shovel-ready" like a sacred oath. On *Meet the Press* on December 7, 2008, Obama got more specific. "I think we can get a lot of work done fast," he told Tom Brokaw as though he meant it. "When I met with the governors, all of them have projects that are shovel ready, that are going to require us to get the money out the door, but they've already lined up the projects, and they can make them work."

On hearing Obama's promise, the taxpayer could not be faulted for envisioning teams of bronzed young workers, freed from the ranks of the jobless, laboring away in the fresh air CCC-style on needed infrastructure projects. The House and Senate may have had the same idea in mind when they passed the American Recovery and Reinvestment Act on February 13, 2009, just three weeks into Obama's presidency. Four days later, Obama signed the bill into law.

A week after that Obama addressed Congress and the nation on the state of the economy. In the speech, Obama specified that more than 90 percent of the new job openings would be in the private sector. The examples Obama cited were all infrastructure jobs—"rebuilding our roads and bridges; constructing wind turbines and solar panels; laying broadband and expanding mass transit"—but he noticeably shied away from using the phrase "shovel-ready."

A report released in late November 2009 by the Department of Transportation showed that "shovel-ready" had already lost all real meaning. Eight months after the bill was passed, less than 1 percent of the stimulus funds had been paid out. A few days later, Obama admitted as much when he told a roomful of local government officials and union reps, "The term 'shovel-ready'—let's be honest, it doesn't always live up to its billing."

Rather than acknowledging failure or even miscalculation, Obama chose to dissemble his way out of the jam. In a speech at the Brookings Institution a few days later, Obama boasted that "more than 10,000" infrastructure projects had been funded through the Recovery Act. "By design," however, he delayed their implementation. He did so for two reasons: one was that the projects would have more economic impact if spread over a two-year period; the second, and more important, was that Obama wanted "to do this right." Worried about the potential for abuse, he asked Joe Biden to make sure that "the investments were sound, the projects worthy, and the execution efficient."

Biden was just the man for the task. He proved it during the 2008 campaign. "Look, [McCain's] last-minute economic plan does nothing to tackle the number-one job facing the middle class," said Biden at a stop in Ohio, "and it happens to be, as Barack says, a three-letter word: jobs. J-O-B-S, jobs." If Biden could reduce the letters in "jobs" by 25 percent, maybe, Obama figured, he could do the same for the numbers of the jobless.

Interest group politics did not help the search for shovel-ready projects. Obama's designated chair for the Council of Economic Advisers, Christina Romer, blithely explained why in an interview she did for the transitional team on January 11, 2009. According to Romer, as she was cowriting a report on the stimulus bill, she kept hearing from women's groups. They told her, in Romer's own words, "We don't want this stimulus package to just create jobs for burly men." She cheerfully agreed. So did Obama. To show their sensitivity, White House planners built into the stimulus lots of non–shovel ready work for non-burly people, women and pajama boys both. The only thing that gesture helped build, unfortunately, was Obama's base.

In September 2010, Obama admitted to the *New York Times Magazine* that, when it comes to public works, "There's no such thing as shovel-ready projects." That much conceded, he offered no apology to the American people for misleading them. His one major regret with the stimulus bill, he told the *Times*, was not getting the Republicans to take ownership of the bill's tax breaks so they could share in the blame.

By June 2011, Obama was able to see the humor in this pricey game of bait and switch. At a meeting with his jobs council, a member explained the inevitable delays on any infrastructure project. "I'm sure that when you implemented the Recovery Act your staff briefed you on many of these challenges," the fellow said. He expected an answer in the affirmative. He did not get one. Replied Obama with a smile, "Shovel-ready was not as . . . uh . . . shovel-ready as we expected." The council members burst out laughing. The unemployment rate at the time stood at 9.1 percent. The jobless likely did not get the joke.

OVER THE NEXT TWO YEARS, THIS PLAN WILL SAVE OR CREATE 3.5 MILLION JOBS

Among the more memorable boasts in President Obama's February 2009 address to the nation was his claim that the stimulus plan would "save or create 3.5 million jobs" over the subsequent two years. Although the projection proved false, Obama's boast represented less an intentional lie than further evidence of his indifference to the truth. Protecting him from a true accounting on job projections, he had to know, was the elusive word "save."

The president would take advantage of that wiggle room. In February 2010, on the first anniversary of the stimulus bill's signing, Obama claimed, "The Recovery Act is responsible for the jobs of about two million Americans who would otherwise be unemployed." He added that the act would "save or create" another 1.5 million jobs in 2010, rounding out—voilà!—to a perfect 3.5 million total. Unfortunately for Obama, the Department of Labor kept sets of hard statistics that tested his talent for finessing the truth.

According to the Department of Labor, the economy lost more than three million jobs between February 2009 and February 2010. In February 2009, there were 141,640,000 employed Americans, seasonally adjusted. In February 2010, that number had plunged to 138,599,000. Nor was the situation about to improve. By February 2011, the total of those employed had increased only to 139,422,000, still more than two million below the February 2009 figure. Even more troubling, the potential workforce had grown by nearly four million in that same period. Typically, job growth tracks with population growth. Not this time.

Despite the transparent shortfall, the media were able to find economists who considered the stimulus something other than a total failure. On the occasion of the Recovery Act's first anniversary, *PolitiFact* labored to explain how liberal economists— *PolitiFact* excluded conservatives from the summary—were able to identify a million jobs created or saved in year one and another million projected for year two. "These numbers are based on a 'counterfactual' study that is an estimate subject to some professional disagreement," said the much too generous *PolitiFact*. "And within this broad range of expert opinion, Obama chose a number on the high side. The numbers could easily be less than what he suggests." The fact that these economists found only half of the two million jobs Obama claimed for year one allowed *PolitiFact* to judge his claim to be "half true."

To be fair to Obama, he never did promise, as accused, that the unemployment rate would stay below 8 percent if the stimulus bill was passed. That number came from the January 2009 report co-written by Romer. *PolitiFact*, however, erred in judging Mitt Romney's 2012 charge that Obama promised to hold unemployment below 8 percent "mostly false." Although Obama did not make that promise himself, he let the report do the promising for him. And that report was about as objective as a Solyndra prospectus. As Romer admitted, she prepared it knowing Obama "wanted some evidence" that the stimulus would work as he promised, specifically that it would create or save more than three million jobs. The report confirmed his expectations—almost exactly.

Romer herself was a true believer. She insisted something dramatic had to be done because "today's [unemployment] number of 7.2 percent is terrible." With the stimulus working its magic, that number reached 10.0 percent eight months after the president signed it into law. The unemployment rate would not drop below 8.0 percent until September 2012—mirabile dictu!—just in time for the election. It would not be until November 2013 that the unemployment rate dipped below Romer's "terrible" 7.2 percent. And even then, the numbers were suspect.

A more meaningful gauge than unemployment rates—and much more reliable than administrative claims of jobs "created or saved"—is workforce participation. According to the US Bureau of Labor Statistics, when the stimulus bill passed in February 2009, 65.8 percent of the civilian labor force held jobs. That number slumped gradually for the next five years, hitting bottom in December 2013 at 62.8 percent before ticking slightly upward in early 2014.

During a real recovery, like President Ronald Reagan's, these numbers move in the opposite direction. Reagan fought the recession he inherited by cutting taxes. On July 29, 1981, the Senate voted 89–11 to support his tax cut plan. Forty-eight House Democrats defied their speaker and crossed the aisle to pass the bill there as well. At the time, 63.8 percent of eligible workers were employed. The numbers moved up incrementally from that point, reaching 65.7 five years later and 66.5 percent during Reagan's last month in office. Reagan never worried about whether jobs were shovel-ready. He understood that the work of creating jobs was not the government's, let alone his, but that of the nation's employers. They would create the jobs that made economic sense, even if only burly men could do them.

THE PRIVATE SECTOR IS DOING FINE

"What about the Republicans saying that you're blaming the Europeans for the failure of your own policies?" Obama was asked at a June 2012 press conference. "The truth of the matter is that, as I said, we've created 4.3 million jobs over the last two—27 months; over 800,000 just this year alone," said Obama. Then he added the summary statement that caught everyone's attention, "The private sector is doing fine."

This statement varied so conspicuously from the true state of affairs that many considered it just another gaffe. At the time Obama said this, the official unemployment rate stood at 8.2 percent. According to the Bureau of Labor Statistics, more than 6.5 million adults who wanted work could not find it, nearly a million more than when Obama took office. And the unemployment rate for those under age twenty stood at nearly 24 percent. Otherwise, the private sector was doing swimmingly.

YOU KNOW, THE DAYS OF JUST PORK COMING OUT OF CONGRESS AS A STRATEGY, THOSE DAYS ARE OVER

On that same edition of *Meet the Press* in which Obama talked about shovel-ready jobs, he also addressed the issue of pork. He vowed that the "old, traditional politics-first way" of choosing stimulus projects was history. His "first-rate economic team" was going about its work methodically, rationally, objectively. "You know, the days of just pork coming out of Congress as a strategy," he told Brokaw, "those days are over."

The White House's pork-free diet barely outlasted the inauguration. Weeks later, in February 2009, the *Washington Post* reported with something like wonder that the stimulus bill was not at all free of targeted pork "despite vows by President Obama that the legislation would be kept clear of pet projects." Five years after the passage of the bill, Elizabeth Harrington of the *Washington Free Beacon* assembled a list of the ten "most outrageous" stimulus projects. It was a tough competition. The winning entries included:

- $1.3 million for signs saying "Project Funded by Recovery and Reinvestment Act."
- $152,000 for a study to prepare lesbians for adoptive parenthood.
- $600,000 to distribute trees in a wealthy Denver neighborhood.
- $384,949 given to Yale University for a study entitled "Sexual Conflict, Social Behavior, and the Evolution of Waterfowl Genitalia."
- $1.2 million for a study of erectile dysfunction in fat San Francisco–area men.
- $100,000 to a Che Guevara–inspired theater in Minnesota to produce "socially-conscious puppet shows."
- $389,357 to pay college students in Buffalo to record their daily malt liquor drinking and marijuana use.
- $3.4 million to build a tunnel for turtles providing "eco-passage" under a Florida road.
- $8,408 to Florida Atlantic University to test whether mice get drunk after consuming alcohol.

The *Washington Free Beacon* pulled most of this information from a report by Senator Tom Coburn of Oklahoma, "100 Stimulus Projects: A Second Opinion." Although projects like the above

deserved attention for their absurdity, others deserved it for their
duplicity, none more so than an Illinois energy project awkwardly
called FutureGen. As a senator, Obama, along with the former
governor and current federal inmate Rod Blagojevich, had lobbied
hard but unsuccessfully to secure funding for the project. Despite
those efforts, administration officials were telling the media that
to show they were "serious about keeping earmarks out," they
would not include funding for FutureGen in the stimulus bill. As
one Obama adviser told a *Politico* reporter, "We don't want any
room for Republicans or Democrats to put earmarks in—even to
worthy projects."

The reporter was much too trusting. All the while Obama was
promising a pork-free bill, his transition team was meeting with
FutureGen's industry partners. Into this mammoth, hastily conceived bill, Illinois senator Dick Durbin slipped a line item to
fund "near zero-emissions power plant(s)." As Coburn observed,
"Everyone familiar with the subject knew that there was only one
shovel-ready project in the entire country that met the criteria for
'fossil energy research and development' listed in the bill." That
just happened to be the FutureGen plant in Mattoon, Illinois. In
the ensuing months, the plant received enough taxpayer money
to pay for more than ten thousand drunken mice studies, a cool
$1.073 billion. This nifty little flimflam did not raise red flags in
America's newsrooms. It scarcely raised an eyebrow.

AND WHEN I'M PRESIDENT, I WILL GO LINE BY LINE TO MAKE SURE THAT WE ARE NOT SPENDING MONEY UNWISELY

"I'm proud that we passed the recovery plan free of earmarks,"
President Obama told Congress in February 2009, "and I want

to pass a budget next year that ensures that each dollar we spend reflects only our most important national priorities." Senator Coburn did not quite agree. In his report on pork, he described the FutureGen project as "the largest earmark in the history of pork-barreling." From Obama's perspective, the fact that Illinois senator Durbin did not claim the project as his own made it something other than an earmark—something sneakier actually, as earmarks come with a certain accountability.

Just a month into the presidency, Obama was less concerned about violating a campaign pledge than about being seen violating one, especially on earmarks. The very word sounded tawdry and unpleasant. In his run for the presidency, he had been quick to denounce them. "The truth is, our earmark system in Washington is fraught with abuse," he told a crowd in Green Bay, Wisconsin, in September 2008. "It badly needs reform—which is why I didn't request a single earmark last year, why I've released all my previous requests for the public to see, and why I've pledged to slash earmarks by more than half when I am president of the United States of America." Four days later, at his first debate with John McCain, Obama redoubled his promise. "Absolutely, we need earmark reform," he huffed. "And when I'm president, I will go line by line to make sure that we are not spending money unwisely."

Just a week or so after Obama signed the stimulus bill, the House passed a pork-heavy $410 billion omnibus spending bill, and he got his chance to go line by line slashing earmarks. According to the *New York Times*, the bill contained more than 8,500 earmarks and reflected "Democratic priorities." These pet projects included $1.7 million for a honeybee lab in Texas, $870,000 for red wolf breeding in North Carolina, $200,000 for gang member tattoo removal in California, and, speaking of pork, $1.8 million for swine odor and manure management in Iowa. Since the bill had been largely assembled while Obama was still a US senator, he got to slip in $7.7 million for the Carl D. Perkins Career and Technical Education Program.

Nor was Obama the only member of his administration to see his or her chosen projects rewarded. Several recent members of Congress including Joe Biden, Rahm Emanuel, and Hillary Clinton, and at least three more cabinet members collectively accounted for nearly $500 million in earmarked projects. With the economy apparently needing more stimulus, Obama decided to holster his veto pen. As a result, the California gangbangers got to erase their tattoos and the Iowa pigs got to gussy up. To help suppress what Tennessee Williams's Big Daddy might have called the "powerful and obnoxious odor of mendacity," House Democrats killed a Republican proposal that would have empowered the House Committee on Ethics to investigate links between political donations and earmarks. Obama signed the omnibus spending bill into law on March 11, 2009, with scarcely a slash mark through it. The age of transparency was in full swing.

WE'RE RUNNING OUT OF PLACES TO DRILL ON LAND

Like so many of his Democratic colleagues, Obama cottoned to projects like the doomed solar plant Solyndra—"a testament to American ingenuity and dynamism" said Obama a bit prematurely—because traditional sources of energy were supposedly being exhausted. In a June 2010 speech regarding the BP oil spill in the Gulf of Mexico, Obama reminded America that "part of the reason oil companies are drilling a mile beneath the surface of the ocean—because we're running out of places to drill on land and in shallow water." In scolding America for its dependence on cheap oil he rolled out all the self-hating green clichés: we consume ten times more than we produce; we need to end our "century-long addiction to fossil fuels; oil is a finite resource." Implicit in the speech was the idea that consuming oil was in itself an evil like, say, shooting heroin or watching Fox News. After listing some alternative approaches to energy production, Obama claimed to be open to new ideas "as long they seriously tackle our addiction to fossil fuels."

Fast-forward two-plus years to the second presidential debate, this one moderated by CNN's Candy Crowley. "So here's what I've done since I've been president," said the anti-oil crusader, "We have increased oil production to the highest levels in sixteen years." In his turn, Romney observed that Obama had done everything he could to block the production of oil, and none of the growth had taken place on federal lands. Obama shot back, "Very little of what Governor Romney just said is true. We've opened up public lands. We're actually drilling more on public lands than in the previous administration." Added Obama, "You need an all-of-the-above strategy, and that's what we're going to do in the next four years." This led to a fiery and telling exchange:

ROMNEY   But that's not what you've done in the last four
             years. That's the problem. In the last four years,
             you cut permits and licenses on federal land and
             federal waters in half.
OBAMA: Not true, Governor Romney.
ROMNEY: So how much did you cut?
OBAMA: Not true.
ROMNEY: How much did you cut them by, then?
OBAMA: Governor, we have actually produced more oil—
ROMNEY: No, no. How much did you cut licenses and
             permits on federal land and federal waters?

Romney had Obama on the ropes. This time Crowley did not intervene. The president lapsed into some tedious detail hoping the bell or something like it would ring. It did not, and Romney kept up the attack.

ROMNEY:	No, no, I had a question and the question was how much did you cut them by?
OBAMA:	You want me to answer a question—
ROMNEY:	How much did you cut them by?
OBAMA:	I'm happy to answer the question.
ROMNEY:	All right. And it is—
OBAMA:	Production is up.
ROMNEY:	—is down.
OBAMA:	No, it isn't.
ROMNEY:	Production on government land of oil is down 14 percent.
OBAMA:	Governor—
ROMNEY:	And production on gas—
[*Crosstalk*]	
OBAMA:	It's just not true.
ROMNEY:	It's absolutely true.

In judging the truthfulness of the participants, *FactCheck* gave the decision to Romney. Obama wrongly denied Romney's claim that the Obama administration cut in half the number of new permits and new leases for offshore drilling. The decrease, said *FactCheck*, was "actually more than half." Obama was also wrong when he said it's "just not true" that domestic oil production on federal lands was down 14 percent. Said *FactCheck*, production "did indeed fall by those percentages as Romney said."

America was not running out of places to drill on land as Obama claimed. Despite the president's best efforts, oil production kept soaring, and he kept bragging. What *FactCheck* missed was this larger deception: Obama was boasting about an energy source that just two years prior he thought both evil and exhausted.

In his 2014 State of the Union address, without any change in policy or direction, Obama felt free to list high among his accomplishments as president: "more oil produced—more oil produced at home than we buy from the rest of the world, the first time that's happened in nearly twenty years." Later in the speech, his woes about our addiction forgotten, Obama bragged that oil and natural gas production were "booming." This avowal represented an extraordinary shift in the gestalt. It was if an antidrug crusader abandoned the cause when, despite his best efforts, an ample supply of home-grown forced the price down.

CHAPTER 6

THE SUNSHINE PRESIDENT

I n March 2013, much to the astonishment of those paying attention, the official White House blog announced that the administration would help celebrate "Sunshine Week" in recognition of the administration's "continued commitment to open and accessible government." For the past five or so years, the Obama camp had been drilling the sunshine meme into the brains of the softheaded. The campaign booklet used in Obama's 2008 campaign, for instance, had its own special section titled quaintly "Restore Trust in Government and Improve Transparency." The booklet promised that, as president, Obama would "restore the American people's trust in their government by making government more open and transparent and by giving regular Americans unprecedented new tools to keep track of government officials, who they are meeting with, who is giving them money and how they are spending taxpayer dollars."

This was more than just boilerplate, or at least it appeared to be. The candidate took this message to the people during the 2008 campaign and energized himself with the promises he was making. He reached maximum charge on the night of September 22 in Green Bay, Wisconsin. There, speaking against a backdrop of crossed American flags, he delivered what might best be titled the "No More Secrecy" speech. At the time, this message did not seem to be entirely fanciful, and it certainly did not seem so to Obama supporters. Those naive enough to take Obama at his word had little reason to doubt that his presidency would be as bright and sunny as promised. And yet, just a few months into the Obama era, this speech resonated among the knowing as emptily as Bush 41's promise of "no new taxes."

TRANSPARENCY WILL BE THE TOUCHSTONE OF THIS PRESIDENCY

Somewhere along the way, Barack Obama got it into his head that he would be a postmodern Prometheus. He would bring to humanity not fire—there was plenty of that already, especially in the precincts Obama dominated—but sunshine. He would project that sunlight into the corners of government that, according to White House aides, had been "secretive, opaque, and closed" under Bush and expose them to the light. If "compassion" was the catchword of Bush's White House, "transparency" would be the catchword of Obama's.

Obama never meant a word of it. There was nothing within the power of Congress or the courts or our enemies abroad to prevent him from honoring his vow. Nor was transparency an incidental promise. So central to his presidency was the pledge of an open administration that he maintained the illusion before his assembled staff on his first full day in office: "Let me say it as simply as I can. Transparency and the rule of law will be the touchstones of this presidency."

A report released by the Committee to Protect Journalists (CPJ) in October 2013 showed just how perversely empty that promise proved to be. In the way of background, a group of foreign journalists founded the CPJ in 1981 to protect their colleagues around the world from harassment by authoritarian governments. The CPJ is not exactly part of the much-bruited "right-wing noise machine." *Au contraire*, over the years its board of directors has included any number of liberal luminaries, among them Christiane Amanpour, Gwen Ifill, Tom Brokaw, Dan Rather, and Clarence Page, and even serious leftists like Victor Navasky, a longtime editor of the *Nation*. The principal author of the report was Leonard Downie Jr., a former executive editor of the *Washington Post*. In the opening paragraph of the report, Downie sliced right to the heart of the issue:

> In the Obama administration's Washington, government officials are increasingly afraid to talk to the press. Those suspected of discussing with reporters anything that the government has classified as secret are subject to investigation, including lie-detector tests and scrutiny of their telephone and e-mail records. An "Insider Threat Program" being implemented in every government department requires all federal employees to help prevent unauthorized disclosures of information by monitoring the behavior of their colleagues.

The climate described in the 2013 CPJ report was a bit cloudier and cooler than the sunny one Obama forecast in 2008. And yet as the atmosphere chilled, the media noticed only slowly. In May 2010, for instance, the president signed the Daniel Pearl Freedom of the Press Act, a piece of legislation that required the State Department to monitor press freedom worldwide and sanction those countries that failed to protect it. Upon signing the bill, Obama denounced "those who would go to any length in order to silence journalists around the world" and blithely excluded himself from "those" who did the silencing.

At the time, few in the media noted any irony deeper than the fact that Obama took no questions after the signing and had not staged a formal press conference in nearly a year. The National Press Club, for instance, headlined its summary of the event with the chirpy "Club Hails Signing of Press Freedom Law." America's reporters and editors were not yet aware, or at least not yet willing to admit, that Obama as president represented the single greatest threat to press freedom in their professional lives. True to his reputation as messiah, Obama would soon make even the willfully blind see.

In May 2013, nearly three years to the day after Obama signed the Daniel Pearl Freedom of the Press Act, the illusion of an unfettered press disappeared. It was in this month that the Associated Press (AP) learned that Obama's Department of Justice had quietly seized the records for twenty AP telephone lines a year earlier. These included the personal and professional lines of several reporters. The seizure had to do with AP's reporting on a covert CIA operation in Yemen. Although only five reporters were involved in that story, more than one hundred reporters used the lines and switchboards whose records were seized. AP president Gary Pruitt wrote to Attorney General Eric Holder that the "government has no conceivable right to know" the content of those records. On *Face the Nation*, Pruitt boldly assessed White House strategy, saying, "I know what the message being sent is: If you talk to the press, we're going after you."

A coalition of some fifty news-gathering organizations promptly came to the AP's defense. In a barely polite letter to Holder, the coalition accused the attorney general of ignoring the Department of Justice's decades-old guidelines governing subpoenas of journalists and news organizations. The authors of the letter reminded Holder, "The approach in every case must be to strike the proper balance between the public's interest in the free dissemination of ideas and information and the public's interest in effective law enforcement and the fair administration of justice." The DOJ did none of the above. Its attorneys went behind the AP's back, failed to negotiate the scope of the subpoena with the AP, and refused to explain what threat to the integrity of the investigation made the subterfuge necessary.

An even more disturbing story broke a week later. It seemed that for the prior three years the DOJ had been secretly dipping into the personal and professional communications of Fox News's Washington correspondent James Rosen. The case involved Rosen's interactions with a State Department contractor monitoring North Korea's nuclear program. What troubled the media community most was the DOJ's use of search warrants to investigate a reporter and the threat to prosecute him under the terms of the Espionage Act as an "as an aider, abettor and/or co-conspirator." "Search warrants like these have a severe chilling effect on the free flow of important information to the public," a First Amendment lawyer, Charles Tobin, told the *Washington Post*. "That's a very dangerous road to go down."

On May 16, 2013, a few days after the story about AP broke but a few days before the story about Rosen did, Obama took a moment during a joint press conference with Turkish prime minister Recep Tayyip Erdogan to say that he would "make no apologies" for investigating national security leaks that threatened the well-being of the American military. "I don't think the American people would expect me as commander in chief not to be concerned about information that might compromise their missions or might get them killed," Obama said defiantly.

This was one of those finesses that served Obama so well with the uninformed. In fact, the probes dug much deeper than "national security." A few weeks later, in June 2013, the McClatchy newspapers broke the story of an "unprecedented" Obama administration initiative launched in 2011 in the wake of the Bradley (or, in *New York Times*–speak, "Chelsea") Manning leaks. Much like Nixon's "plumbers," the operatives of the Insider Threat Program, as it was known, worked to suppress leaks in the national security agencies. Unlike the plumbers, however, the Insider Threat people extended their mission into the seemingly benign regions of education, agriculture, and Social Security. Scarier still, in the Maoist spirit of the Obama administration, everyone was expected to plumb. The administration obligated employees to turn themselves and their coworkers in for failing to report leaks. Specifically, the program's strategic plan mandated supervisors to "penalize clearly identifiable failures to report security infractions and violations, including any lack of self-reporting."

None of this, of course, stopped Edward Snowden, the NSA contractor who first went public with his massive document dump a week before the McClatchy article. What the Internal Threat Program could do, however, was discourage employees from reporting routine waste and corruption. "You don't get people speaking up when there's wrongdoing," said Ilana Greenstein, a former CIA case officer. "You don't get people who look at things in a different way and who are willing to stand up for things. What you get are people who toe the party line, and that's really dangerous for national security."

Just as troubling, the Internal Threat Program discouraged disgruntled employees from talking to the media. "The suspicion has to be that maybe these 'leak' investigations are less about deterring leakers and more about intimidating the press," opined the *Wall Street Journal*. The liberal First Amendment lawyer James Goodale was harsher still. In a *New York Times* op-ed, he declared that "President Obama will surely pass President Richard Nixon as the worst president ever on issues of national security and press freedom"

Unlike Richard Nixon, who had good reason to distrust the media, Obama had no apparent motive for his secrecy other than to give himself the space to do as he pleased. "They feel entitled to and expect supportive media coverage," admitted the veteran correspondent Josh Meyer in speaking of the White House press office. For all the love that the media showered on the Obama administration, what they got in return, said Meyer, was "across-the-board hostility."

In the age of Obama, however, many in the media had a hard time holding a grudge, and Obama knew it. Weeks after the story about Rosen broke, the president made what the *New York Times* called a "ringing affirmation of press freedom." The *Times* reported that Obama was "troubled" by the revelations of DOJ mischief and that Holder "shared those concerns." The *Times* summarized the speech with the redemptive headline "Obama, Offering Support for Press Freedom, Orders Review of Leak Investigations." Obama's reaction fitted a well-established pattern: upon revelation of a scandal, feign outrage, promise an investigation, and hope the media bite.

Obviously, not everyone in the media was as easily appeased as the *Times'* editors, but too many were. Six months after Goodale's blistering op-ed and three months after the release of the devastating CPJ report, David Remnick went unchallenged on the *Charlie Rose Show* when he listed as one of Obama's many accomplishments "the fact that there's been no scandal, major scandal, in this administration, which is a rare thing in an administration." For all its merits, the CPJ report did not use the word "scandal" or any of its derivatives. It has been said that a political incident becomes a scandal only when the *Times* calls it a "scandal" on the front page, and despite Obama's shocking disregard of his commitment and the media's acknowledgment of the same, the *Times* editors chose to reserve the "S" word for bigger things like, say, a lane closure on the George Washington Bridge.

The Snowden affair alone would have qualified as a scandal were George Bush president. Although the mission of the NSA demands careful attention to leaks and Bush deserves some share of the responsibility for allowing that mission to grow, the proverbial buck for the mission's mushrooming stops at the desk of the "no secrecy" president. That Obama could have allowed extensive and gratuitous surveillance of the telephone and e-mail traffic of ordinary citizens made a lie of all those empty campaign promises. National security may not have been his motivation. As a result of the Snowden revelations, the CPJ report acknowledged that government officials were "reluctant to discuss even unclassified information" with reporters for fear that government surveillance would blow their cover. Maybe that was the point after all.

NO MORE SECRECY

The CPJ report notes that Obama took office promising to undo what he called the "excessive secrecy" of the Bush years. On day one of his presidency, Obama issued directives to various government agencies to respond more quickly to Freedom of Information Act (FOIA) requests and to create "Open Government Initiative" websites to keep the public informed of their activities. This was all theoretically well and good, but the websites proved to be anything but open. According to Leonard Downie Jr., they served primarily to dispense "favorable information and images" and otherwise limit Obama's exposure to probing questions from the press. "When you call the White House press office to ask a question or seek information, they refer us to White House websites," confirmed Chris Shlemon, the Washington producer for Britain's ITV Channel 4 television news network. "We have to use White House website content, White House videos of the president's interviews with local television stations and White House photographs of the president."

Say what one will about Barack Obama, but it is hard to deny him his boldness. He promised to create not just a transparent and accountable administration but rather the *"most* transparent and accountable administration in *history"* (italics added). That was not the bold part. Anyone can make promises. What impressed about Obama in this regard was how quickly, flagrantly, and unapologetically he broke every transparency promise he made.

Obama was talking transparency right out of the chute. "To seize this moment we have to use technology to open up our democracy," he told his friends at Google in November 2007. To purge America of the bad taste left by "one of the most secretive administrations in our history"—presumably Bush's—he promised to put a whole mess of government data online in "universally accessible formats" so citizens could track the business of government. To make this work, Obama would hire the nation's first chief technology officer (CTO). After seven years of media propaganda about the cryptic and duplicitous Bush administration, the Google crowd had to welcome this apostle of open government.

For those paying attention, the transparency era did not last long. Among Obama's specific promises, one that he made in Green Bay and elsewhere, was the pledge "When there is a bill that ends up on my desk as President, you will have five days to look online and find out what's in it before I sign it." Again, this was one of those promises that no external force prevented him from fulfilling. And yet it took Obama all of nine days to disregard what he had said not just once on the campaign trail but multiple times.

On January 27, 2009, the House voted to approve the Lilly Ledbetter Fair Pay Act of 2009, a trivial and convoluted piece of Democratic feel-good legislation that extended the period in which employees could sue their employers. Just two days later, without the bill's being posted, let alone vetted by a curious public, the president signed it into law. The fact that he would be violating the spirit of this equal pay bill by paying female White House employees at least 12 percent less than male ones did not seem to trouble him, nor did the fact that he had not bothered to post the bill. *PolitiFact* was one of the very few news operations to notice how speedily Obama had ignored a significant campaign promise. "We asked the White House about this and if they planned to begin posting laws to the Web site for comment soon, but we got no response," wrote *PoliFact*'s Angie Holan at the time.

A week later, Obama signed into law his second bill, an expansion of the State Children's Health Insurance Program. On this occasion, he signed the bill just hours after it was approved in Congress. The day this bill was signed, Holan got a response to her earlier e-mail from a White House spokesman, Tommy Vietor. "We will be implementing this policy in full soon," Vietor, a gifted obfuscator, wrote back. "Currently we are working through implementation procedures and some initial issues with the congressional calendar."

Weary perhaps of documenting every violation, Holan waited until May to weigh in again. On this occasion, Obama signed the Credit Card Accountability, Responsibility, and Disclosure Act of 2009 just two days after the bill was authorized in Congress, not five as promised. The White House apparently posted a form for public comment sometime during the bill's passage through Congress, but as Holan conceded, it was not easily accessed. "When we finally discovered the undated comment area for the credit card bill through a global search of the White House site," she wrote, "it wasn't clear where it was located on the site or where people should go for future comments."

In April 2009, Obama finally got around to appointing his CTO, a young Indian American named Aneesh Chopra. Among Chopra's tasks, said Obama, was to make the government more effective, efficient, and, yes, "transparent." In December 2009, after a sunshine-free year at the White House, Chopra was featured along with Chief Information Officer Vivek Kundra on an in-house web program with the overblown title, "Open *for* Questions: Comprehensive Open Government Announcement"—the nifty italicization of the word "for" being in the original. With cameras rolling, Chopra and Kundra tried to explain a recent White House directive on open government. Unlike the Bush administration, which Kundra described as "secretive, opaque, and closed," the Obama administration was committed to being "transparent, open, and collaborative."

The presentation had some unusual flaws, most memorably Chopra's failure to keep a straight face. For instance, after boasting that the administration was "focused on results," he turned to Kundra and started giggling. It was so thoroughly weird that channel surfers might have thought they had stumbled on a sneak preview of *Harold and Kumar Go to the White House*. Still, this silliness would not have been a big deal if the transmission had remained within the friendly confines of whitehouse.gov, but it did not. Somehow, the Chopra and Kundra show found its way to Comedy Central's Jon Stewart, who showed clips of the giggling Chopra and mocked him as only Jon Stewart can.

For all the seeming hilarity, the business of government remained as secretive, opaque, and closed after the launch of the Open Government Initiative as it had been before. The CPJ report quoted the ABC News White House correspondent Ann Compton as saying, "There is no access to the daily business in the Oval Office, who the president meets with, who he gets advice from." Compton, who had been covering presidents since Gerald Ford, claimed that many of Obama's important meetings with major figures from outside the administration on issues like health care, immigration, or the economy were not even listed on his public schedule. This effectively prevented the media from reporting on how the president made decisions and who was helping shape them.

As Compton related, Obama's predecessors allowed reporters to hear the president's remarks at the beginnings of meetings and to see who was in the room. Afterward, the reporters were free to talk to the participants outside the White House. "This president has wiped all that coverage off the map," Compton told Leonard Downie Jr. "He's the least transparent of the seven presidents I've covered in terms of how he does his daily business." David E. Sanger, the veteran chief Washington correspondent of the *New York Times*, was even harsher than Compton. Said Sanger, "This is the most closed, control freak administration I've ever covered."

Three months after the debut of the Open Government Initiative, the degree of the administration's opacity became apparent with the passage of Obamacare. On Tuesday, March 9, 2010, House Speaker Nancy Pelosi perfectly captured the perversion of the whole process when she spoke to a gathering at the Legislative Conference for the National Association of Counties. "It's going to be very, very exciting," she said, referring to the massively complex Patient Protection and Affordable Care Act then working its way through Congress. Pelosi then added the priceless statement, "We have to pass the bill so you can find out what's in it."

Pelosi steamrollered the bill through the House and watched it pass narrowly on Easter Sunday, March 21. By this time, the very idea that the White House should post the bill and let the public read it, let alone comment on it, seemed like a vestigial pipe dream from some distant past. Those who wanted to review the 2,400-page epic *before* its passage would have had to find a hard copy and speed-read it. Just two days after the bill's passage, Obama signed his signature piece of legislation into law, unread by mortal man.

AND WE WILL PUT EVERY CORPORATE TAX BREAK AND EVERY PORK BARREL PROJECT ONLINE FOR EVERY AMERICAN TO SEE

Barack Obama made many a specific promise in his Green Bay speech. Among the more appealing promises was that he would keep citizens informed about every spending bill before Congress. They would be able to see the corporate tax breaks in the bill, the names of the corporations that would benefit, and all the pork barrel projects included. So confident was Obama in his hold on the media that he repeatedly made vows this specific with no apparent intention of honoring them. More impressive still, he dishonored these vows within weeks of taking office.

The House and Senate each passed the American Recovery and Reinvestment Act on February 13, 2009, three weeks into Obama's presidency. Four days later, Obama signed it into law. To be sure, Obama did not wait until the fifth day or post the bill online as pledged. In the spirit of consistency, he also violated his pledge to provide citizens information as to who would benefit from a bill laden with pork and corporate goodies. They got not even a whiff of that.

Three years after the fact, the academics James Gimpel, Frances Lee, and Rebecca Thorpe published an article in the *Political Science Quarterly* in which they assessed the fate of the stimulus funds. The authors discovered that the money did not, as promised, "assist those most impacted by the recession." Rather, it assisted those most favorably disposed to the Obama presidency. On the positive side, the stimulus did not necessarily go to the districts of powerful Congress members as traditional pork tended to do. As the authors acknowledged, however, the pork did show "a distinct tilt toward counties that were stronger for the Democratic Party in 2008."

The argument could be made that since the passage of this bill was presented as something of an emergency, there was no time to create the promised reporting apparatus. That same argument, however, could not be made for every subsequent tax or spending bill to be passed in years to come. This promise, unlike some others, was one the White House did not even pretend to honor.

WE NEED TO CLOSE THE REVOLVING DOOR THAT LETS LOBBYISTS COME INTO GOVERNMENT FREELY

In November 2007, as Obama struggled to gain a toehold in Iowa, he warmed up a Des Moines crowd with one of his favorite tirades: "I am running to tell the lobbyists in Washington that their days of setting the agenda are over. They have not funded my campaign. They will not run my White House, and they will not drown out the voices of the American people when I am president."

The message resonated. Obama won the Iowa caucus and shocked the Clintons, the ultimate insiders, in so doing. Lobbyists made such a tempting target that Obama fired away at them from one primary state to the next, embellishing his stump speech as he went. In some versions, lobbyists would not be allowed to "work in" or "get a job in" Obama's White House, let alone "run" it. As he got closer to taking office, Obama made his promises about lobbyists more specific, not less. In his campaign's "ethics plan," the candidate laid out his lobbyist-less vision of America's future:

No political appointees in an Obama-Biden administration will be permitted to work on regulations or contracts directly and substantially related to their prior employer for two years.

And no political appointee will be able to lobby the executive branch after leaving government service during the remainder of the administration.

It is possible that no campaign promise has ever been so flagrantly broken so quickly as Obama's promise to exclude lobbyists from his administration. Just ten days after his election, more than two months *before* he would take office, the *New York Times* ran a cautiously damning article on the shape of things to come. "Among the full roster of about 150 staff members being assigned to government agencies between now and Inauguration Day are dozens of former lobbyists and some who were registered as recently as this year," wrote the reporter David Kirkpatrick. As Kirkpatrick pointed out, many more members of the transitional staff had close associations with the lobbyist community as well.

As Obama must have known, to set up a new administration without using scores of veteran influence-peddlers would be well-nigh impossible. According to the *Times*, the "vast majority" of those on the transition team were former Clinton administration officials, virtually all of whom spent the eight years between Democratic administrations "capitalizing on the connections and expertise they developed in the Clinton years." In the face of all the obvious conflicts, an Obama spokeswoman, Stephanie Cutter, continued to insist that Obama was committed "to change the way Washington does business and curb the influence of lobbyists on our government." Soon, even the true believers would have a hard time believing.

Obama did not make it easy for them. That he would retain the services of Sandy Berger, a former national security adviser to Bill Clinton, troubled all but the most devoted. When last in the news, just three years earlier, Berger was pleading guilty to the unauthorized removal and retention of classified 9/11 documents, a crime that a House committee called "a disturbing breach of trust and protocol that compromised the nation's national security." Nearly as compromising from Obama's perspective, Berger spent the subsequent years running Stonebridge International, a consulting and lobbying firm that "speaks the language of government."

This was one lie that the media noticed. Angie Holan of *Politi-Fact* scored Obama's promise about lobbyists "broken" less than two months after the inauguration. "Of the 513 promises we're tracking," wrote Holan, "this one has become the most controversial." It was controversial not just because Obama broke it so quickly, but because it was "the cornerstone" of his campaign against special interests.

The problem would only grow, but the controversy would fade. In his 2013 semicomic best seller, *This Town*, the *New York Times Magazine*'s Mark Leibovich shone a little ironic sunshine on the "antilobbyist, anti-revolving-door Obama White House." Leibovich observed that scores of Obama hires quickly left for lobbying jobs without the media pointing out the hypocrisy. "If it was noted at all," wrote Leibovich, "the news was treated as a natural turn within the revolving door." Leibovich cited as an example a *Politico* article by Amie Parnes about three legislative affairs staffers who left the White House in 2011 to become lobbyists. According to Leibovich, Parnes spoke of their new jobs as just reward for hard work without mentioning at all "Obama's public antipathy to K Street and his vow to slow the city's revolving door." Leibovich may have been too close to see the obvious. With 2012 the next flip of the calendar, the president had a race to run, and those old promises just slowed him down.

BARACK OBAMA WILL STRENGTHEN WHISTLE-BLOWER LAWS TO PROTECT FEDERAL WORKERS WHO EXPOSE WASTE, FRAUD, AND ABUSE OF AUTHORITY IN GOVERNMENT

In his official campaign documents, candidate Obama presented himself as a whistle-blower's best friend: this in contrast to his predecessor, who "stifled" the "courage and patriotism" of those who dared speak out. As Thomas Drake can attest, Obama has fallen rather spectacularly short of his promises.

Drake was precisely the kind of guy a taxpayer would hope to see working in government. He specialized in intelligence during his ten-year stint with the Air Force, served as a CIA analyst and a contractor for the NSA for twelve years, and then joined the NSA full-time in 2001. In 2002, Drake objected, as did others, to an NSA data collection program known as TrailBlazer. For reasons obvious only to dead-eyed bureaucrats, management had rejected a comparable program that was more efficient than TrailBlazer and more protective of citizens' privacy.

Although not one of the original complainants, Drake testi-fied honestly when the accusations of waste, fraud, and misman-agement reached the inspector general's office in the Department of Defense. The subsequent report confirmed Drake's testimony, but that did not stop the NSA's management from persisting with TrailBlazer and punishing Drake with a purgatory of petty as-signments. The unhappy Drake walked his concerns through the proper channels but got nowhere. Frustrated, he started talking to the *Baltimore Sun* in 2006. None of the information he provided to *Sun* reporters was classified, but it was enough to generate a series of articles about this $1.2 billion boondoggle.

In November 2007, Drake's life took a turn for the Kafkaesque when a dozen FBI agents raided his house, not because he had talked to the *Baltimore Sun*, but because he had allegedly leaked info about the NSA's warrantless wiretap program. As a result, Drake was forced out of the NSA and ended up working at, of all places, an Apple Store. Despite threats of a lifetime in prison, he refused to plead guilty to anything, and his case idled.

Given Obama's professed affection for whistle-blowers, Drake "had reason for hope," as he would relate in an op-ed a few years later. In the op-ed, which he wrote with a fellow whistle-blower, Jesselyn Radack, Drake quoted Obama's campaign promises about supporting "acts of courage and patriotism" by whistle-blowers like himself and Radack. Unfortunately, the authors noted, "Obama's actions have not matched those words." In the unkindest cut of all, they added, "His administration's reaction to national-security and intelligence whistle-blowers has been even harsher than the Bush administration's was." If the theorists were comparing Obama with Adams and Jefferson, the realists were comparing him with Nixon and Bush, and unfavorably at that.

Drake saw that reality up close. More than two years after the FBI searched his home and more than a year after Obama was sworn in, Obama's Department of Justice chose to indict Drake on ten felony counts. These included violations of the 1917 Espionage Act, one of Democratic president Woodrow Wilson's more flamboyant assaults on civil liberties. "The Espionage Act was meant to help the government go after spies, not whistle-blowers," wrote Radack and Drake. "Using it to silence public servants who reveal government malfeasance is chilling at best and tyrannical at worst."

In March 2011, as prosecutors prepared to try Drake in a US district court in Baltimore, he was awarded the Ridenhour Truth-Telling Prize, the highest honor accorded to whistle-blowers. The media attention was getting to Obama's DOJ. After several more months of waffling, prosecutors dropped the ten-count indictment on espionage charges and allowed Drake to plead guilty to one misdemeanor count of "exceeding authorized use of a government computer." Although no fan of Drake's, the former NSA and CIA director Michael Hayden spoke out publicly against the DOJ's "prosecutorial overreach." It was so heavy-handed, he said, "that it collapsed under its own weight."

The DOJ's arbitrary execution of justice troubled United States District Judge Richard Bennett even more. He cited the absurdly disparate treatment received by the aforementioned Obama adviser Sandy Berger. "[Berger] certainly is able to bounce back from this kind of situation far more quickly than someone who winds up having to work at the Apple Computer Store, correct?" asked Bennett rhetorically.

Happily, Drake fared better than the Socialist Party presidential candidate Eugene Debs. During World War I, Wilson's DOJ prosecuted Debs for making a speech that "obstructed recruiting." Debs served nearly three years in prison before Wilson's Republican successor, Warren G. Harding, commuted his ten-year sentence. By Wilson's standard, Drake did not do half badly. Although broken and bankrupted by the proceedings, he escaped without imprisonment or even a fine. Said Judge Bennett in conclusion, "Somebody somewhere in the US government has to say to somebody in the Department of Justice that the American public deserves better than this." When last heard from, Drake was still waiting for his invitation to a White House beer summit.

CHAPTER 7

THE CONSTITUTIONALIST

T he headline on the article the McClatchy chain fed to its affiliates after the 2014 State of the Union speech summed up the drift of the Obama presidency rather concisely: "Obama to Congress: Help the Poor, or I Will." With that headline, the editor intended to praise the gesture and flatter the president. Again, the "I" commands. Again, the president "wills" an outcome. Again, the editorialists cheer.

In fact, President Obama was not being quite as imperious as the headline suggested. "I'm eager to work with all of you," he said to Congress, specifically the Republican-controlled House. "But America does not stand still—and neither will I. So wherever and whenever I can take steps without legislation to expand opportunity for more American families, that's what I'm going to do." Unchastened by a threatened Republican lawsuit, Obama continued to insist on his own prerogatives. A June 28, 2014, *Washington Post* headline nicely captured the spirit of that day's radio address— "Obama: Congress Obstructs, So I Act Alone." Constitutionally, in fact, the president could not do much "alone," domestically at least, beyond rearranging the furniture of the White House, but by 2014 the president had long since forsaken the Constitution.

It wasn't supposed to be this way. The historian and adviser to President Kennedy, Arthur Schlesinger Jr., introduced the phrase "imperial presidency" during the Nixon era as a handy caution against presidents who overreached. In the years that followed, the chattering classes used the phrase as needed to chastise those presidents, invariably Republican, "who had assumed more power than the Constitution allows and circumvented the checks and balances fundamental to our three-branch system of government." So said Congressman John Conyers in a *Washington Post* op-ed introducing his 486-page jeremiad, "Reining in the Imperial Presidency."

Conyers, like many sunshine constitutionalists on the left, once believed that the Nixon administration represented "a singular embodiment of the [imperial] idea." That, of course, was before W blundered in from Texas. "Unfortunately," wrote Conyers, "it is clear that the threat of the imperial presidency lives on and, indeed, reached new heights under George W. Bush."

Conyers was hardly alone in his anxiety. In the first eight years of the decade, the left fretted openly about the outsize ambitions of President Bush. In 2005, Andrew Rudalevige wrote a book titled *The New Imperial Presidency: Renewing Presidential Power after Watergate*. In 2006, the populist folk hero Jim Hightower penned an essay titled "Bush's Imperial Presidency." Wrote Hightower, "Now comes the Bush-Cheney regime, pushing the most massive and rapid expansion of presidential might America has ever known." In 2007, the *New York Times* weighed in with a piece by Adam Cohen titled "Just What the Founders Feared: An Imperial President Goes to War." Huffed Cohen, "The war is hardly the only area where the Bush administration is trying to expand its powers beyond all legal justification."

No one agonized more openly or, in retrospect, more comically about the imperial presidency of George Bush than did Barack Obama himself. "The biggest problem that we're facing right now has to do with George Bush trying to bring more and more power into the executive branch and not go through Congress at all," Obama said at a campaign stop in late March 2008. "And that's what I intend to reverse when I am president of the United States." Spoiler alert: he lied.

TRANSPARENCY AND THE RULE OF LAW WILL BE THE TOUCHSTONES OF THIS PRESIDENCY

On his first day in office, Obama promised his assembled staff that "transparency and the rule of law will be the touchstones of this presidency." This was a pledge Obama made often on the stump in one form or another, in regard both to transparency and to the rule of law. In *The Audacity of Hope*, Obama questioned whether Bush was sincere when he raised his hand on Inauguration Day and swore "to uphold the Constitution." Obama, a constitutional scholar *imaginaire*, went on to praise "the rejection of absolutism implicit in our constitutional structure."

As Obama or his ghostwriter argued, this rejection of an imperial presidency, "for most of our history" at least, "encouraged the very process of information gathering, analysis, and argument that allows us to make better, if not perfect, choices, not only about the means to our ends but also about the ends themselves." In other words, as a planned result of the separation of powers, the president must persuade Congress of the rightness of his choices, and that is the way it should be. "In sum," wrote Obama, "the Constitution envisions a road map by which we marry passion to reason, the ideal of individual freedom to the demands of community. And the amazing thing is that it's worked."

Well, that is at least the way it used to work before those rascally Republicans took control of the House of Representatives. As to the date their insurgency began, Obama wasn't quite sure. At a November 2013 press conference, he traced this "unprecedented pattern of obstruction" back some "five years." That would place its beginning in 2008. The Republicans did not take control of the House until 2011. No one seemed to notice Obama's three-year miscalculation.

As Obama told his radio audience in January 2014, "Where Congress isn't acting, I'll act on my own to put opportunity within reach for anyone who's willing to work for it." Obama reiterated the message in a June 2014 radio address. "Republicans in Congress keep blocking or voting down almost every serious idea," he pontificated. "And as long as they insist on doing it, I'll keep taking actions on my own."

So much for the "information gathering, analysis, and argument" of yesteryear. Obama and his advisers had been calling this the "pen and phone" strategy. The *Washington Post* described it "as actions that he and his administration can take unilaterally without seeking approval from the Republican-controlled House, which remains hostile to his agenda."

As has been seen, Obama clearly lied about transparency. As shall be seen, he lied just as spectacularly about the rule of law. One would think that his allies, indignant as they were about Bush's mischief against the constitution, would insist that Obama honor that venerable document—but this presumes much too much integrity on the part of Obama's allies. To the degree that they have noticed Obama's assumption of imperial powers, they have applauded it.

In early 2014, David Remnick wrote about his experience accompanying Obama on a West Coast fund-raising tour. At one stop, when Obama walked out onstage, "It happened again: another heckler broke into Obama's speech. A man in the balcony repeatedly shouted out, 'Executive order!,' demanding that the President bypass Congress with more unilateral actions." Obama confirmed to the audience that, yes, people did want him to sign more executive orders and "basically nullify Congress." At that point, wrote Remnick, "Many in the crowd applauded their approval. Yes! Nullify it!" These were not wild-eyed tent dwellers on Wall or some lesser street. These were potential donors.

If this new breed of activist urged Obama to hammer away at the Constitution, old-school civil libertarians lamented its demolition. The longtime *Village Voice* columnist Nat Hentoff had fought many a battle for civil liberties and had scars enough to speak his mind. "Apparently he doesn't give one damn about the separation of powers." said Hentoff of Obama after the president's "pen and phone" remarks. "Never before in our history has a president done these things."

CITIZENSHIP MEANS STANDING UP FOR EVERYONE'S RIGHT TO VOTE

In December 2013, Nicholas Rosenkrantz, a professor of law at Georgetown University Law Center, testified at a House Judiciary Committee hearing on the president's constitutional powers. In testifying, Rosenkrantz called attention to the clause of the Constitution that he thought most relevant. This was the one specifying the president "shall take Care that the Laws be faithfully executed." The founders, Rosenkrantz noted, added this clause to rebut the idea that kings had the power to suspend laws unilaterally. The clause did not so much grant power, Rosenkrantz explained, as it did impose a duty. That duty was to make sure the laws were faithfully executed, the key word here being "faithfully." The enforcement of a given law could be delegated, but the duty could not be. That remained the sole province of the president. He had to ensure the law was enforced, all laws. Ignorance was no excuse.

For Obama, ignorance was never an excuse. Ignorance was a strategy. His appointees to the Department of Justice were employing it before their business cards were printed. They had a case to fix. On Election Day 2008, two New Black Panthers in paramilitary gear intimidated would-be voters at a Philadelphia polling place. One carried a nightstick. Both were abusive. "You are about to be ruled by the black man, cracker!" one of them yelled at a white voter. Bartle Bull, a former civil rights lawyer and a onetime publisher of the left-wing *Village Voice*, was among the witnesses to see and hear them.

Given what Bull and others reported, much of which was captured on video, the Justice Department filed a civil lawsuit against the New Black Panther Party and three of its members for violating the 1965 Voting Rights Act. The DOJ filed the suit during the first week of January 2009, before Obama was sworn in or Eric Holder was confirmed as attorney general. Bull submitted an affidavit in support of the lawsuit. J. Christian Adams, one of the six career attorneys involved, called the Panthers' actions, "the simplest and most obvious violation of federal law I saw in my Justice Department career." None of the accused filed any response, and it appeared that the Department of Justice would prevail by default.

As president, Obama had the duty to see that the laws were faithfully executed. In this instance, he did the opposite. In February 2009, Holder assumed office. In March, the Senate confirmed Obama's appointee Thomas Perrelli as associate attorney general. In May 2009, Perrelli, or someone under him, overruled the six attorneys and let the Panthers walk. To what degree Obama involved himself in this case will likely never be known. Clearly, though, all participants understood that in the Obama DOJ, race would factor into the calculation of justice.

As to motive, Obama never felt secure in his identity as an African American. The old bulls of the vestigial civil rights movement knew his vulnerability and applied pressure as needed. It seems likely they did so here. Thomas Perez, the assistant attorney general for civil rights, would testify that the "facts and law" did not support the original lawsuit. Adams and other attorneys vehemently rejected that argument. "That claim is false," said Adams. "If the actions in Philadelphia do not constitute voter intimidation, it is hard to imagine what would." Then too, if Perez had confidence in what he was saying, Congress would not have had to drag him and his colleagues kicking into various hearings.

It was harder still to believe Perez's claim under oath at a US Commission on Civil Rights hearing that there was no political involvement in the decision to drop the case. Nor was he the only one to make this claim. Holder testified before a House Appropriations subcommittee in March 2011 that "the decisions made in the New Black Panther Party case were made by career attorneys in the department."

United States District Court judge Reggie Walton was not buying. In ruling on a related case, he had received several relevant documents, including a series of e-mails between Perrelli and a colleague. "The documents reveal that political appointees within DOJ were conferring about the status and resolution of the New Black Panther Party case in the days preceding the DOJ's dismissal of claims in that case," wrote Walton in his ruling. He added that this "would appear to contradict Assistant Attorney General Perez's testimony that political leadership was not involved in that decision." As punishment for misleading Congress, and possibly even lying under oath, Perez was named secretary of labor in January 2013.

As expected, the media would not let the narrative stand as Adams described it. They did what they often did in such cases, especially early in the presidency—attack the whistle-blower. Adams made a tempting target. Although not a political appointee, he was a conservative. *Main Justice*, a progressive legal blog and a source for many left-leaning journalists, chronicled Adams's sins against progressive dogma. He once filed an ethics complaint against Hillary Clinton's brother. On another occasion, he asked a question at a meeting of the Federalist Society "that appeared skeptical of affirmative action." And, most damning of all, Adams worked on a 2005 federal lawsuit that accused black officials in Noxubee County, Mississippi, of violating the civil rights of white voters.

For the record, at the conclusion of that case, US District Court judge Tom S. Lee ruled against the Noxubee County Democratic Party leader, Ike Brown, a twice-convicted felon. Working with the Noxubee Democratic Executive Committee, said Lee, "[Brown] manipulated the political process in ways specifically intended and designed to impair and impede participation of white voters and to dilute their votes." Although Adams was not a major player in this case, his involvement was enough to draw a race-baiting taunt from Andrew Cohen, writing for the *Atlantic*. Adams's "claim to fame as a federal lawyer," said the sanctimonious Cohen, "seems to be his penchant for accusing black people of discriminating against whites."

Cohen did not mention Adams's primary partner on the New Black Panthers case, Christopher Coates, and for good reason. As the *Washington Post* acknowledged, Coates had a "pedigree different" from Adams's. In fact, the DOJ hired Coates during the Clinton administration in 1996, and he had worked before that for the American Civil Liberties Union. As the former head of the voting section that brought the case, Coates testified before the US Commission on Civil Rights in defiance of his supervisor's orders. To do so, he sought and was granted whistle-blower protection. "I had people who told me point-blank that [they] didn't come to the voting rights section to sue African American people," said Coates. "When you are paid by the taxpayer, that is totally indefensible."

Coates testified that the Obama Justice Department was resist-

ing "race neutral" enforcement of the law. "We had eyewitness testimony. We had videotape. One of [the Panthers] had a weapon.
They were hurling racial slurs," Coates testified. "I've never been
able to understand how anyone could accuse us of not having a
basis of law in this case."

The irony of all this, of course, was that Obama had long pos-
tured as a champion of voting rights. He taught a course in the
same at the University of Chicago and once proposed to write a
book on the subject. As a US senator in 2007, Obama showily introduced a bill with Chuck Schumer to protect voters from intimidation. "There is no place for politics in this debate," Obama
testified in March 2007. "Both parties at different periods in our
history have been guilty in different regions of preventing people
from voting for a tactical advantage. We should be beyond that."

The *New York Times* promptly recognized Obama as the friend
of voting rights he feigned to be with the now-amusing headline,
"Obama-Schumer Bill Proposal Would Criminalize Voter Intimidation." And yet in the case that Bartle Bull called "the most bla-
tant form of voter intimidation I've ever seen," Obama's Justice
Department showed itself *beyond* neither politics nor racial propaganda. When called to testify about this case in 2011, Holder
blasted Bull. He claimed that by failing to understand the historical context of the case, Bull insulted "my people." For all its implicit racism, Holder's "my people" comment may have been the
most honest remark to come out of the DOJ in the whole case.

Obama could offer no competition in an honesty contest.
During the 2014 State of the Union speech, he summoned the
nerve to say, "Citizenship means standing up for everyone's right
to vote." So saying, he cast himself and his own DOJ beyond
the pale of good citizenship and rendered silly once again his
claim that "there's not a black America and white America and
Latino America and Asian America; there's the United States of
America."

I BELIEVE THAT MARRIAGE IS THE UNION
BETWEEN A MAN AND A WOMAN

On the trip back from Rick Warren's Saddleback Church in Orange County, California, in August 2008, Barack Obama had to be bitch-slapping the scheduler who had set him up with that gig. Several of Obama's more memorable quotes came out of the Saddleback appearance, and none of them would prove helpful.

One of them went like this: "I believe that marriage is the union between a man and a woman. Now, for me as a Christian, it's also a sacred union. God's in the mix." To be sure, there has been some debate about whether Barack Obama *is* a Christian. He found Jesus, after all, in a place only slightly more celestial than Westboro Baptist, the church of Jeremiah Wright.

The biographer David Mendell, who knew Obama back when, wrote that in his pursuit of a US Senate seat in 2004, "Obama, without fail, would mention his church and his Christian faith when he was campaigning in black churches and more socially conservative downstate Illinois communities," but he did not want to talk to Mendell about either. When Obama eventually did share his views, they had the theological gravitas of a Wayne Dyer book on tape. "Many of the impulses that I had carried with me and were propelling me forward," he told Mendell, "were the same impulses that express themselves through the church." Obama's belief in the teaching of Jesus proved no deeper than his belief in the teachings of Madison—or of Marx for that matter. His Christianity was as calculated as his politics. He could lie about one as glibly as he could lie about another.

Given his stated philosophy on marriage, whether Muslim or Christian, it made sense that for the first two years of the presidency he would enforce the Defense of Marriage Act (DOMA). Designed to protect traditional marriage from progressive encroachment, this bill cleared the Senate on an 85–14 vote. Democratic president Bill Clinton signed it into law in September 1996, right after welfare reform and just in time to ensure reelection. In its essence, DOMA defined the word "marriage" to mean only "a legal union between one man and one woman as husband and wife."

In February 2011, however, Obama shocked the legal community—and much of the Christian community—when he and Holder came willy-nilly to the conclusion that the marriage law they had been honoring was not "constitutional." Going forward, Obama decided, the Justice Department would no longer enforce DOMA. That simple. Those who took Obama at his word that the "rule of law" would be the touchstone of his administration were not particularly pleased. "It is a transparent attempt to shirk the department's duty to defend the laws passed by Congress," said Lamar Smith, the Republican chairman of the House Judiciary Committee. "This is the real politicization of the Justice Department—when the personal views of the president override the government's duty to defend the law of the land."

Smith could be excused here for not quite knowing what the president's personal views were. In 2011, at least according to the ever credulous *New York Times*, Obama "oppose[d] same-sex marriage but has said repeatedly that his views were 'evolving.'" In truth, "whipsawing" might be a better word for Obama's views. In 1996, less than a decade after finding Jesus chez Reverend Jeremiah Wright, Obama told a gay newspaper, "I favor legalizing same-sex marriages, and would fight efforts to prohibit such marriages." By 1998, with an eye on Congress, he was now "undecided" on the issue. By 2004, the would-be US senator was telling that same gay newspaper, "I am not a supporter of gay marriage."

In *The Audacity of Hope*, Obama told the story of how one

of his lesbian supporters called to lament his stand against gay marriage. Her call reminded him that "as a Christian" he had to remain "open to the possibility that my unwillingness to support gay marriage is misguided," that perhaps he "had been infected with society's prejudices and predilections and attributed them to God." Translation: he was prepared to change positions as soon as he got the sign. God never gave it, but in 2011 Gallup did, and that was omen enough for Obama.

Jonathan Turley, the holder of the prestigious Shapiro Chair for Public Interest Law at George Washington University, testified before the Senate Judiciary Committee on the same December 2013 day as Rosenkrantz. Although personally a supporter of same-sex marriage, Turley had a hard time making legal sense out of Obama's left-field decision to ignore DOMA. For one, Turley found the timing curious. The Obama administration had been defending the law for the previous two years, and the president, publicly at least, had not changed his personal stance on gay marriage. As Turley noted, many observers questioned "a decision to abandon the law 'mid-stream' without any clear advocate with standing to argue the law's merits."

The decision to abandon DOMA troubled Turley for another reason as well. Obama was basing this policy change on an interpretation "that had thus far remained unsupported by direct precedent." When the Supreme Court did address this issue two years later in *United States v. Windsor*, the decision was a close one, five to four, and, as Turley noted, "the decision was more nuanced than the one indicated by the administration."

By refusing to enforce DOMA, Obama was setting a precedent, and not a good one, namely, that a president could refuse to defend a law and could base the refusal on a legal interpretation that no court had ever accepted. Given this precedent, Turley wondered what would happen if a president chose not to defend a law in defiance of a lower court's rulings. At the current rate of constitutional drift, that answer will likely be known by 2016.

Holder, surely with Obama's approval, continued to flout the Constitution on this issue, perhaps above all others. In February 2014, he encouraged state attorney generals to ignore state bans on same-sex marriage. "Engaging in that process and making that determination is something that's appropriate for an attorney general to do," argued Holder. The *New York Times*, with much too straight a face, called this move "the latest manifestation of the Obama administration's evolving position on gay rights." Alan Wilson, the chairman of the Republican Attorneys General Association, described Holder's call to action with considerably more precision than the *Times*: "This administration is repeatedly ignoring the rule of law."

WE'RE NOT GOING TO USE SIGNING STATEMENTS AS A WAY OF DOING AN END RUN AROUND CONGRESS

At a May 2008 town hall meeting in Billings, Montana, a fired-up Barack Obama slammed then-president Bush for trying "to accumulate more power in the presidency." The "theory" guiding the Bush administration, as Obama saw it, was that the president could "make laws as he's going along." The nerve! At the time, the subset of that theory that alarmed Obama most was the president's use of "signing statements." This was an odd choice of target for Obama. Few people even knew what a signing statement was, and fewer cared. The very obscurity of it, though, brought out the sanctimony in the pious young constitutionalist.

To illustrate his point, Obama did an ungainly imitation of Bush contemplating a signing statement: "Well, I can basically change what Congress passed by attaching a letter saying, 'I don't agree with this part or I don't agree with that part, I'm going to choose to interpret it this way or that way.'" Obama rejected this strategy outright. "That's not part of his power," he told the friendly audience, and Obama was in a position to know. He recalled his teaching of the Constitution as showily as John Kerry recalled his service in Vietnam. "I believe in the Constitution," he said proudly, "and I will obey the Constitution of the United States." To make certain the audience got the message, Obama spelled out his intentions specifically: "We're not going to use signing statements as a way of doing an end run around Congress." A promise does not get much more definitive than that.

Nor does a lie get more dazzling than when a president breaks a promise this definitive so casually, contemptuously, and often. In December 2011, the *New York Times* took notice. Shortly before Christmas that year, Obama signed a budget bill. Upon doing so, he issued a signing statement in which he listed dozens of provisions in the bill that he planned to bypass. These included a congressional funding ban on bringing Guantánamo detainees to the mainland, a thirty-day presidential alert to Congress of major planned military operations, restrictions on receiving certain foreign dignitaries, and many more hindrances to Obama's exercise of presidential powers.

As Obama explained, he issued the signing statement only because he had "many well-founded constitutional objections" to the provisions therein. What Congress heard him say, of course, was, "I don't agree with this part or I don't agree with that part, I'm going to choose to interpret it this way or that way." Had Obama been a mere mortal, one could forgive him for changing his mind. But Obama knew the law like a Pharisee. He had been teaching it, he bragged, for ten years. He knew before he took office what signing statements were, and while campaigning he talked about them largely to show off what he knew.

Having lied about using signing statements, Obama apparently felt free to lie about how he would use them. According to the *Times*, Obama had earlier said he would issue a signing statement only if he had not already registered an objection to that provision elsewhere. "But his statement on Friday," the *Times* protested gently, "*repeated* several objections" (italics added). Obama wanted a climate change czar. What president wouldn't? Congress did not want to fund that position. As the *Times* noted, Obama had challenged that same anti-czar provision with a signing statement eight months earlier in April 2011.

Lies inevitably beget more lies. When questioned back in April, White House Press Secretary Jay Carney did his best Baghdad Bob imitation. "He never said he was opposed to signing statements," said Carney about the man who insisted, in 2008, "We're not going to use signing statements as a way of doing an end run around Congress." Carney patiently explained to his former colleagues, "[Obama's] concern was with what he saw was abuse of the signing statement by the previous administration." Here again was the Obama governing strategy in full flower: no need to admit fraud or failure when you can blame Bush.

All of this might have remained an obscure footnote in the Obama legacy had it not been for one Sergeant Bowe Bergdahl. In June 2009, Private First Class Bowe Bergdahl vanished from a remote military outpost in Paktika Province of Afghanistan, leaving behind a note that told of his disillusionment with the US Army and its mission in Afghanistan. Five years later, the Obama administration covertly negotiated his release in exchange for five high-ranking Taliban detainees who had been held at Guantánamo.

One problem beyond the obvious security threat, as the CNN legal analyst Jeffrey Toobin pointed out, was that Obama failed to give Congress at least thirty days' notice before releasing the prisoners. "I think he clearly broke the law," Toobin said. "The law says 30-days' notice. He didn't give 30-days' notice." Toobin did not buy Obama's claimed exemption from this law due to a signing statement. A signing statement, he told the CNN anchor Wolf Blitzer, "is not law."

Taken aback by the comments of the generally liberal Toobin, Blitzer replied, "You realize, of course, you're accusing the President of the United States of breaking the law." Toobin didn't flinch. "I do think that his critics have a very good point here," he said. "It matters whether people follow the law or not." Jonathan Turley was even more blunt in his assessment: "Barack Obama is really the president Richard Nixon always wanted to be."

I BELIEVE IN THE CONSTITUTION, AND I WILL OBEY THE CONSTITUTION OF THE UNITED STATES

Yes, President Obama refused to enforce the Defense of Marriage Act, but at least in that case he deemed the law unconstitutional. On the subject of illegal immigration, he didn't bother. He chose not to enforce many perfectly valid immigration laws because they did not poll well among Hispanic voters. It would get no deeper than that.

Since year one of the Bush administration, Congress had been trying to pass the awkwardly titled Development, Relief, and Education for Alien Minors Act, better known as the DREAM Act. This was an idealized acronym concocted to paper over what was essentially a crime, a geopolitical breaking and entering. Democrat Dick Durbin and Republican Orrin Hatch first introduced the bill in the Senate in August 2001. This was still another bipartisan fandango in the allegedly polarizing Bush era. In a nutshell, this bill would have provided permanent residency to those illegal aliens who had arrived in the United States as minors and behaved themselves well enough not to get their mug shots plastered on the post office wall. Although President Bush supported immigration reform, as did President Obama, neither the DREAM Act nor any major immigration bill made it to their desks. The reason was simple enough: no variation of such a bill could muster adequate congressional support.

In 2009, eight powerful US senators sponsored still another version of the DREAM Act. Among the sponsors were two Republicans, Richard Lugar and Mel Martínez, as well as the independent senator Joseph Lieberman. During this two-year period, Democrats controlled both houses of Congress. Still, the will was not there, nor was the White House leadership, to pass this bill out of the Senate.

As late as 2006, the reader will recall, candidate Obama saw such robust debates as a sign of a healthy system of checks and balances, one that "encouraged the very process of information gathering, analysis, and argument." Once Obama ascended to the presidency, all those checks and balances just made it harder for him to transform America. His constituencies, especially labor and the Hispanic lobby, wanted action, not gathering and arguing. They started leaning on him to ignore Congress and act unilaterally. One minor obstacle stood in the way, and that was article I, section 7, of the Constitution. For the previous 220 years—"400 years" according to Representative Sheila Jackson Lee—that article informed Congress in some detail on how to turn an idea into a law.

Obama could not enforce the DREAM Act, said Nicholas Rosenkrantz, "by pretending that it passed when it did not." As late as March 2011, Obama the legal scholar seemed to agree. "America is a nation of laws, which means I, as the President, am obligated to enforce the law," he told a Univision audience. "With respect to the notion that I can just suspend deportations through executive order, that's just not the case, because there are laws on the books that Congress has passed."

By June 2012, what Obama said in March 2011 seemed as stale as a morning-after bowl of tortilla chips. The president had lost his taste for all that legislative analysis and argument given that the result was "an absence of any immigration action from Congress." Five months before the presidential election he knew the media would give him a pass, and he hoped that Latinos would give him their vote. So he decided to dispense with debate and fix immigration policy by his own lights, confident he could make that policy "more fair, more efficient, and more just." This fix started with a presidentially guaranteed relief from deportation for the so-called Dreamers. On top of that came the right to apply for a work authorization, both guarantees in full defiance of existing federal law.

The speech that introduced this change of immigration policy was littered with enough lies and half-truths to stir Joe Wilson from the grave, let alone his seat. It was only "temporary," not "immunity," not a "path to citizenship," said Obama. Not surprisingly, the premise on which Obama proposed to relax enforcement was fundamentally false. He boasted that by "putting more boots on the southern border than at any time in our history," he was able to reduce illegal crossings to the lowest level in the past forty years. Yes, there were fewer border crossings than in the past. In fact, the number had fallen precipitously since 2005, but that had almost nothing to do with prioritized security and almost everything to do with what the Pew Research Center described as "weakened U.S. job and construction markets." Like so many of the "successes" of the Obama era, this one was inadvertent.

On August 23, 2013, in a move that the major media barely noticed, the Obama administration subtly expanded the list of those who would be excluded from deportation. Deep in a nine-page memo from the US Immigration and Customs Enforcement headquarters to its field offices was an order that "prosecutorial discretion" be shown to parents or guardians of United States citizens and lawful permanent residents, a.k.a. Dreamers.

The news scarcely troubled the media, let alone the citizenry, but at least a few Republicans noticed. "President Obama has once again abused his authority and unilaterally refused to enforce our current immigration laws," said House Judiciary Committee Chairman Bob Goodlatte. Jonathan Turley agreed. "In ordering this blanket exception," said Turley. "President Obama was nullifying part of a law that he simply disagreed with. There is no claim of unconstitutionality." Said Rosenkrantz, "Exempting as many as 1.76 million people from the immigration laws goes far beyond any traditional conception of prosecutorial discretion."

What troubled Turley even more was the willingness of so many participants in this debate to accept Obama's "transparent effort to rewrite the immigration law." These included Dick Durbin, the Democratic senator from Illinois who sponsored the original DREAM Act. "Because the House has refused to consider the DREAM Act and a filibuster blocked it in the Senate," said Durbin as casually as if he were the senator from Swaziland, "this presidential action was absolutely necessary to serve the cause of justice." More understandably, given his nation's historical lapses into lawlessness, Mexican president Felipe Calderón endorsed the move as well. "We believe this is very just," said Calderón through an interpreter. "Thank you for the valor and courage that you had in implementing this action."

In all fairness to Obama it should be noted that he has no monopoly on presidential dishonesty—or hypocrisy for that matter. Consider the following exchange between CNN's Wolf Blitzer and Calderón in 2010:

BLITZER: So in other words, if somebody sneaks in from Nicaragua or some other country in Central

America, through the southern border of
Mexico, they wind up in Mexico, they can go get
a job. . . .

CALDERÓN: No, no.

BLITZER: They can work.

CALDERÓN: If—if somebody do [sic] that without permission,
we send back—we send back them.

BLITZER: You find them and you send them back?

CALDERÓN: Yes.

In March 2014, appalled by Obama's open indifference to the law, the House of Representatives passed the Enforce the Law Act, a bill that would give both the House and the Senate standing to sue the president in federal court if the president failed to enforce a given law. Five Democrats crossed the aisle to join 228 Republicans in its passage. Representative Trey Gowdy reminded the House of the spirit that South Carolinians bring to the job with a rousing speech in defense of the Constitution. "That is a lot of power," said Gowdy after citing the legitimate powers of the president. He then asked the question of the day: "What are we to do when the power is not enough?"

By May 2014, the consequences of Obama's unilateral action were becoming too apparent to ignore. Reuters was among the first to notice that "tens of thousands of children unaccompanied by parents or relatives" were flooding across the southern U.S. border illegally, ten times more per year than just three years prior. "Usually you have to pass an ill-considered law before the 'unintended consequences' come knocking," opined Steven Hayward in *Human Events*, "but in this case the consequences are already parked in emergency shelters in Texas, costing the American taxpayer $252 apiece per day."

CHAPTER 8

THE REGULATOR

Edgar Allan Poe called it "the imp of the perverse," that willful, self-destructive voice within that impels us to do things or say things that cause our undoing. Nearly two centuries after Poe's coinage, the imp has found a permanent home in the psyche of America's progressives. The imp does not urge them to throw themselves in front of subway cars or jump off observation towers or even (see: Obama) bicycle without a helmet. The imp doesn't have to. He has convinced them to disarm themselves, then proudly move into urban neighborhoods where the unarmed are prey. They then prod the rest of America toward the same madness.

In the ongoing debate over guns, the would-be controllers face opponents who shoot guns, understand their value, and respect the constitutional history that protects their right to own them. To this debate Obama and his allies bring little knowledge and no passion save for the political advantage they may gain. Only a media-endorsed mendacity gives them a fighting chance.

This set of circumstances leads the more heartless on the left to welcome mass shootings. These are the best opportunities they and their media allies have to make their case. The fact that they have not been able to pin any recent mass shootings on a right-winger never stops them from trying.

I HAVE NEVER FAVORED A BAN ON HANDGUNS

At an ABC News–hosted presidential primary debate in April 2008, Charlie Gibson said to Obama, "In 1996, your campaign issued a questionnaire that said you favored a ban on handguns." This remark put Obama in something of a corner. In the primary campaign he had been quietly reaffirming his belief in the Second Amendment while adding enough qualifiers to keep the base in line.

Cornered or not, Obama seemed well prepared for Gibson's question. He promptly shot back, "No, my writing wasn't on that particular questionnaire, Charlie. As I said, I have never favored an all-out ban on handguns." The lie stood, at least for the moment, and in a televised debate, the moment is about all that counts. Once again, Obama was being strategically deceptive. Once again, *FactCheck*, a left-leaning operation funded by the Annenberg Foundation, was forced to call him on it. Said the fact-checker: "He was wrong about that—his handwriting appears on a small part of the document."

A clumsily named Chicago nonprofit, Independent Voters of Illinois–Independent Precinct Organization, had sent out the questionnaire. As *FactCheck* noted, Obama admitted his handwriting may have been on the questionnaire, but he insisted "that a campaign aide filled out the bulk of it." This included the "yes" answers on the handgun ban and other gun control measures as well. Obama submitted that questionnaire during his first run for state senate in 1996. The idea that an aspiring low-level candidate like himself would trust "a campaign aide" to fill out an important questionnaire passes no known smell test. Hillary Clinton did not believe him for a Chicago minute. Shortly after the debate, her campaign put out a flyer in rural Indiana, the front of which asked the question "Where does Barack Obama really stand on guns?" and the back of which answered, "Depends on who Barack Obama is talking to."

MORE THAN 90 PERCENT OF THE GUNS RECOVERED IN MEXICO COME FROM THE UNITED STATES

Three months into his presidency, Barack Obama took his international apology tour to Mexico. At an April 16 news conference in Mexico City, Obama addressed the drug wars ravaging the country. "This war is being waged with guns purchased not here but in the United States," said Obama. He elaborated, "More than 90 percent of the guns recovered in Mexico come from the United States, many from gun shops that lay in our shared border."

The global intelligence company Strategic Forecasting, better known as Stratfor, had been watching the Mexican drug wars with a sharper eye than that of either Obama or the Mexican political class. As Scott Stewart noted in a February 2011 intelligence report, the Mexican government has made a practice of deflecting responsibility for its internal chaos to the United States, in regard to both drug purchases and gun sales. In the case of the latter, the needs of the Mexican government and the Obama administration meshed well. Obama and his allies were perpetually on the lookout for issues or incidents that would enable them to push for more stringent gun control.

As to the "oft-echoed 90 percent," said Stewart, that was "more political rhetoric than empirical fact." The number, Stewart explained, was derived from a US Government Accountability

Office (GAO) report to Congress. According to that report, the
US Bureau of Alcohol, Tobacco, Firearms and Explosives (ATF)
was able to trace 4,000 of the guns seized in 2008 whose data the
Mexican authorities provided. Of those 4,000, some 3,480—or 87
percent—were traced back to the United States. That 87 percent
was likely rounded off to 90 percent and then Obama's "more than
90 percent."

The deep deception lay not in the rounding but in the calculating. In fact, Mexican authorities seized roughly 30,000 firearms
in 2008 but sent information on just 7,200 of them to the ATF. Of
that 7,200, only about 4,000 could be traced. The 3,480 guns posi-
tively traced to the United States represented less than 12 percent
of the total firearms seized and less than 48 percent of all those
submitted by the Mexicans to ATF for tracing. In other words,
almost 90 percent of the guns in question were *not* traced back to
the United States. As Stewart clarified, many of the guns Mexican authorities seized had no serial numbers and the numbers on
some others had been erased. Others clearly came from the Mexican defense department. Others were lost through bureaucracy
and theft. Still others had a provenance from a third country.

Stratfor was not the only organization to question the GAO's
figures. In June 2009, Jerald E. Levine, an official in the Department of Homeland Security, sent a letter to the GAO's director of
international affairs and trade, Jess Ford. "DHS officials believe
that the 87 percent statistic is misleading," said Levine. After
citing the same figures as Stewart, he concluded, "Numerous
problems with the data collection and sample population render
this assertion as unreliable."

Here too, one lie demanded another for cover. When Fox News
asked the Obama administration to clarify how it came up with
the figure 90 percent, already widely discredited, senior National
Security Council spokesman Denis McDonough told Fox, "By
recovered, he means traceable, guns traced back to the United

States." This was, of course, pure gibberish. A big lie demanded big, clean numbers. Little ones would not do, nor would big ones with asterisks. A number like "90 percent" could change hearts. A number like "12 percent" could not. "We feel good about these numbers and that's why the president uses the word recovered," added McDonough, clarifying nothing. The ATF and the Obama administration were not through politicizing the gun trafficking business. They would be back with a vengeance soon enough.

THE FAST AND FURIOUS PROGRAM WAS A FIELD-INITIATED PROGRAM BEGUN UNDER THE PREVIOUS ADMINISTRATION

"Last point I would make is that there are going to be some opportunities where I think we can build some strong consensus," said President Obama to President Calderón on the occasion of his April 2009 visit to Mexico. "I'll give you one example, and that is the issue of gun tracing. The tracing of bullets and ballistics and gun information that have been used in major crimes."

DOJ officials, working under then–deputy attorney general David W. Ogden, Eric Holder's number two man, got right to work. Six months later, in October 2009, they made good on Obama's promise to Calderón with a nine-page memo called "Department of Justice Strategy for Combating the Mexican Cartels." The memo instructed ATF offices near the Mexican border to broaden their scope in order to "identify, investigate and eliminate" the cartels. This approach, the memo added, would ensure "that scarce ATF resources are directed at the most important targets."

Operational tactics were left to the field offices, in this case the ATF field office for Arizona and New Mexico headed by the special agent in charge, Bill Newell. For no particularly good reason, the office named its new program Fast and Furious after the movie franchise. Newell ran the operation out of his Phoenix field office and kicked it off in November 2009. At the time, the ATF reported to Eric Holder's Department of Justice. The bureau had been moved from the Treasury to the Justice Department in 2003, in no small part because of a history of management problems.

As some field officers noticed, the ATF had begun to exhibit the symptoms of regulatory mission creep even before Obama came to power. With Obama's political operatives fully in place, that creep turned into a sprint. All the major political players responsible for Operation Fast and Furious were outspoken champions of gun control. They included a senior federal prosecutor for Arizona, Dennis Burke; his boss Eric Holder; Burke's former Chicago buddy Rahm Emanuel, now the White House chief of staff; and the president himself.

Agents could not help sensing the unspoken mission of the ATF. "When I came on the job, ATF wasn't about gun control," said Jay Dobyns, the former ATF agent who famously infiltrated the Hell's Angels. "It was about enforcing the federal firearm laws. And now [2011] the agency is about denying honest people their second amendment rights."

Holder does not appear to have been involved in the creation of Fast and Furious. It seems more likely that Newell, Burke, and others in the hierarchy hoped to impress their new bosses much the way the ATF of 1993 tried to impress the newly installed Clinton administration. That burst of creative nonsense led to the horrors of the Waco assault, in which more than eighty people died. A comparable burst in 2009, Operation Fast and Furious, has already killed more, and the body count continues to mount. Five years after the operation was first launched, no one has successfully explained what the ATF and the Department of Justice hoped to accomplish. One thing they did prove, however, was just how profound was the lie that transparency would be the touch-stone of the Obama administration.

As the operation worked, ATF agents leaned on licensed gun dealers in Arizona to ignore traditional restraints and sell weapons to buyers they knew to be straw purchasers for the cartels. The ATF proposed to track these sales and then, at some point, find their way to the bosses in the Mexican cartels and bust them. The problem was that for the first year at least ATF did no busting, and as many as two thousand guns flowed across the border into the hands of the cartels. Carlos Canino, the acting ATF attaché in Mexico, would call the operation a "perfect storm of idiocy."

Meanwhile, DOJ officials kept supplying fresh grist for the gun control propaganda mills. In 2010, for instance, while Fast and Furious was well under way, Burke took the occasion to slam the gun dealers. "We have a huge problem here," said Burke at the time. "We have now become the gun locker of the Mexican drug cartels." To be sure, Burke did not mention that the dealers had been all but forced to participate in the program.

In the early morning hours of December 15, 2010, more than a year after the program was launched, the one thing wary ATF agents feared would happen did happen. Drug dealers used one of the Fast and Furious guns to kill an American border patrol agent, Brian Terry. Before that fatal December day was through, e-mails flew between Phoenix and Washington, DC. Several were exchanged between Burke and Monty Wilkinson, Holder's deputy chief of staff. Wrote Burke in one of them, "The guns found near the murder [sic] BP officer connect back to the investigation we were going to talk about—they were AK-47s purchased at a Phoenix gun store."

ATF officials knew they had a mess on their hands and started mopping up immediately. They began by arresting Jaime Avila Jr., a known straw man. Avila had purchased the guns used to kill Terry nearly a year earlier and, incredibly, had been allowed to purchase hundreds more weapons under the surveillance of the ATF for the next eleven months. ATF agents arrested Avila, however, on a stand-alone charge unrelated to Fast and Furious lest they call attention to the operation. If nothing else, they had more success in suppressing the news than they did in arresting cartel members. The media would not catch on to Fast and Furious for months. They might not have caught on at all had not some bloggers and whistle-blowers prompted them.

A few of these ATF whistle-blowers had found their way to Republican senator Charles Grassley, the ranking minority member of the Senate Judiciary Committee. In late January 2011, Grassley asked the Department of Justice if it was true that ATF had allowed guns to "walk" into Mexico. On February 4, 2011, Assistant Attorney General Ronald Weich responded forcefully, "At the outset, the allegation described in your January 27 letter—that ATF 'sanctioned' or otherwise knowingly allowed the sale of assault weapons to a straw purchaser who then transported them into Mexico—is false." Weich tried to bury the Fast and Furious debacle under the larger banner of Operation Gunrunner, an e-tracing weapons interdiction system launched in 2006. He also claimed that there had been no attempt to retaliate against any whistle-blowers, a claim the ATF agent John Dodson would thoroughly refute in his 2013 book, *The Unarmed Truth*, and the Department of Justice's inspector general would confirm. Specifically, as Senator Grassley noted, "The administration leaked Privacy Act protected documents to the press in an effort to discredit Mr. Dodson with half-truths even though those documents had been withheld from Congress."

A little more than a month after Weich denied that guns had crossed the border, Obama answered a question from a Mexican journalist, Jorge Ramos, about Fast and Furious by admitting that "a serious mistake may have been made." In this Univision interview, Obama denied that either he or Holder had anything to do with Fast and Furious, but he noted that Holder had assigned his inspector general to investigate. "And you were not even informed about it?" asked an incredulous Ramos. "Absolutely not," said Obama; "this is a pretty big government, the United States government. I have got a lot of moving parts." Please note: not "It has," but "I have."

WHEN ERIC HOLDER FOUND OUT ABOUT IT, HE DISCONTINUED IT

Ronald Weich apparently did not see the Univision interview or CBS's reporting on it. On May 2, 2011, he sent Grassley another letter confirming his statement in the first one. "It remains our understanding," Weich wrote, "that ATF's Operation Fast and Furious did not knowingly permit straw buyers to take guns into Mexico." On that same May 2, Holder accompanied the head of the DHS, Janet Napolitano, to a White House meeting with Obama. No reason was given for this meeting, but the threesome almost certainly discussed Holder's scheduled appearance the following day before the House Judiciary Committee. That appearance set a new standard for willful cluelessness. When the committee's chair, Darrel Issa, asked Holder when he first knew about the program, Holder replied, "I probably heard about Fast and Furious over the last few weeks."

The last few weeks? The reader will recall that Brian Terry had been killed six months prior, and Holder's office had been informed that same day as to the reason why. Six weeks before Holder's testimony, Obama told a Mexican audience that Holder had already plunged deep into an investigation. When Issa asked whether Deputy Attorney General James Cole authorized the operation, Holder answered, "My guess would be no." My guess?

When Issa asked if the head of DOJ's criminal division, Lanny Breuer, authorized it, Holder answered, "I'm not sure whether Mr. Breuer authorized it." In fact, Breuer would later admit to the Senate Judiciary Committee that he was aware of the gunwalking tactics of Fast and Furious as early as April 2010, more or less putting a lie to every letter that the DOJ sent to Grassley thereafter. "The Justice Department had publicly denied to Congress that ATF would ever walk guns," said Grassley. "Yet the head of the Criminal Division, Mr. Breuer, knew otherwise and said nothing."

By December 2011, enough facts had emerged about the operation that the Justice Department could no longer sustain the obvious falsehoods in Weich's two letters. On December 2, Cole sent Grassley still another letter, this time acknowledging that the "February 4 letter contains inaccuracies." As a result, wrote Cole, "the Department now formally withdraws the February 4 letter." From this point, the story gets too involved and byzantine to explain in detail. In brief, the Republicans in the House and in the Senate wanted to know who in the Department of Justice authorized the operation and who attempted to conceal its implosion. They showed particular interest in the likely butt-covering communications between the first letter sent by Weich and Cole's retraction of it. In June 2012, just as the House Committee on Oversight and Government Reform was about to cite Holder for contempt of Congress for withholding subpoenaed documents, Obama asserted executive privilege. The House was not impressed. A week later, its members voted to cite Holder for contempt anyhow; he was the first cabinet member ever cited.

In September 2012, in the midst of a tightly contested reelection race, Barack Obama responded to one of the few media people who dared to challenge him on Operation Fast and Furious, Jorge Ramos. Ramos had reason to be disturbed by the operation. The weapons sold under the supervision of ATF's agents had killed as many as three hundred Mexican citizens. At a Univision forum, Obama unblushingly told Ramos, "The Fast and Furious program was a field-initiated program begun under the previous administration." This was a strategic lie that Obama surely knew was a lie. Three months earlier, White House Press Secretary Jay Carney made the same bogus claim virtually word for word at a press conference. The White House correspondent Jake Tapper, then with ABC, called him on it. "It began in fall 2009," said Tapper. Carney kept stonewalling. "The tactic began in the previous administration," he insisted, but as he knew, and as the president knew, the "tactic" driving Fast and Furious had no precedent. Yes, there had been other interdiction programs in the past, but none so bewilderingly open-ended as the one launched in October 2009.

Obama had more nonsense to tell Ramos about the operation. "When Eric Holder found out about it, he discontinued it. We assigned an inspector general to do a thorough report that was just issued, confirming that in fact Eric Holder did not know about this, that he took prompt action and the people who did initiate this were held accountable." In fact, six months after Brian Terry's death, as seen in Weich's second letter, the Department of Justice was denying that Operation Fast and Furious had even allowed guns to walk into Mexico. And if Holder had anything to do with shutting it down, or getting it started, Congress still does not know.

As of this writing, the House Committee on Oversight and Government Reform is suing the Department of Justice to acquire the relevant documents, and the ever transparent Obama administration is resisting Congress in a way that Nixon only wished he could have used. "Starting today, every agency and department should know that this administration stands on the side not of those who seek to withhold information, but those who seek to make it known," Obama told his staff on his first full day in office. Apparently, Holder did not get this memo.

THE PEOPLE WHO DID INITIATE THIS
WERE HELD ACCOUNTABLE

Despite the deaths of two American agents and hundreds of Mexican citizens, the White House held no one accountable for Fast and Furious. Dennis Burke resigned without mentioning it. At the time of his resignation, Holder issued a statement praising his "dedication and service." Acting ATF head Kenneth Melson was reassigned. Improbably, Bill Newell was promoted, as was the supervisor of the operation, David Voth. No Department of Justice official was so much as publicly reprimanded. Protected as they were by the White House, those who knew the score had no reason to tell anyone what they knew.

Between the operational absurdity of Fast and Furious and the ritualistic obstruction of its overseers, this should have been disgrace enough to deny Obama reelection. In 2012, though, the major media set an extraordinarily high bar for presidential scandal. Their eagerness to protect Obama's candidacy was never more obvious than in the second presidential debate, the town hall–style tag team event hosted by CNN's Candy Crowley.

When an audience member asked Obama, "What has your administration done or [what does it] plan to do to limit the availability of assault weapons?" Obama responded with some prescripted blather: of course, he believed in the Second Amendment, but he wanted a "comprehensive strategy" to deal with gun violence. On the same question, Romney started with generalities but then made a natural segue to Fast and Furious.

ROMNEY: I'd like to understand who it was that did this, what the idea was behind it, why it led to the

> violence—thousands of guns going to Mexican drug lords.
>
> OBAMA: Candy!

True to form, Crowley, right after her notorious Benghazi intervention, jumped into the ring to body-slam Romney once more:

> CROWLEY: Governor, Governor, if I could, the question was about these assault weapons that once were banned and are no longer banned. I know that you signed an assault weapons ban when you were in Massachusetts. Obviously with this question, you no longer do support that. Why is that? Given the kind of violence that we see sometimes with these mass killings, why is it that you've changed your mind?

In fact, the questioner never used the word "ban" or any of its synonyms. She spoke directly to the Obama administration's practices, not Romney's. Romney's discussion of Operation Fast and Furious was a perfectly legitimate response to the question asked, but it was obviously one that neither Crowley nor Obama wanted to hear during a critical debate. Crowley much preferred to share Romney's seeming vacillation on this issue.

Emboldened by his reelection, Obama headed to Mexico in May 2013 to scold his fellow citizens once again for corrupting our peace-loving amigos south of the border. For its sheer brazenness and dishonesty, this one passage needs to be read in full:

> And we also recognize that most of the guns used to commit violence here in Mexico come from the United States. [*Applause.*] I think many of you know that in America, our Constitution guarantees our individual right to bear arms, and

as President I swore an oath to uphold that right and I always will. But at the same time, as I've said in the United States, I will continue to do everything in my power to pass common-sense reforms that keep guns out of the hands of criminals and dangerous people. That can save lives here in Mexico and back home in the United States. It's the right thing to do. [*Applause.*] So we'll keep increasing the pressure on gun traffickers who bring illegal guns into Mexico. We'll keep putting these criminals where they belong—behind bars.

Toward the conclusion of her book, *Fast and Furious: Barack Obama's Bloodiest Scandal and Its Shameless Cover-Up*, Katie Pavlich posed the question that has puzzled everyone who was paying attention: "What was the purpose of Fast and Furious?" As she noted, although the guns could be traced to crime scenes after a crime had been committed, there never was a way to trace them to cartel bosses. Then too, if the purpose was to arrest the straw buyers, the ATF could have easily done that before the guns crossed the border. Asked Pavlich, "Was Fast and Furious designed to help build a case for new gun control measures that could not otherwise pass Congress?" Three years after the scandal first came to light, this question still baffles.

ONLY A MORE CIVIL AND HONEST PUBLIC DISCOURSE CAN HELP US FACE UP TO OUR CHALLENGES AS A NATION

Three weeks after Brian Terry was killed, and about sixty miles away, a deranged young man in Tucson, Arizona, embarked on a shooting spree that left six people dead and more than a dozen injured. Prominent among the injured and the likely target was

Democratic congresswoman Gabrielle Giffords, a woman about whom the shooter had been obsessing for years.

Although neither Obama nor Eric Holder attended any memorial for Brian Terry—Holder never so much as called the family—President Obama promptly descended on Tucson for a feint at national healing. His speech at the memorial service was a curious thing. For one, it was so fraught with scriptural references—four uses of the "G" word alone—that had a Republican given it, Bill Maher would have flogged him that evening on HBO. More to the point, the president who just a few years earlier was urging his followers to bring guns to a knife fight was now passing himself off as the great American peacemaker.

"Rather than pointing fingers or assigning blame," said Obama in Tucson, "let us use this occasion to expand our moral imaginations, to listen to each other more carefully, to sharpen our instincts for empathy, and remind ourselves of all the ways our hopes and dreams are bound together." If Obama had given this speech three years earlier, even three days earlier, he might have convinced America that his call for "a more civil and honest public discourse" was sincere. But even before the Tucson police had drawn the chalk marks, Democratic operatives triggered a fury of finger-pointing almost unprecedented in its dishonesty and incivility. The headline of a Michael Daly column in the liberal New York *Daily News* three days before the speech captured the gist of what appeared to be a coordinated strike: "Rep. Gabrielle Giffords' Blood Is on Sarah Palin's Hands after Putting Cross Hair over District."

A slightly more sober article in the *Washington Post* that same day made a direct connection between the shooting and a map that Palin's political action committee had posted months before. It showed twenty congressional districts targeted with either the crosshairs of a gun sight or a surveyor's symbol, depending on who interpreted it. "[Giffords] was very much troubled that Sarah Palin put her in the crosshairs," Congressman James Moran told the *Post*. To reinforce the link between Palin and a would-be assassin, Moran added that "a substantial percentage" of Giffords's district was "anti-government and pro-gun." This, the *Post* reporters editorialized, was "a potentially dangerous mix." In the days leading up to Obama's Tucson speech, virtually every major news outlet ran a story along these very same lines. In the absence of any hard information about the shooter, this narrative worked.

In fact, the shooter, Jared Loughner, may not have known who Sarah Palin was. A deeply disturbed schizophrenic with a fondness for drugs and satanic music, Loughner had been suspended from community college, rejected by the army, and abandoned by his friends. To the degree that he had political leanings of consequence, he veered left. The media should have known this immediately. On the same day as the shooting the alternative *Phoenix New Times* identified Loughner as a "Left-Wing Pothead" in its headline. One friend cited in that article described him as "left wing, quite liberal," even "radical." Another friend said that the sight of George Bush would make him "well up" in anger. In the days after the shooting, however, it was not the right pointing fingers at the left. It was almost exclusively the left pointing fingers at the right, most specifically at an entirely innocent individual, Sarah Palin. Obama knew this. When he told the Tucson crowd, "It's important for us to pause for a moment and make sure that we're talking with each other in a way that—that heals, not in a way that wounds," his own people, as Sarah Palin could attest, were doing the wounding. He likely approved of it. He did nothing to stop it. In Tucson, he failed to identify the culprits, and in so doing, quietly reinforced the false media narrative that incivility was the province of the right. So much for "honest public discourse."

I MEAN, GUN CONTROL, WE HAD 80, 90 PERCENT OF THE COUNTRY THAT AGREED WITH IT

Appearing on ABC's *This Week* in September 2013, Barack Obama bristled when the host, George Stephanopoulos, asked why he had accomplished so little since his November 2012 reelection. "So the question then is not whether or not the ideas that we've put forward can garner a majority of support, certainly in the country," snapped Obama. "I mean gun control, we had 80–90 percent of the country that agreed with it."

True to form, Stephanopoulos declined to question the numbers. Given a free pass, the man who had rejected "pointing fingers" in Tucson proceeded to point fingers at those who, he thought, deserved the blame. "The problem we have is we have a faction of the Republican Party, in the House of Representatives in particular, that view compromise as a dirty word," said Obama before adding a narcissistic touch, "and anything that is even remotely associated with me, they feel obliged to oppose." Obama had some advice for those congressmen too stubborn to yield to the seeming wave of popular support for gun control: "That's not why the people sent you here."

At the time, the memory of the Sandy Hook shooting was still raw in the public consciousness. In December 2012, a deeply disturbed young man had shot and killed twenty first graders and six of their teachers at a Connecticut public school. Knowing the political capital inherent in dead schoolchildren, Obama and his allies worked to keep the memory fresh. Given the moral weight of their cause, they did not feel obliged to stick to the facts. Three months after the shooting, for instance, at a San Francisco fundraiser, Obama told a group of Democratic donors that those twenty children were "gunned down" by "a fully automatic weapon." This was a purposefully distorted locution. The act of gunning some-one down is naturally attributed to an individual or individuals, not to a weapon. In addition to removing all human agency from the shooting, Obama lied about the weapon used. He knew the gun was a semiautomatic. He said as much before correcting him-self and converting it into an automatic. Something about San Francisco seemed to embolden Obama on the subject of guns. It was at a comparable fund-raiser five years earlier that he made his "bitter clinger" remarks.

For those who took their facts from Obama, Republicans who resisted gun control must have seemed as suicidal as polar bears who deny climate change. But like the polar bears, the congress-men had a better grasp of the facts on the ground. Two months before Obama's appearance on ABC, Pew Research Center ran the numbers on gun control. If anything, they were skewing slightly more sharply than they might have been because of Sandy Hook.

On the most basic gun control question—"What do you think is more important: to control gun ownership or to protect the right of Americans to own guns?"—the numbers in the Pew study broke in favor of gun control 50 to 48 percent, nowhere near the 80 to 90 percent Obama promised. On the question of whether stricter gun laws "give too much power to the government over average citizens," 57 percent agreed. This was clearly not a nation clamoring for new gun laws.

As expected, Republicans were less enthusiastic about gun control than Democrats. Only 19 percent of Republicans thought gun legislation was "essential this year," and 53 percent said gun legislation "should not be done" at all. The passion on this issue strongly favored gun rights. Its partisans were four times more likely to contribute to their cause than were gun control support-ers. As an avowed constitutionalist, one who championed the marriage of "passion to reason," Obama should have appreciated that the founders created a republic, and not a democracy, for just such an occasion as Sandy Hook. The reality, of course, was that Obama respected the whole of the Constitution no more than he did the Second Amendment.

CHAPTER 9

THE STATESMAN

Barack Obama began his run for the White House just two years after leaving his post as a state senator in the provincial backwater of Springfield, Illinois. Despite that limitation, Obama promptly began promoting himself as a man to the international stage born, a savant, a statesman unlike any America had produced since Woodrow Wilson.

The one gesture that made his candidacy viable, in fact, was a speech he made as a state senator in 2002 that went well beyond the pale of his local brief. This was the speech in which he denounced as "dumb" a war in Iraq—a war that had not yet started; a war that all of his major primary opponents voted to authorize; a war whose unfolding confirmed, to the Democratic base at least, Obama's strategic foresight. On the subject of Iraq, alas, Obama was not quite the savant that he and his followers thought him to be. His premature withdrawal of American troops from an allegedly "sovereign, stable and self-reliant Iraq" in 2011 proved to be at least as "dumb" as anything he had accused his predecessor of doing.

In 2008, however, Iraq was still intact and so was Obama's reputation. His Chicago speech enabled him to flank senators Hillary

Clinton and John Edwards to the left and secure a stake in the Democratic primaries. Propelled by that speech, Obama would go on to win the nomination, the general election, and a Nobel Peace Prize, all before he had the chance to target a single American citizen for a drone strike.

I KNOW MORE AND UNDERSTAND THE WORLD BETTER THAN SENATOR CLINTON OR SENATOR McCAIN

"Foreign policy is the area where I am probably most confident that I know more and understand the world better than Senator Clinton or Senator McCain," said an overconfident Barack Obama in April 2008 at still another fund-raiser in San Francisco. This strategic jab at the two people who stood between him and the White House was less a lie than an empty, unverifiable boast. If there was a lie involved, it was one of omission, a past omission that Obama seemed to correct at that same fund-raiser.

Obama took particular aim at Hillary Clinton. He countered her claim of having met leaders from eighty foreign countries with his real-world experience in several key outposts. "I traveled to Pakistan when I was in college," said Obama in the way of illustration. "I knew what Sunni and Shia was [*sic—Obama has always had problems with noun-verb agreement*] before I joined the Senate Foreign Relations Committee."

This declaration took the ABC reporter Jake Tapper by surprise. He thought it odd that he had not heard of this trip, especially "given all the talk of Pakistan during this campaign." Indeed, Obama introduced the general subject of Pakistan as early as August 1, 2007. As Tapper observed at the time, Obama talked about US-Pakistan policy as a way of challenging Hillary's perceived strength on foreign affairs. Yet despite the strategic edge his personal experience in Pakistan may have given him, Obama failed to mention his Pakistan adventure in that August 2007 speech or for the next eight months.

Had Tapper inquired further, he would have learned that Obama did not mention the visit to Pakistan in either of his books, the 1995 *Dreams from My Father* or the 2006 *Audacity of Hope*. Given that Obama used both of those books, especially *Audacity*, to emphasize his precocious political wisdom, the omission of his Pakistan experience perplexes. When Tapper asked the Obama campaign staffers about the trip, they described it as a casual stopover to see friends on the tail end of a visit with his mother in Indonesia. In fact, Obama spent three weeks in Pakistan, during Ramadan at that, more time than he spent in Indonesia. This should have spurred reporters to question Obama's previous silence. Had they been half as curious as their counterparts on HBO's *The Newsroom*, they might have blown open one of the great underreported stories of the 2008 campaign, a story that broke just two weeks prior to Obama's Pakistani epiphany.

This story involved the recent breaches of the presidential candidates' passport records. On March 22, 2008, the *Washington Post* headline about the event read, "Rice Apologizes for Breach of Passport Data; Employees Looked at Files on Obama, Clinton, McCain." The "Rice" in question was Secretary of State Condoleezza Rice. The offended party in the *Post*'s story was Barack Obama. Obama told reporters that he expected "a full and thorough investigation."

Not until the thirteenth paragraph of the *Post*'s article did the reader learn that one of the three contract employees caught in the act worked for the Analysis Corporation, whose CEO was a certain John Brennan. The *Post* did report that Brennan donated $2,300 to the Obama campaign but suggested no deeper tie. That information was offset by the revelation that the other two culpable contract employees worked for Stanley Inc., whose CEO, Philip Nolan, had contributed $1,000 to the Clinton campaign. Stanley, however, had been handling passport work for fifteen years and had just been awarded a five-year, $570 million contract. The company had no reason to play favorites in the 2008 campaign. It promptly fired the two employees, neither of whom, almost assuredly, worked at the directive of Nolan or of the Clinton campaign.

Unlike Stanley Inc., a huge government contractor, Analysis Corporation had fewer than one hundred employees, and its one culpable employee escaped discipline. The *Post*'s article reported only that this unnamed person's employment status was "under review." Nor was Brennan a casual donor to the Obama campaign. To its credit, *CNN Politics* saw the real news angle in the passport scandal: "Chief of Firm Involved in Breach Is Obama Adviser." As CNN reported, also on March 22, Brennan "advises the Illinois Democrat on foreign policy and intelligence issues." Lucky guy: Brennan went on to advise the president as the director of the CIA.

After its initial article on the passport breach, the *Post* said not a single word about the incident or Brennan's connection to it. Incredibly, the *Post* remained mute on the subject even in its thirteen-hundred-word front-page article of January 9, 2009, "Obama Taps CIA Veteran Brennan as Counterterror Adviser." The fact that one of Brennan's employees breached Obama's passport files just months earlier held no interest for the newspaper whose dogged reporting of an arguably lesser offense brought down the Nixon White House.

NO HOLY WAR CAN EVER BE A JUST WAR

On October 9, 2009, the Norwegian Nobel Committee stunned the world by naming Barack Obama the recipient of the Nobel

Peace Prize for "his extraordinary efforts to strengthen international diplomacy and cooperation between peoples." If Barack
Obama needed confirmation of his emergence as international
statesman he got it in spades. He joined Jimmy Carter, Theodore
Roosevelt, and, yes, Woodrow Wilson as the only American presidents to have won the award.

The Norwegians, as they say at the craps table, were betting
on the come. Obama, after all, had taken office on January 20 of
that very same year. Nominations closed a few weeks later. It was
as if the National League had nominated a rookie for the MVP
award after his third at bat and given it to him after the twelfth.
Still, said the fawning Norwegians, "Only very rarely has a person
to the same extent as Obama captured the world's attention and
given its people hope for a better future." The Norwegians praised
Obama for his commitment to arms reduction, human rights, democracy, and, of course, "climactic challenges." These were the
same people, one recalls, who gave the climate guru Al Gore the
Nobel Prize just two years prior.

At the same time the Norwegians were puffing Obama up, they
were setting him up. They obviously thought Obama a fellow glo-
balist and wanted him to know their expectations. Announced
the Nobel committee none too subtly, "His diplomacy is founded
in the concept that those who are to lead the world must do so on
the basis of values and attitudes that are shared by the majority of
the world's population." This presumption rankled those Americans who thought it was their values and attitudes the president
was expected to share.

The award put Obama in an awkward position. He knew he did
not deserve it. So did just about every other thinking person on the
planet, friend and foe alike. Joked *Wonkette*'s Anna Maria Cox with
some accuracy, "Apparently Nobel prizes are now being awarded to
anyone who is not George Bush." Elaborated *RedState*'s Erick Erick-
son, "Obama is becoming Jimmy Carter faster than Jimmy Carter

became Jimmy Carter." Said Kristina Hernandez of CRC Public Relations, "It was the Beer Summit that put Obama over the edge." Indeed, the diplomatic highlight of Obama's first nine months had been the awkward "beer summit" he staged between a Cambridge cop and the black Harvard intellectual the cop had arrested.

With all this as background, Obama journeyed to Norway in December 2009 and gave perhaps the most thoughtful speech of his presidency on America's role in the world. To give credit where it's due, he also spoke humbly about himself. Said Obama, in the most honest moment of his presidency, "My accomplishments are slight." He got no argument on that, even from his fans.

To pacify the internationalists, however, Obama had to reassert one of the foundational falsehoods of his presidency, namely that Islam was a "great religion" whose principles were being "defiled" by all the various wars and insurgencies fought under its banner. In a comparable way, suggested Obama, the "cruelties of the Crusades" defiled Christianity. In a grand gesture of moral equivocation, Obama concluded, "No holy war can ever be a just war." In fact, a compelling case can be made that the Crusaders descended on the Holy Land only in response to Muslim assaults on Christian pilgrims. And surely the defensive battles by Christians against would-be Muslim invaders at Tours, Lepanto, and Vienna were as morally justified as the American battle against the Taliban. Unfortunately, as he often did during his presidency, Obama felt compelled to distort the Christian past to rationalize the Islamic present.

WHEN THE CHIPS ARE DOWN I HAVE ISRAEL'S BACK

"Let me be absolutely clear," Senator Barack Obama said in a July 2008 press conference in Amman, Jordan. "Israel is a strong friend of Israel's. It will be a strong friend of Israel's under a McCain . . . administration. It will be a strong friend of Israel's under an Obama administration. So that policy is not going to change." It is a good thing that Israel has a strong friend in Israel because it has no other friend in the region and, at least since January 2009, no reliable friend in the White House.

All gaffes aside, the very existence of Israel remains perilous and all the more so because its people cannot trust Barack Obama. In order to shore up that trust and to offset Republican criticism during an election year, the president told the American Israel Public Affairs Committee in March 2012, "There should not be a shred of doubt by now: When the chips are down, I have Israel's back."

Two days later, at a White House press conference, Jake Tapper asked Obama what exactly he meant when he said, "I have Israel's back." Lest his pledge be taken too seriously, Obama qualified his support. "It was not a military doctrine that we were laying out for any particular military action," said the president. "It was a restatement of our consistent position that the security of Israel is something I deeply care about, and that the deeds of my administration over the last three years confirms [sic] how deeply we care about it."

The Israelis could not have cared less about what the royal "I" claimed to care about. What troubled them were those very "deeds." In October 2013, Caroline Glick, managing editor of the *Jerusalem Post*, spoke as bluntly as an Israeli editor can about an American president: "US President Barack Obama views lies as legitimate political tools. He uses lies strategically to accomplish through mendacity what he could never achieve through honest means."

THIS ADMINISTRATION HAS DONE MORE
FOR THE SECURITY OF THE STATE OF ISRAEL THAN
ANY PREVIOUS ADMINISTRATION

In terms of outright lies, few match the claim that President Obama made to influential Jewish supporters at a New York City fund-raiser in late November 2011. "I try not to pat myself too much on the back," said Obama in the first and lesser of his two untruths, "but this administration has done more for the security of the state of Israel than any previous administration." Even if one excludes the support Truman lent during Israel's founding, Johnson's support during the Six-Day War, Nixon's support during the Yom Kippur War, George H. W. Bush's support during the Gulf War, and George W. Bush's support during the Iraq War, Obama's boast still wouldn't fly. As Mark Tapson argued in a *FrontPage* editorial, "The reality is that no administration has done *less* to secure Israel from Muslim aggression."

Tapson had no trouble finding examples to support his claim. Just three days after the Obama fund-raiser in New York, for instance, Secretary of Defense Leon Panetta gave a speech at the Brookings Institution that netted the Fox News headline, "Panetta Scolds Israel on Peace Talks." During the talk, he put the onus on Israel to "reach out and mend fences" with the newly Islamist state of Egypt and the ever volatile Turkey, as though Israel had done something to merit fence-mending. As to the Palestinians, Panetta all but ordered Israel "to get to the damned table." Both in tone and in content, Panetta mirrored what Obama had been saying—when not at fund-raisers—for the previous three years.

Throughout his tenure, Obama warned Jews not to build homes in Jerusalem. He compelled Israel to negotiate with Hamas despite the group's sworn vow to annihilate Israel. He pressured Israel to apologize to Turkey for intercepting a terrorist arms flotilla. And, most problematically, he demanded that Israel withdraw to its indefensible 1967 borders. Said Tapson in conclusion, "This tiny sliver of a pro-American democracy is surrounded by a swelling tide of genocidal hostility. You would never know it, however, from listening to Obama's smug self-congratulation."

Obama might have warmed up to Israel if its citizens returned to power someone other than the conservative Benjamin Netanyahu just two months after Obama's inauguration. From the outset, Obama could barely conceal his discomfort with Israel's new prime minister. That unease bubbled to the surface less than a month before his New York speech when Obama got caught in an epic Kinsley gaffe. A live microphone caught him telling French president Nicolas Sarkozy, "You're fed up with [Netanyahu], but I have to deal with him every day!"

Once reelected, Obama squeezed Israel even harder. In March 2014, immediately before a visit from Netanyahu, Obama set the stage in an interview with the *Atlantic*'s Jeffrey Goldberg. He said ominously that a failure by Netanyahu to make the concessions could limit America's "ability to manage international fallout, and that has consequences." For Israel, the word "consequences" has an existential ring to it.

In April 2014, Secretary of State John Kerry squeezed harder still. In a private address to an international group of high-level officials at the Trilateral Commission, Kerry argued that unless Israel accepted a two-state solution it risked becoming an "apartheid state." Once he realized his off-the-record remarks had been recorded and reported by the *Daily Beast*, Kerry apologized for his choice of words, but the Israelis had no trouble interpreting his intent.

WE'VE BEEN ABLE TO MOBILIZE UNPRECEDENTED, CRIPPLING SANCTIONS ON IRAN

In her October 2013 article in the *Jerusalem Post*, Caroline Glick cited, among other deceptions, Obama's shifting stance on nuclear sanctions against Iran. Glick, who was born in Obama's Hyde Park neighborhood and graduated from Columbia University, was not just some Israeli outlier on this issue. Many in Congress felt much as she did, the most prominent of them being Democratic senator Robert Menendez, chairman of the Senate Committee on Foreign Relations. Menendez had reason to be upset. Late in 2011 the US Senate attempted to pass a tough sanctions bill against an Iranian administration eager to go nuclear. At the president's request, the Senate softened its original demands and tried to create a balanced bipartisan agreement. When the Senate succeeded in doing just that, the White House set about undermining even this watered-down version. Although underreported at the time, Menendez's criticism of the White House was unsparing. Calling its behavior "outrageous," he said to a State Department deputy, "It would have been more honest to say, We don't want any amendment whatsoever."

As the *Washington Post*'s Jennifer Rubin observed, Menendez delivered "perhaps the most critical words spoken by any senator in recent memory." Rubin overstated the case, but Menendez's rebuke of the White House on the subject of the sanctions was among the most forceful internecine smackdowns of the Internet era. The president's opposition notwithstanding, the Senate passed Menendez's sanctions bill by a rather convincing 100–0.

Left with little choice, Obama signed the bill into law. He did so on New Year's Eve, all the better to bury any news coverage it might have mustered. The political dynamics, however, soon changed. The likely Republican nominee for president, Mitt Romney, was insisting that restraining Iran should be America's "highest national security priority." Obama made a tactical response. By March 2012, he was boasting, "We've been able to . . . mobilize unprecedented, crippling sanctions on Iran." In fact, the sanctions were not crippling. They were not unprecedented, and Obama's contribution to the "we" was to get in the way.

In late July 2012, Romney took his message to Israel and there adopted what the *New York Times* described as "the language of Israel's leaders." Two days after the *Times* reported on Romney's trip, Obama issued by executive order new sanctions against two Iranian financial institutions. That same day, the White House announced further restrictions on the purchase of Iranian petrochemical products. "If the Iranian government continues its defiance, there should be no doubt that the United States and our partners will continue to impose increasing consequences," blustered Obama. As the *Washington Post* noted, the White House's announcement preceded by hours a bipartisan congressional measure that would lay still more economic sanctions on Iran. It was just enough of a time gap to squeeze out a headline or two—e.g., the *New York Times'* "White House and Congress Are in Step over Iran Sanctions"—and pacify some of Obama's major Jewish donors. These headlines did not begin to pacify Glick. "The mendacity at the heart of Obama's political playbook," she wrote, "is something that Israel needs to understand if it to survive his presidency without major damage to its strategic viability."

WITH REGARD TO THE KIND OF THING YOU'RE TALKING ABOUT ON A GOVERNMENT-TO-GOVERNMENT LEVEL: NO

Duplicity is a great procreator. It has a seemingly inevitable way of spawning future generations of lies, deceptions, and evasions. So it was in the case of Obama's Iran policy. In February 2013, Fox News's chief Washington correspondent, James Rosen, the same Rosen who had been singled out for surveillance by the NSA, asked the then–state department spokesperson Victoria Nuland about reports of "direct, secret bilateral talks with Iran." Answered Nuland, "With regard to the kind of thing you're talking about on a government-to-government level: no." Nuland was lying. What made this unique among the hundreds of other White House lies was that the administration eventually owned up to it—in a limited kind of way.

In December 2013, Rosen returned to the State Department's briefing room to confront spokesperson Jen Psaki about reports that senior American officials had been engaging in a series of meetings with equally senior Iranian officials. Asked Rosen, "The question today is a simply [sic] one: when the briefer was asked about those talks and flatly denied them, that was untrue, correct?" After some awkward equivocating by Psaki, Rosen asked if it was State Department policy "to lie" to preserve the secrecy of certain negotiations. "There are times when diplomacy needs privacy in order to progress," Psaki conceded. "This is a good example of that."

In fact, the reports that Rosen cited were accurate. For the previous two years, American officials had been meeting with their Iranian counterparts in Oman, an Arab state on the southeast coast of the Arabian Peninsula. They met to conclude an agree-

ment on Iran's nuclear policy. "The lie matters less than the investment in the talks themselves," argued the journalist Major Garrett
in the *National Journal*. Garrett made the case that Obama had
blocked sanctions so that these secret negotiations could proceed
unimpeded. Garrett did not account, however, for Obama's quick
embrace of sanctions once he realized Romney's tough talk was
eroding his donor base. Ever hopeful, Garrett or his editors titled
his article, "The Obama Administration's Useful Lie about Iran
Talks."

Israeli prime minister Benjamin Netanyahu, for one, did not
think the talks were "useful" to Israel at all. "What was concluded
in Geneva last night is not a historic agreement, it's a historic mistake," said Netanyahu in late November 2013. The deal, he argued,
has Iran "taking only cosmetic steps which it could reverse easily
within a few weeks, and in return, sanctions that took years to
put in place are going to be eased." Naftali Bennett, the Israeli
minister of trade and industry, was among many in the Israeli
leadership unconvinced that Obama had Israel's back. "If in five
years, a nuclear suitcase explodes in New York or Madrid," said
Bennett, "it will be because of the agreement that was signed this
morning."

The Iranian nuke deal proved useful to Obama at least in the
short haul. He took the occasion of his 2014 State of the Union
speech to boast of his administration's diplomacy, which, he
claimed, "halted the progress of Iran's nuclear program—and
rolled back parts of that program—for the very first time in
a decade." He attributed this success in no small part to "the
sanctions that we put in place," the same congressionally driven
sanctions that he once attempted to sabotage. To clarify his own
position going forward, he insisted, "If this Congress sends me a
new sanctions bill now that threatens to derail these talks, I will
veto it."

In an ironic spin of the wheel, Iran promptly accused Obama

of lying about how the tentative deal was reached. Said Iran's foreign ministry spokeswoman, Marzieh Afkham, "The delusion of sanctions having an effect on Iran's motivation for nuclear negotiations is based on a false narration of history." Showing the world just how reliable a negotiating partner Iran would be, Afkham insisted, "America considers preventing Iran from obtaining a nuclear weapon to be its biggest achievement, but it is wrong since Iran has never sought to obtain a nuclear weapon and will never do so in future." Of course not.

"The key to phase one of the Iran deal is for the White House to tell no lies to itself now about Iran's actions," wrote an insufficiently jaded Major Garrett in the *National Journal*. "It's equally important the administration not lie to itself about the value of its cloak-and-dagger diplomacy." This seems unlikely. Going forward, both Iran and the Obama administration have every incentive to lie: Iran to protect its nuclear program, Obama to protect his legacy. Unfortunately, both also have a well-documented history of doing just that. Caroline Glick made this case in the summary of her mischievously titled article "Obamacare Victims and Israel." If Congress does not call Obama on his lies, she worried out loud, "Israel becomes the foreign corollary to the Americans whose health insurance Obama canceled."

Israeli leadership will not likely let that happen. On the occasion of Holocaust Remembrance Day in late April 2014, several key figures in the Israeli national security establishment, including Prime Minister Netanyahu, spoke out strongly about the imminent peril Israel faced in the absence of projected American power. "Anyone who thinks that a U.S. administration would respond immediately to an Iranian agreement violation, without negotiations, is deluding himself," wrote the former national security adviser General Yaakov Amidror. "Israel cannot accept the existential threat caused by this delusion."

WHEN YOU WERE ASKED, WHAT'S THE BIGGEST GEOPOLITICAL THREAT FACING AMERICA? YOU SAID RUSSIA—NOT AL-QAEDA. YOU SAID RUSSIA.

In his third and final debate with Mitt Romney, this one on foreign policy, Osama-killer Obama presumed he had the upper hand. "I'm glad that you recognize that al-Qaeda's a threat," he said mockingly, implying that this was a new position on Romney's part. "A few months ago," Obama continued, "when you were asked what's the biggest geopolitical threat facing America, you said Russia—not al-Qaeda." Here, Obama was being deceptive. Regardless of what he may have said about Russia, Romney never suggested that al-Qaeda was anything less than a serious threat. On the FIG scale, however, Obama's remarks would not have pushed the needle past the "finesse" range. They were the kind of misrepresentations one would expect during a debate.

What made Obama's comments memorable were subsequent world events. The Nobel Peace Prize winner mocked the provincial Massachusetts governor prematurely with a prescripted barb. "You know, the Cold War's been over for 20 years," Obama taunted him. "Governor, when it comes to our foreign policy, you seem to want to import the foreign policies of the 1980s, just like the social policies of the 1950s and the economic policies of the 1920s."

In a March 2014 article in the liberal online publication *Slate*, David Weigel explained the advantage Obama hoped to secure with his intentional deception. "He was playing to the cheap seats," wrote Weigel. "Voters do not fear Russia, or particularly care about its movements in its sad, cold sphere of influence. They do care a lot about terrorism." By "cheap seats" Weigel meant low-information voters. Weigel rightly called this a "cheap trick."

In his response, Romney attempted to unwind Obama's conscious spin. He explained that Russia was the most serious "geopolitical foe" and that Iran was America's "greatest national security threat." The clarification that followed has become a YouTube staple for its prescience. "I have clear eyes on this," said Romney, "I'm not going to wear rose-colored glasses when it comes to Russia, or Mr. Putin. And I'm certainly not going to say to him, I'll give you more flexibility after the election. After the election, he'll get more backbone."

Romney here alluded to Obama's March 2012 exchange in South Korea with Russian president Dmitri Medvedev that was picked up by a live microphone

MEDVEDEV: Yeah, I understand. I understand your message about space. Space for you . . .

OBAMA: This is my last election. After my election I have more flexibility.

MEDVEDEV: I understand. I will transmit this information to Vladimir.

Speaking of South Korea, the former secretary of state Dean Acheson failed to place the Korean peninsula within America's "defense perimeter" in a critical January 1950 speech. Many believe this failure encouraged Soviet honcho Joseph Stalin to greenlight the communist invasion of South Korea. There are many now who wonder whether Obama's indiscreet remark on his second-term ambitions encouraged Putin to threaten Ukraine. Words do have consequences.

I DIDN'T SET A RED LINE

President Obama never quite knew what to do about Syria, and his indecision showed in the way he handled a crisis that will not be resolved anytime soon. The blundering climaxed in August 2012, when intelligence reports suggested that the Syrian government may have been planning to use chemical weapons against the rebel opposition. Working frenetically behind the scenes, the administration tried to get intermediaries like Russia and Iran to warn President Bashar al-Assad that the use of such weapons would be a very bad idea.

Although usually anchored to his teleprompter, Obama wandered into uncharted semantic waters on August 20 at an impromptu press conference in the White House briefing room. There, a reporter asked the president about the intentions of the Syrian government. Specifically, the reporter wanted to know "whether you envision using U.S. military [for], if simply for nothing else, the safekeeping of the chemical weapons."

Obama gave a long and rambling answer in response. In the critical part of that answer, he established that he not yet ordered "military engagement," but that the security of chemical and biological weapons concerned him. "We have been very clear to the Assad regime, but also to other players on the ground," said the president emphatically, "that a red line for us is we start seeing a whole bunch of chemical weapons moving around or being utilized. That would change my calculus. That would change my equation." The *New York Times* took Obama at his word and described his "red line" remark as "Mr. Obama's first direct threat of force against Syria."

With his unscripted remarks, Obama had ventured where his

security advisers wished he had not. "The idea was to put a chill into the Assad regime without actually trapping the president into any predetermined action," one anonymous adviser told the *Times*, but trapped the president was, or so he seemed. Rather than contradict the president publicly, administration officials more or less backed him up. The day after the press conference, when asked about the "red line," the White House spokesman Josh Earnest said that "any use or proliferation of efforts related to those chemical weapons is something that would be very serious and it would be a grave mistake."

In April 2013, the White House legislative affairs director Miguel Rodriguez reinforced the red line policy in a letter to members of Congress. "Because of our concern about the deteriorating situation in Syria," wrote Rodriquez, "the president has made it clear that the use of chemical weapons—or transfer of chemical weapons to terrorist groups—is a red line for the United States of America." The following day in a conference call with reporters and White House officials, the red line was confirmed anew. "It's precisely because we take this red line so seriously," said one official, "that we believe there is an obligation to fully investigate any and all evidence of chemical weapons use within Syria."

In September 2013, a dithering President Obama turned to Congress on the Syrian issue. He needed someone to share the public relations burden of a potential military strike against a Syrian government that stood accused of using chemical weapons. Administration officials did not want this to be made "Obama's war" the way they and their colleagues had coldly made Iraq "Bush's war." To diffuse responsibility, they had to pull the administration back from the red line Obama had so memorably drawn.

Secretary of State John Kerry rolled out the strategy before the Senate on September 3, 2013. "Some have tried to suggest that the debate we're having today is about President Obama's red line," said Kerry in a carefully prepared statement. That notion he said was "plain and simply wrong." Rather, the debate was about "the world's red line," a red line "that anyone with a conscience ought to draw." Then Kerry reminded Congress about the ten-year-old Syria Accountability Act. The act addressed the Syrian government's support of terrorism in Lebanon, but it also included a few sentences about Syrian chemical weapons in its preamble. The crafty Kerry called this obscure act "Congress's own red line."

The following day at a press conference in Stockholm, a reporter asked the president about Syria: "Is a strike needed in order to preserve your credibility for when you set these sort of red lines?" Off the teleprompter, an Obama performance could be excruciating, and this was one such performance. Obama managed to recite all the talking points Kerry recited the day before: the Syria Accountability Act, the congressional red line, the rejection of chemical weapons by 98 percent of the world's people. But before he found his groove, he did instinctively what he often did when challenged. He denied his own earlier comments. "First of all, I didn't set a red line," he scolded the reporter. He recovered quickly and added, "The world set a red line," but by then it was too late: no amount of qualifiers could erase so bold a red line.

WE KNOW THE ASSAD REGIME WAS RESPONSIBLE

On September 10, 2013, President Obama got ready to address the nation on Syria. In this speech he would explain how he authorized a targeted air strike against Assad's government, thought better of it, turned to Congress for approval, and then asked Congress to postpone a vote while he pursued a "diplomatic path." That was the easy part. The hard part was making this waffling, wavering, wildly disingenuous performance look like a strategy.

The reason given for the proposed—but now deferred—attack

was that Assad's government had allegedly crossed the mythical red line and "gassed to death over a thousand people." In fact, the evidence for this charge was always shaky. It was possible, though unlikely, that Assad did, in fact, order such an attack. What was beyond doubt was that Obama misled the nation on the state of existing intelligence. "We know the Assad regime was responsible," said Obama in his September 10 address. As shall be seen, "we" did not know that. "The facts cannot be denied," Obama insisted. Yes, they could be credibly denied and would be.

Despite the critical nature of the issue at hand, the major media, particularly the *New York Times*, were largely content to let Obama get away with this shadow boxing. Following the president's September 10 address, the *Times* published a series of articles that seemed to confirm Obama's thesis that Assad was responsible for the sarin gas attacks. Particularly helpful to the administration was a United Nations report that sarin gas had been used in a chemical weapons attack near Damascus on August 21, 2013. Although the report did not say who used the gas, the White House and the media quickly satisfied themselves that the forensic details "strongly implicated the Syrian government."

There were not many independent journalists capable of short-circuiting this happy information loop, but one who could did. That was Seymour Hersh, a veteran Pulitzer Prize–winning reporter with pristine liberal credentials. Indeed, in the first major scoop of his career Hersh exposed the previously well-concealed My Lai massacre. In a lengthy article published in the *London Review of Books* Hersh carefully deconstructed the Syrian fables the Obama administration had been telling.

Unlike many in the American media, Hersh did not feel the need to tiptoe around Obama's delicate narrative. "Barack Obama did not tell the whole story this autumn," wrote Hersh, "when he tried to make the case that Bashar al-Assad was responsible for the chemical weapons attack near Damascus on 21 August." According to Hersh, Obama omitted important intelligence, presented assumptions as facts, and, most critically, failed to acknowledge that the Syrian army was not the only player in the civil war with access to sarin. "The cherry-picking," continued Hersh in a sentence designed to wound Obama's anti–"dumb war" sensibilities, "was similar to the process used to justify the Iraq war." One of Hersh's sources, a former intelligence officer, rubbed in the salt when he compared Obama's intelligence gathering to that used by Lyndon Johnson after the Gulf of Tonkin incident.

Like Johnson, Obama was willing to go to war to back up his public threats, said Hersh, "without knowing for sure who did what." At every step, officials let the gullible media think the White House knew more than it actually did. Few were more gullible than Joby Warrick of the *Washington Post*. For his August 31, 2013, article, Warrick repeated the administration's talking points as confidently as if they had come from a burning bush. "Unknown to Syrian officials," reported Warrick, "U.S. spy agencies recorded each step in the alleged chemical attack, from the extensive preparations to the launching of rockets to the after-action assessments by Syrian officials."

Administration officials had masterfully created the illusion that its operatives had monitored Syrian preparations in the lead-up to the attack. They did so good a job, in fact, that they created a backlash. Observers wondered out loud why team Obama failed to intervene in an attack it saw coming. "Let's be clear," an intelligence official was forced to say, "the United States did not watch, in real time, as this horrible attack took place."

The administration also felt free to inflate the body count. A week after the attack, the White House released a four-page report specifying the number of dead as exactly 1,429. This prompted Kerry to proclaim, "The primary question is really no longer, what do we know. The question is what are we—we collectively—what are we in the world going to do about it." In fact, there were many questions about what was known, including the number of people actually killed. As Hersh reported, a Syrian human rights group counted 502 deaths, and a French report listed as few as 281.

Hersh wasn't through yet. "The White House's misrepresentation of what it knew about the attack, and when," he wrote, "was matched by its readiness to ignore intelligence that could undermine the narrative." The intelligence Obama was most keen on ignoring concerned al-Nusra, an Islamist rebel group designated as a terrorist organization. Hersh made a strong case not only that al-Nusra had attacked rival resistance groups and Christians, but also that it had developed a working familiarity with sarin gas. The administration, said Hersh, routinely disregarded reports on the same. Kerry, in fact, dismissed al-Nusra as a serious actor, a claim he later was forced to retract.

As Hersh observed, this intel legerdemain has consequences. If by some miracle Assad destroys his weapons stockpile as promised, al-Nusra could end up as the only faction inside Syria with access to sarin, a strategic game-changer for a group outside the law to begin with. As Hersh concluded ominously, "There may be more to negotiate."

BUT THE DEBATE IS SETTLED. CLIMATE CHANGE IS A FACT.

In the current age, the portfolio of any respectable statesman, especially a Nobel Peace Prize winner, inevitably includes a brief on "climate change." In fact, the Norwegians awarded President Obama the Nobel Peace Prize in no small part because of his willingness to confront the world's "great climatic challenges." The problem was that by 2014 no one was quite sure what those challenges were. Indeed, the earth had not warmed in sixteen years, and this had inspired the savvier environmentalists, Obama among them, to at least shift the branding of the seeming crisis from "global warming" to "climate change."

To defend the indefensible, George Orwell once observed, political figures employ language that consists largely of "euphemism, question-begging and sheer cloudy vagueness." On the subject of climate, Obama has been among the cloudiest and vaguest of all the world's statesmen and easily its most vainglorious west of Pyongyang. No other leader in a nation with a free press would have dared to insist, as Obama did in June 2008, that his nomination represented "the moment when the rise of the oceans began to slow and our planet began to heal."

All presidents have dealt with the weather, and most undoubtedly have speculated about it. Obama, however, has transformed his speculation into policy in ways none of his predecessors thought to do. As a candidate, for instance, Obama pledged to establish a cap-and-trade system. In a rare honest movement with the *San Francisco Chronicle*'s editors in January 2008, he admitted that under his plan, "Electricity rates would necessarily skyrocket." As structured, this jerry-rigged system would have capped the amount of carbon emissions companies could produce but would have also given them the opportunity to trade for more permits as needed. Obama actively promoted the House version of this bill, known as the American Clean Energy and Security Act of 2009.

In promoting the bill, Obama threw out promises and statistics as carelessly as he did for Obamacare. The trick, as he explained back in San Francisco, was to make the case for long-term economic benefit "persuasively enough" that Americans would accept higher prices. To get the bill passed, Obama and the House leadership, then Democratic, violated just about every transparency pledge Obama had ever made. They brought this fifteen-hundred-page opus to the floor unposted and unread by anyone and allowed just three hours for debate. Fortunately, Americans never got to see the final price tag. Although the bill passed the House, several moderate Senate Democrats, fearing voters' backlash, killed it in legislative utero. The hard left criticized Obama for failing to deliver on a promise, but its troops could not rightly accuse him of a "lie." The Senate thwarted his will. That happens. But a lesson was learned: telling consumers they have to pay more does not help a bill get passed.

The falsehood Obama has consistently shared about climate is comparable to the one he told about Syria, namely that there was no dispute about the evidence. The MIT climatologist Richard Lindzen has explained how a false "consensus" has seemed to emerge. "When you have an issue that is somewhat bogus, the opposition is always scattered and without resources," said Lindzen. "But the environmental movement is highly organized. There are hundreds of NGOs. To coordinate these hundreds, they quickly organized the Climate Action Network, the central body on climate. There would be, I think, actual meetings to tell them what the party line is for the year, and so on." In fact, more than thirty thousand scientists—nine thousand of them PhDs—have signed the Global Warming Petition, challenging the evidence for global warming. This petition alone should have warned Obama off the claim in his 2014 State of the Union speech, "The debate is settled. Climate change is a fact." Like so many on the left, including most of America's mainstream media, he felt no need to examine contrary evidence.

Instead, Obama has continued to speak in the kind of gassy platitudes about which Orwell warned us. His definitive speech on climate, delivered at Georgetown University in June 2013, is a case in point. There, Obama repeatedly referred to carbon emissions as "pollution," knowing full well that carbon dioxide is the sine qua non of life on earth. This conscious corruption of the language offered further proof, if any were needed, of Orwell's claim "that the decline of a language must ultimately have political and economic causes."

At Georgetown, Obama also claimed, "The twelve warmest years in recorded history have all come in the last fifteen years." Even if this was true, he failed to mention that world temperatures had defied all computer models and remained flat for the previous sixteen years. He claimed too that "ice in the Arctic shrank to its smallest size on record," but by the time of the 2014 State of the Union, Arctic ice had increased 50 percent from the previous year. That rebound went unmentioned in the State of the Union, as did the fact that Antarctic ice was at its highest level in thirty-five years. Obama was cherry-picking, just as he did with the Syria evidence.

"Now, we know that no single weather event is caused solely by climate change," said Obama at Georgetown in a tautology worthy of Joe Biden. "But we also know that in a world that's warmer than it used to be, all weather events are affected by a warming planet." This equally empty-headed remark would have at least some weight if the earth were warming and if there were hard evidence that warming was bad for the planet, but as of this writing, there is apparently not enough evidence for either to convince even Senate Democrats.

CHAPTER 10

THE REVENUER

There is something about the Internal Revenue Service and the collection of taxes in general that brings out President Obama's inner totalitarian. This came to light in a classic Kinsley gaffe during an April 2008 presidential primary debate. The moderator, ABC's Charlie Gibson, noted that when the rates of taxation on capital gains drop, revenues almost invariably increase. Conversely, when the rates are increased, the revenues drop.

"So why raise it at all," asked Gibson, "especially given the fact that 100 million people in this country own stock and would be affected?" Said Obama, "Well, Charlie, what I've said is that I would look at raising the capital-gains tax for purposes of fairness." Obama took another several minutes trying to squirm out of the political mess he had just made, but the implications were clear. "Fairness," whatever that is, had priority in Obama's economic philosophy over results. This soft-core Marxism was not an easy philosophy to sell, and it would lead to any number of deceptions in the years that followed.

RIGHT NOW, WARREN BUFFETT PAYS A LOWER
TAX RATE THAN HIS SECRETARY

In his 2012 State of the Union speech, President Obama echoed the sophistry that Warren Buffett himself first introduced, namely that "Warren Buffett pays a lower tax rate than his secretary." To illustrate the point, the secretary in question, Debbie Bosanek, sat next to Michelle Obama throughout the speech.

There was little that wasn't false about this whole setup. The *Forbes* contributor Paul Roderick Gregory ran the numbers. If Bosanek actually paid a higher effective rate than Buffett's claimed 17.4 percent, Gregory calculated she would have to be earning more than $200,000 a year. Given her longtime service to the multibillionaire Buffett, a salary in that range was probable. This would put Bosanek well into the top 5 percent of all income earners. Buffett could call Bosanek a secretary if he liked, but she was not quite the "barely getting by" worker bee Dolly Parton sang about in her anthemic "Nine to Five."

There was a more fundamental dishonesty about Obama's claim. Buffett paid a 17.4 percent rate only because a great percentage of his income came from capital gains. There was no reason to believe he paid a lower percentage on his earned income than Bosanek or anyone else in his employ. To increase the amount Buffett or any other 1 percenter would pay, Obama would have had to ask for an increase in the capital gains tax, and that would lead back to the conundrum in which he found himself in the ABC debate.

This was not, however, how Obama framed the issue. He insinuated that Buffett's lower rate was a result of Bush's tax cuts. "Do we want to keep these tax cuts for the wealthiest Americans?"

Obama asked. "Or do we want to keep our investments in every-thing else?" This line of reasoning too was based on a false assump-tion, as was the deceptive word "investments." In fact, Bush's tax cuts increased the amount of revenue collected by more than 30 percent from his first year as president to his last, just as Reagan's and Kennedy's tax cuts increased federal revenue after they were passed. As economist Thomas Sowell argued, "Obama knew then that tax rates and tax revenues do not automatically move in the same direction. In other words, he is lying when he talks as if tax rates and tax revenues move together."

UNDER MY PLAN, NO FAMILY MAKING LESS THAN $250,000 A YEAR WILL SEE ANY FORM OF TAX INCREASE

In early September 2008, energized by a successful convention, Republican John McCain edged in front of a surprised Barack Obama in the presidential polls. "McCain leads Democrat Barack Obama by 50%–46% among registered voters," wrote Susan Page in *USA Today* on September 8, "the Republican's biggest advan-tage since January and a turnaround from the *USA Today* poll taken just before the convention opened in St. Paul. Then, he lagged by 7 percentage points."

McCain owed much of that surge, if not all, to the dazzling per-formance at the convention of a running mate few Americans had even heard of two weeks earlier. What Alaskan governor Sarah Palin brought to the ticket in addition to her plentiful charm was a powerful populist appeal. Her husband, she reminded the audi-ence, was a lifelong commercial fisherman. Her sister Heather and her sister's husband had just opened a small-town service station. As Palin explained, she and her kin did not "quite know what to make of a candidate who lavishes praise on working people when they are listening, and then talks about how bitterly they cling to their religion and guns when those people aren't listening."

With no feel for the lives of ordinary working people, Palin explained, Obama felt free "to make government bigger, take more of your money, give you more orders from Washington." Palin then got specific. Obama, she argued, "planned to raise income taxes, raise payroll taxes, raise investment income taxes, raise the death tax, raise business taxes, and increase the tax burden on the American people by hundreds of billions of dollars." How, she wondered, would Heather and her husband, and millions of other small-business people as well, "be any better off if taxes go up?"

By the time Obama spoke in Dover, New Hampshire, on September 12, four days after the disturbing poll results were released, the Obama camp saw a need to reassure America's middle class that Obama, not Palin, was its true friend, even if to do so he had to make promises he had no intention of keeping. "I can make a firm pledge," he told the New Hampshire crowd. "Under my plan, no family making less than $250,000 a year will see any form of tax increase. Not your income tax, not your payroll tax, not your capital gains taxes, not any of your taxes."

There was nothing impromptu about this pledge. Obama's running mate, Joe Biden, repeated it himself, tellingly, in his October 3 debate with Palin. "No one making less than $250,000 under Barack Obama's plan," said Biden even more emphatically, "will see one single penny of their tax raised whether it's their capital gains tax, their income tax, investment tax, any tax." Obama repeated the pledge before a joint session of Congress on February 24, 2009, this time upping the deductible from a penny to a dime: "If your family earns less than $250,000 a year, you will not see your taxes increased a single dime. I repeat: not one single dime." Just five weeks later, he and his Democratic Congress made hash out of that pledge when they raised cigarette taxes 62 cents a pack. In that an estimated 55 percent of all smokers fall into the category "working poor," the tax had the much-maligned "disparate impact" on the bitter clinger crowd.

Speaking of disparate impact, Obama and his Democratic allies also imposed a tanning tax, the most racially targeted "revenue enhancement" since poll taxes were banned. Snooki Polizzi took the news personally. "I don't go tanning anymore because Obama put a 10 percent tax on tanning," she said at the outset of summer 2010. "And I feel like he did that intentionally for us." By "us," she did not mean her fellow cast members on *Jersey Shore*. The tanning tax was the first of the many dictated by Obamacare to go into effect. Other new taxes included a tax on high medical bills, a tax on flexible spending accounts, a tax on early retiree health insurance plans, and, of course, the individual mandate penalty under Obamacare that Supreme Court Chief Justice John Roberts ruled a "tax."

In 2013, his antitax pledge long since forgotten, Obama endorsed the Marketplace Fairness Bill, which, if passed, is expected to produce $24 billion a year in Internet sales tax revenue, the overwhelming majority of which will come from the middle and working classes. The Obama camp can argue that its man did not raise *income* taxes on those making under $250,000, but he and Biden promised no increase on "any" tax, not even on Snooki's tanning.

NOT EVEN A SMIDGEN OF CORRUPTION

On February 2, 2014, just before kickoff time at the Super Bowl, Bill O'Reilly of Fox News interviewed President Obama live on the air. When O'Reilly asked about the still-unresolved IRS scandal, Obama blew him off. "They—folks have, again, had multiple hearings on this," said Obama dismissively. "I mean these kinds of things keep on surfacing, in part because you and your TV station will promote them."

O'Reilly persisted. "You're saying no corruption?" At this point, Obama admitted only to "some boneheaded decisions." Not content with his evasion, O'Reilly suggested the possibility of mass corruption. "Not even mass corruption," said Obama awkwardly before clarifying, "not even a smidgen of corruption, I would say." If there were not even a smidgen of corruption, it is hard to understand what outraged Obama when news of the IRS scandal first broke. "It's inexcusable, and Americans are right to be angry about it, and I am angry about it," he said of the inspector general's report on the IRS in May 2013. "I will not tolerate this kind of behavior in any agency, but especially in the IRS, given the power that it has and the reach that it has into all of our lives." To be sure, Obama routinely expressed anger at the news of some new scandal erupting on his watch—IRS, the failed Obamacare website, the VA scandal, Fast and Furious—but never before had he purged the memory of his anger so quickly and thoroughly.

A Tea Party activist, Catherine Engelbrecht, remembered all too well. Prior to the 2008 election, Engelbrecht kept to the political sidelines. She and her husband, Bryan, had been busy running a small manufacturing plant in Rosenberg, Texas, a majority Hispanic town about thirty-five miles southwest of Houston. Upset by the banality of the 2008 election debates and disturbed by the fraud she witnessed as an election judge, Engelbrecht started two new political organizations. One, the King Street Patriots, sought to educate citizens about economic freedom and related subjects. The second, True the Vote, worked to prevent voter fraud. To give her organizations credibility with potential donors, Engelbrecht filed with the IRS for tax-exempt status in July 2010. That, said Engelbrecht, is when she walked "through the looking glass" and into the wonderland of the Obama administration.

Prior to 2010, no government agency had audited or investigated the Engelbrechts' business in the two decades of its existence. That would change in a hurry. Sometime in the winter, following Engelbrecht's IRS applications, the FBI showed up at her door. Its agents inquired about an individual who had attended a King Street Patriots meeting—once. In January 2011, the IRS visited the Engelbrechts' shop and conducted an exhaustive audit of both their personal and their business returns. Two months later, the IRS started in on an invasive round of questions about True the Vote. A second round followed a few months later.

In February 2012, the IRS subjected Engelbrecht and True the Vote to a third round of questions. Its agents wanted to see every Facebook post and every tweet she had ever written. As Engelbtrecht testified before the House Oversight and Government Reform subcommittee in February 2014, the IRS also wanted to know "the names of groups that I had spoken with, the content of what I had said and every word I intended to speak in the coming year."

The IRS started hectoring the King Street Patriots as well. At about the same time, the ATF dropped by unscheduled to audit the Engelbrechts' facility under the pretext that they had a permit to manufacture gun components. OSHA took its place in the audit queue and hit up the business with $17,500 worth of fines on what Engelbrecht called "little Mickey Mouse stuff." Soon after, Texas's environmental agency showed up for an unscheduled audit based on a complaint whose source the agency would not reveal.

In September 2012, Congress weighed in. California Democratic senator Barbara Boxer wrote to Thomas Perez, the same assistant attorney general who quashed the New Black Panther Party case, saying, "As you know, an organization called 'True the Vote,' which is an offshoot of the Tea Party, is leading a voter suppression campaign in many states. I don't believe this is 'True the Vote.' I believe it's 'Stop the Vote.'" In October 2012, with the election around the corner, Representative Elijah Cummings, another Democrat, sent a letter to True the Vote asking whether it was part of a "criminal conspiracy to deny legitimate voters their constitutional rights." Not easily intimidated, Engelbrecht filed an ethics complaint against Cummings.

If this were not oppression enough for one American, the IRS subjected Engelbrecht to two more rounds of inquisition, and the ATF dropped by again for an unscheduled audit. At that time, more than two years after she'd first filed, Engelbrecht still had not received tax-exempt status for either organization. Although the harassment of Engelbrecht was extreme, the targeting was not exceptional. The IRS stalled or rejected the applicants of comparable groups. The Treasury Department's inspector general conceded as much in a May 2013 report: "The IRS used inappropriate criteria that identified for review Tea Party and other organizations applying for tax-exempt status based upon their names or policy positions instead of indications of potential political campaign intervention." The report's predictably anodyne prose did not begin to capture the brute tyranny that Engelbrecht and others experienced. In concluding her testimony, Engelbrecht asked Congress "to end this ugly chapter of political intimidation. There was a time when people of good will were encouraged to participate in the processes of government, not targeted because of it."

LINE IRS EMPLOYEES IN CINCINNATI IMPROPERLY SCRUTINIZED 501(c)(4) ORGANIZATIONS

In May 2013, White House Press Secretary Jay Carney blamed the targeting of conservative groups on "line IRS employees in Cincinnati." In a half-honest moment, he admitted that these rogue

agents singled out groups by using words like "tea party" and
"patriot." This admission alone would refute Obama's claim that
there was not even a smidgen of corruption involved in the IRS's
targeting practices. In fact, though, the IRS had spawned not a
smidgen of corruption, but a veritable culture of corruption.

As was customary in this administration, Carney was just one
of many to pile onto the same hapless scapegoats. Lois Lerner, the
director of the IRS's Exempt Organizations division, also blamed
the "line people in Cincinnati." So too did Obama during the
O'Reilly interview. In a dazzling bit of chutzpah, he traced IRS's
"boneheaded decisions" to an unnamed "local office." The only
candidate for this unhappy designation was Cincinnati. Indeed,
the Cincinnati crew played much the same role in the IRS scandal as filmmaker Nakoula Bassely Nakoula would play in the
Benghazi one. Each was condemned to absorb the wrath of low-
information voters until the media could distract them with news
kinder to Obama.

Congressional hearings into the IRS's misbehavior began in
May 2013. As it turned out, the Cincinnati boneheads were none
too happy with their assigned role. One of them, Elizabeth Hofacre, explained that her superiors had her send all Tea Party applications to Washington, specifically to the IRS attorney Carter
Hull. This was not the norm. "I was frustrated because of what
I perceived as micromanagement with respect to these applications," said Hofacre. Hull, in turn, told Congress he had to send
along some of the Tea Party applications for further review to the
IRS's chief counsel, William Wilkins, a political appointee. This
was not the norm either.

When Wilkins testified before the House Oversight Committee in November 2013, he used the phrase "I don't recall" eighty
times. He was a model of transparency, however, compared with
Lerner, who took the Fifth, an unusual move in a corruption-free

agency. Lerner would take the Fifth again in March 2014. In May 2014, the House of Representatives voted to hold Lerner in contempt of Congress. Congressional confidence in the IRS plummeted further in June of that year upon the revelation that an alleged computer crash had erased two years' worth of Lerner's e-mails. The knowledge that the computer crashed just ten days after the first Republican query into the targeting of political activities did little to restore that confidence.

What was being learned in 2014, however, could not undo what had been done in 2012. From the administration's perspective, the IRS's wasteful, vindictive multilevel review of the Tea Party movement served a highly useful purpose. It sabotaged the get-out-the-vote efforts of people Obama had casually slurred as "tea baggers" in a handwritten letter to a Texas schoolteacher. Hull's testimony took the scandal only so high up the chain of command, but that was a long way above Cincinnati.

In May 2014, Judicial Watch, a right-leaning legal watchdog group, received a wealth of papers from the IRS that confirmed the scandal's reach. A series of e-mails showed the Washington-based attorney Steven Grodnitzky acknowledging that Tea Party applications were considered part of a "Sensitive Case Report" project. Apparently, none of these applications could be resolved without approval from the attorney in charge of IRS "rulings and agreements" in the agency's DC headquarters. "Most liberal groups applying for the same status were swiftly approved," summarized the UK's *Daily Mail*, "including one application from President Obama's half-brother, whose application was back-dated so he could claim tax advantages retroactively for a foundation he had set up in the name of their common father."

Even more damning were the e-mails that showed Lerner contacting the Justice Department about the potential criminal prosecution of Tea Party groups. Lerner agued that if just one conservative activist was imprisoned, that action might chill the movement and "shut the whole thing down."

Thanks to a continuing investigation by the House Ways and Means committee, America also learned that the IRS was harassing existing conservative groups as well as applicants. Committee chair Dave Camp of Michigan said that the IRS had flagged dozens of conservative 501(c)(4) organizations for surveillance. This included monitoring their activities, their websites, and a variety of other public information. Of the groups selected for surveillance, Camp claimed, 83 percent were right-leaning. Of the groups selected for audit, 100 percent were.

Unrepentant, Obama and his congressional allies continued to seek out inventive new ways to undermine their opposition. Even more straightforward in its subversion than the White House was a group of seven Senate Democrats led by Chuck Schumer. In March 2012, the group sent a letter to the IRS demanding that the agency "impose a strict cap on the amount of political spending by tax-exempt, nonprofit groups." When last heard from in early 2014, Schumer was urging the White House to circumvent Congress and use the IRS and other government agencies to check the power of the conservative grass roots. The Tea Party groups, Schumer claimed, "gained extraordinary influence by being able to funnel millions of dollars into campaigns with ads that distort the truth and attack government." Fearing for the future of the Democrat-media monopoly on truth distortion, he singled out "the Tea Party elites" for abuse. In the process, he created both a new benchmark for oppression and a memorable new oxymoron.

Also in March 2012, Michigan senator Carl Levin, a Democrat, sent his first letter to then–IRS commissioner Douglas Shulman, in which he emphasized the "urgency" of reviewing the political activity by nonprofit applicants. Levin cited ten specific groups needing review, at least nine of which were clearly conservative.

Given the irrefutable evidence of mischief up and down the IRS hierarchy and in Congress as well, a reporter asked Jay Carney whether Obama misspoke when he said there was not a "smidgen" of corruption in the IRS. Said Carney, now seemingly immune to the truth, "What we've learned from an independent inspector general and through the testimony we've seen completely backs up what the president said."

CHAPTER 11

THE COMMANDER IN CHIEF

Barack Obama gave the world its first glimpse of how he would operate as commander in chief at an unusual time and in an unusual place. The date was October 2, 2002. The place was a windy square in downtown Chicago. At a hastily planned rally staged by a few senescent Chicago SDSers, the obscure state senator Barack Obama laid out his philosophy of war and peace. Unlike the playwright Lillian Hellman, herself a socialist and serial fabulist, Obama showed just how prepared he was to cut his conscience to fit that year's fashions. He would do a good deal of conscience-cutting as presidential candidate and as president. This Chicago speech set the pattern.

Urged toward caution by his political advisers, Obama chose not to risk his future to please a bunch of old hippies. While opposing the impending war in Iraq as "dumb," Obama laid the groundwork for his future by grandly insisting he was "not opposed to war in all circumstances." This future Nobel Peace Prize winner cited the American Civil War and World War II as wars to which he could have given his blessing.

As president, Obama would pick and choose among military engagements with no greater clarity or commitment than he showed in Chicago. His dovish base pulled one way. The hawk-ish national security establishment pulled another. And he would calculate the nation's trajectory, as in Chicago, largely on the basis of his own perceived best interests. To cover his insincerity, Obama would do what he usually did in such circumstances—make stuff up.

I SAID THERE'S NO DOUBT THAT ADDITIONAL US TROOPS COULD TEMPORARILY QUELL THE VIOLENCE

As a US senator in 2007, Barack Obama opposed "the surge," the controversial strategy that saved Iraq from chaos. On January 10, 2007, on MSNBC, he predicted that the surge would fail. "I am not persuaded that 20,000 additional troops in Iraq is going to solve the sectarian violence there," he said, again failing to make sub-ject and verb agree. "In fact, I think it will do the reverse." As his-tory records, the surge succeeded. On *Meet the Press* in July 2008, confronted with a clip of his errant prediction, Obama countered, "I [also] said there's no doubt that additional U.S. troops could temporarily quell the violence." ABC's Fact Check Desk could find no evidence that Obama said anything like that when it mat-tered. The closest he came was a throwaway comment that there had been "improvement in certain neighborhoods." Obama said this, however, after the surge had started working. Even then, he concluded, "You hadn't seen any real significant difference over what we've seen in the last year."

One could forgive Obama his faulty memory here were it honestly faulty, but his history suggests otherwise. The former defense secretary Robert Gates, in one of the more revealing pas-sages of his book *Duty: Memoirs of a Secretary at War*, described a conversation he witnessed between President Obama and then–

secretary of state Hillary Clinton. When Clinton said she opposed the Iraq surge to counter Obama's solid antiwar credentials in the run-up to the Iowa caucuses, Obama conceded that he opposed the surge for political reasons as well. Wrote Gates, "To hear the two of them making these admissions, and in front of me, was as surprising as it was dismaying." Undoubtedly, all presidents factor the personal and the political into national security decisions. For Obama, the "me" factor has been the primary one, if not the only one. This is what makes acknowledging error so very difficult for him and lying so very easy.

I INTEND TO CLOSE GUANTÁNAMO, AND I WILL FOLLOW THROUGH ON THAT

Twelve days after his election in November 2008, Obama granted CBS's Steve Kroft an interview to air on *60 Minutes*. "There are a number of different things that you could do early pertaining to executive orders," suggested Kroft. "One of them is to shut down Guantánamo Bay." Obama agreed: "Yes, I have said repeatedly that I intend to close Guantánamo, and I will follow through on that."

Indeed, Obama had been promising to close the Guantánamo Bay detention camp since he first launched his campaign in 2007. How could he not? For his allies on the left, here and abroad, Guantánamo was the essence of "Bush's evil," "an American gulag," "America's Auschwitz." Although his language was more temperate, Obama seemed to share his fellow travelers' indignation. On January 22, 2009, his second full day in office, Obama gathered a group of retired generals to watch him sign an executive order committing the administration to shut down Guantánamo within one year. "This is me following through on not just a commitment I made during the campaign," said Obama piously at the time of the signing, "but I think an understanding that dates back to our Founding Fathers, that we are willing to observe core standards of conduct, not just when it's easy, but also when it's hard."

At the time of the signing, critics warned about the NIMBY factor: it would be much easier to sign an order than it would be to ship hundreds of hard-core terrorists to someone's stateside backyard. Then too, critics argued, shutting down the prison served no more practical purpose than to pacify those activists who had developed a Tourette-like fixation on the word "Guantánamo." Undeterred by logic, Obama moved forward with his plans—but not very far, or very fast. In July 2009, Obama granted the Guantánamo closing commission an extra six months to do a study. In December 2009, he gave orders to purchase a state prison in Illinois for $350 million. In January 2010, the one-year deadline came and went, and the 240 well-fed detainees at Guantánamo were still living large in their air-conditioned gulag.

In May 2010, despite Democratic control of both the Senate and the House, the planned prison closing stalled badly. In a rare display of bipartisan spirit, the House Armed Services Committee voted unanimously to prohibit any replacement facility from being located within the United States. To help Obama save face on a flagrantly broken promise, the *Times'* Charlie Savage cited generic "political opposition" and Republican "demagoguery" for the failure. "The president can't just wave a magic wand to say that Gitmo will be closed," an unnamed administration official told Savage. This likely surprised *Times* readers who did not know that messiahs needed magic wands.

By the time of the 2014 State of the Union speech, the executive order had just passed its fifth anniversary, and 155 prisoners remained at Club Gitmo. In the speech, Obama put the blame where he decided it belonged. "This needs to be the year," preached Obama, "Congress lifts the remaining restrictions on detainee transfers and we close the prison at Guantánamo Bay." Despite Democratic control of the Senate, Obama and the media used "Congress" as shorthand for "Republican." Understanding the word game, the Democrats applauded.

For the most part the media played their expected role and helped Obama project the blame elsewhere. The *Miami Herald*, for instance, headlined its story "Obama to Congress: Close Guantánamo Prison." The *Huffington Post* ran an article head-lined "Obama Is Right: Close Guantanamo—It's Anti-American." If the soft left was willing to oblige Obama one more time, the hard left proved less pliable. A few months earlier *Firedoglake* nailed the issue in its headline, "Obama's Deluded Remarks Ignore His Role in Keeping Prisoners at Guantanamo."

As with so many of Obama's other broken promises, he simply didn't care enough to keep this one. *Firedoglake*, at least, remem-bered it was Obama who promised to close Guantánamo, Obama who insisted on doing it by executive order, and Obama who failed to push it through Congress when Democrats controlled both houses. Obama liked the way the promise sounded, but once again he lacked the will to fulfill it.

QADDAFI THREATENS A BLOODBATH THAT COULD DESTABILIZE AN ENTIRE REGION

In his March 28, 2011, address to the nation, Barack Obama laid out the case for America's surprise military intervention in Libya. "We knew that if we . . . waited one more day," said Obama, "Benghazi, a city nearly the size of Charlotte, could suffer a mas-sacre that would have reverberated across the region and stained the conscience of the world." Two days earlier in a radio address, Obama used the word "bloodbath" to describe Benghazi's likely fate at the hand of strongman Muammar Qaddafi. Ever the man of action, Obama continued, "*I* refused to let that happen" (italics added). Instead, he authorized military action "to stop the killing" and enforce U.N. Security Council Resolution 1973.

At the time, there was a good deal of debate about Obama's motives and especially about a passive-aggressive strategy known by the curious sobriquet "leading from behind." Instead of directing the attack against Qaddafi, an old-school Arab tyrant no one much liked, Obama deferred to NATO and then employed America's ample air power to aid the Libyan insurgency. Given all the balderdash about Bush's "illegal war" in Iraq, some questioned why Obama had not asked Congress for authorization as Bush had for both the war on terror and the war in Iraq. Many others wondered, "Why Libya?"

Less than two months before America went to war, Obama had not so much as mentioned this benighted country in his State of the Union address. The last time Qaddafi had gotten much play in the America media was in 2003, when he was persuaded to abandon his program of weapons of mass destruction. As recently as April 2009, Qaddafi's son had a friendly meeting with Hillary Clinton in Washington. In September 2009, John McCain and a small Senate delegation met with Qaddafi in Tripoli. There former Democratic vice presidential candidate Senator Joe Lieberman described his regime as "an important ally in the war on terrorism." Then just eighteen months later, in a special address to the nation, Obama justified his takedown of Qaddafi in part because he "terrorized innocent people around the world—including Americans who were killed by Libyan agents." In a casual lie of omission, Obama failed to mention that these killings occurred years earlier, before Qaddafi had become an ally in the war on terror, an "important" ally at that.

In early 2011, the goodwill Qaddafi had mustered, however tenuous, suddenly lost all value. Obama asked Americans to believe Qaddafi was about to smear a Rwanda-size stain on "the conscience of the world." As happened with Kosovo in 1999, the major media refused to challenge a Democratic president's account of impending genocide. Goaded by the French and the British, Obama inflated the horror and assigned blame to just one of the two culpable parties, much as President Bill Clinton did in Kosovo.

If Obama had studied the 1999 action in Kosovo—and Hillary was there to help him—he would have known how the media would react if a Democratic president launched an unauthorized air war. At the time, Yugoslavia was fracturing. To hold the country together, the mostly Serbian authorities were attempting to suppress an insurrection by ethnic Albanians in the province of Kosovo. Like Obama, President Clinton had not bothered getting congressional approval before unleashing America's air power. To bolster public support, Clinton and his people began a drumbeat about mass graves, ethnic cleansing, and even genocide. As in Libya, there was not a stated reason for this war other than to prevent genocide. Yugoslavia had no WMDs, no terror arm, no ambitions against its neighbors, no grudge against the United States, no sheltered terrorists, not even any oil.

The State Department's David Scheffer was the first to claim a six-figure death count, specifically "upwards of about 100,000 [Islamic] men that we cannot account for" in Kosovo. A month later, the State Department upped the total to 500,000 Kosovo Albanians missing and feared dead. On CBS's *Face the Nation*, Secretary of Defense William Cohen repeated the 100,000 figure and claimed that the war "was a fight for justice over genocide." President Clinton compared the work of the Serbs in Kosovo to the German "genocide" of the Jews during the Holocaust and assured America that "tens of thousands of people" had been murdered. The *New York Times* helped Clinton amplify his message. No fewer than 375 articles would contain the combination of the words "Kosovo" and "genocide"; most of the articles would make a direct equation between the two.

In the war's wake, however, international teams could find no signs of genocide. The ethnic Albanian dead numbered in the hundreds, not in the hundreds of thousands. The Spanish forensic surgeon Emilio Perez Pujol would tell the British *Sunday Times* that the talk of genocide was "a semantic pirouette by the war propaganda machines, because we did not find one—not one—mass grave." In 2001, a United Nations court ruled, as the BBC noted, that "Serbian troops did not carry out genocide against ethnic Albanians."

For the Libya conflict, Alan Kuperman, a professor of public affairs at the University of Texas and author of the book *The Limits of Humanitarian Intervention*, did the calculations that the media refused to do. Writing in the *Boston Globe* just two weeks after the president's address on Libya, Kuperman made a simple point: "The best evidence that Khadafy did not plan genocide in Benghazi is that he did not perpetrate it in the other cities he had recaptured." He cited the data from Human Rights Watch concerning Misurata, a city of 400,000 inhabitants that Qaddafi's forces had recently seized. There, in nearly two months of war, only 257 people had been killed, including combatants. In Rwanda, by contrast, more than 800,000 Tutsi were killed in just ninety days. In Misurata, less than 3 percent of the wounded were women. This was not at all what one would expect to find in the sort of indiscriminate bloodbath Obama had projected. As Kuperman also noted, the ubiquitous cell phone cameras failed to capture any images of a massacre. Kuperman had no obvious political grudge. He had previously served as a legislative assistant to Democratic House speaker Tom Foley and legislative director for then-congressman Chuck Schumer.

What did happen in Libya, Kuperman explained, is that rebel forces, fearing imminent defeat, followed the Kosovo playbook and faked a humanitarian crisis. On March 14, Soliman Bouchuiguir, president of the Libyan League for Human Rights in Geneva, told Reuters that if Qaddafi attacked Benghazi, there would be "a real bloodbath, a massacre like we saw in Rwanda." Four days later, the US military started bombing. Bouchuiguir had ample help in reordering reality to fit the rebels' needs. On March 22, the *New York Times*' David Kirkpatrick reported, "The rebels feel no loyalty to the truth in shaping their propaganda, claiming nonexistent battlefield victories, asserting they were still fighting in a key city days after it fell to Qaddafi forces, and making vastly inflated claims of his barbaric behavior."

A month after the bombing started in Libya, Obama, along with French president Nicolas Sarkozy and British prime minister David Cameron, sent a letter to the international press. They now claimed that "the bloodbath that he had promised to inflict on the citizens of the besieged city of Benghazi has been prevented." In the retelling, the "he" doing the promising was Qaddafi. In reality, the only people who promised bloodbaths were the rebel spokesmen and the Western leaders. This absurd self-fulfilling fabrication would have been amusing were it not so lethal. By this time, Obama had to know the rationale for war was false, but he would continue to pursue it for another six deadly months.

As 2011 sped by, the insurgency dragged on, and the only sure casualty was the truth. Among the most hateful myths spread by the insurgents, one that the *Times* conceded had "racist overtones," was that Qaddafi had been using African mercenaries. This falsehood, said the *Times*, "rebels repeat as fact over and over." To reinforce the myth, the rebels put captured black men on public display, itself an illegal act, and claimed they were mercenaries working for Qaddafi. They were not. Amnesty International investigated and discovered the men were hapless undocumented laborers from Chad, Mali, and West Africa—the Libyan equivalent of Dreamers—who were showcased and then set free.

The Libyan National Transitional Council (NTC) designed its propaganda for internal consumption, and the locals believed it. They did not usually bother themselves with reports from Amnesty International or the *New York Times*. Fired up by rumors of black mercenaries on Viagra-fueled rape sprees, the rebels did some ethnic cleansing on their own. Patrick Cockburn of the UK newspaper the *Independent* saw the evidence up close. "Any Libyan with a black skin accused of fighting for the old regime may have a poor chance of survival," he concluded. Obama chose not to notice.

On October 20, 2011, NATO planes attacked a convoy among whose passengers was a desperate Qaddafi. He was hoping to find refuge in his birthplace, the Jarref Valley. That was not to be. Qaddafi fled the shattered convoy on foot and hid in a drainpipe while his bodyguards tried and failed to hold off a local militia. The militia members took Qaddafi prisoner, indelicately sodomized him with a knife, and captured it all on video. They then threw Qaddafi, still breathing, onto a pickup truck. When the truck pulled away, he promptly fell off. This Keystone Cops–meet–Mad Max muddle was not quite the image of a new Libya the NTC was hoping to project, so the NTC prime minister claimed his troops killed Qaddafi in a cross fire. Its agitprop had worked well in the past. Why stop now?

A *Guardian* headline captured the giddy mood in Washington: "Obama Hails Death of Muammar Gaddafi as Foreign Policy Success: President Warns Other Middle Eastern Dictators, Particularly Syrian President Bashar al-Assad, That They Could Be Next." Said Obama in a Rose Garden speech, "The dark shadow of tyranny has been lifted." Joe Biden claimed the strategy a "prescription" for the future and contrasted it with the costly Republican-led war in Iraq. In claiming victory, Obama and Biden championed the victors and made Libya their personal success story. This would have consequences not too far down the road.

If the major media were willing to endorse Obama's narrative, Alan Kuperman was not. Writing for the Harvard Kennedy School's journal *International Security* in 2013, Kuperman unspun the web of deception that the Libyan rebels and their NATO enablers had woven. "The biggest misconception about NATO's intervention," wrote Kuperman, "is that it saved lives and benefited Libya and its neighbors."

As Kuperman clearly documented, Qaddafi did not attack peaceful protesters. The rebels had started the violence, and Qaddafi responded. Barely six weeks after the rebellion began, Qaddafi had all but suppressed it at the cost of about one thousand lives. Then NATO intervened. That intervention prolonged the war seven months and cost roughly seven thousand more lives. At war's end, rebels killed scores of former enemies in reprisal and exiled some thirty thousand black Africans under the pretext that they might have been mercenaries. Many of those refugees headed home to Mali, a relative model of peace and democracy, and launched a rebellion there. Islamist forces and al-Qaeda promptly hijacked the rebellion and imposed Sharia law on the vast northern stretches of the country.

French troops would later oust al-Qaeda from northern Mali, but before they could do so, Islamic jihadists in Mali would provide training for their ideological brethren to the south, the child-snatching barbarians known as Boko Haram. "This group is armed, with heavy weapons of an unimaginable sophistication and the ability to use them," said French president François Hollande of Boko Haram. According to Hollande, the weapons came from a "chaotic Libya."

Things did not work out all that well in Libya either. During the insurrection, the Obama administration had been funneling money to Qatar to help arm Libyan rebels. As the *New York Times* reported more than a year after the fact, "The weapons and money from Qatar strengthened militant groups in Libya, allowing them

to become a destabilizing force since the fall of the Qaddafi government." "Militant" was *Times*-speak for the radical Islamists
whom Qaddafi had suppressed. After the fall of Qaddafi, these
groups refused to disarm and continued to resist the transitional
government's authority.

In the midst of this mess, in early April 2011, an American special representative, Christopher Stevens, arrived in Libya on board
a Greek freighter. His job was to research the various groups involved in the opposition to Qaddafi and report back to Washington. Obama would reward his loyalty and courage with the most
disturbing lies of his long, dishonest career.

WE ARE BRINGING OUR TROOPS HOME FROM AFGHANISTAN. . . . WE WILL HAVE THEM ALL OUT OF THERE BY 2014.

In a glowing December 2009 article in the *New York Times*, Peter
Baker wrote about a potential "turning point" in the history of the
Obama presidency. He referred to an all-day November meeting
at which "a young commander in chief set in motion a high-stakes
gamble to turn around a losing war." The Obama that Baker described was methodical, thorough, rigorous, bold. Obama's leadership style, said one awed participant, fell somewhere between
that of "a college professor and a gentle cross-examiner."

Ever since his emergence on the national scene five years earlier, Obama had been using Afghanistan as a prop. This was the
good war, a "war of necessity" unlike Bush's "war of choice" in
Iraq, the "dumb war." At the convention a year earlier, Obama
had promised to "finish the fight against al-Qaeda and the Taliban in Afghanistan." By the time of that December 2009 meeting,

however, the war was no closer to being finished than it was a year earlier. Five years later it would remain equally unfinished.

Early in his presidency Obama began to sense that war was more complicated than it might seem around a Hyde Park dinner table. In March 2009, he announced a new counterinsurgency strategy for Afghanistan and sent an additional 21,000 troops. "I want the American people to understand," he announced. "We have a clear and focused goal: to disrupt, dismantle and defeat Al Qaeda in Pakistan and Afghanistan."

In May 2009, claiming the war against the Taliban needed "new thinking," Obama appointed General Stanley McChrystal to replace General David McKiernan as commander in Afghanistan. He had not met McChrystal before the appointment. Despite the gravity of the situation, their first meeting was a ten-minute photo op. McChrystal found, not the focused commander in chief of Baker's imagination, but a distracted dabbler in things military. "Obama clearly didn't know anything about him, who he was," an adviser to McChrystal told the late Michael Hastings, then writing for *Rolling Stone* magazine. "Here's the guy who's going to run his fucking war, but he didn't seem very engaged. The Boss was pretty disappointed." What the adviser failed to realize at the time, as did Peter Baker and the rest of the media, was that the war was never really about the future of Afghanistan. The war was about the future of Obama.

When McChrystal arrived in Afghanistan he did not like what he saw. He prepared a policy report in which he concluded that if Obama did not send another forty thousand troops, there was a real danger of "mission failure." This report somehow found its way to the media and put enormous pressure on Obama to respond. It was this leak that precipitated the strategy sessions about which Baker wrote so glowingly.

After all of Obama's professorial musings, the outspoken Mc-

Chrystal got pretty much what he wanted. At West Point on December 1, 2009, Obama announced he would send thirty thousand additional troops to Afghanistan "to break the Taliban's momentum." In more of a political than a military gesture, Obama told the cadets, "After eighteen months, our troops will begin to come home." This was something of a first. Historically, commanders in chief committed troops "until the job was done." As the doughboys in World War I sang, "We won't come back till it's over over there." The unspoken Obama version was, "We won't come back until shortly before the 2012 election."

At the time Obama learned of the *Rolling Stone* article in June 2010, the war was not going noticeably better than it had been before the surge. In the article, Michael Hastings faulted McChrystal's flawed counterinsurgency strategy as well as the "diplomatic incoherence" of the Obama administration. That incoherence "jeopardizes the mission," Stephen Biddle, a senior fellow at the Council on Foreign Relations, told Hastings. "The military cannot by itself create governance reform."

The conundrum that Obama faced was not lost on Hastings. "The president finds himself stuck in something even more insane than a quagmire," he wrote, "a quagmire he knowingly walked into, even though it's precisely the kind of gigantic, mindnumbing, multigenerational nation-building project he explicitly said he didn't want." Acting decisively on at least one front, Obama fired the irreverent McChrystal before the magazine even hit the newsstands. Ever ready to find a silver lining in the Obama presidency, the *New York Times* called the firing "a MacArthur moment, a reassertion of civilian control."

To replace McChrystal, Obama chose the hero of the Iraqi surge that he had once scorned, General David Petraeus. Petraeus, however, had no more success than McChrystal. By 2011, Secretary of Defense Robert Gates was beginning to grasp a character flaw in Obama that was undermining the war effort, namely the shallowness of his professed beliefs. Wrote Gates about a March 2011 meeting in his memoir, *Duty*, "As I sat there, I thought: The president doesn't trust his commander, can't stand Karzai, doesn't believe in his own strategy and doesn't consider the war to be his. For him, it's all about getting out." Lacking conviction, Obama betrayed no core value when he misled the electorate about his exit strategy. In that the major media so very rarely acknowledged his failings, these deceptions worked to his advantage. If they did not impress the Taliban, they impressed enough of the US electorate to get him reelected in 2012.

In the eight years of the Bush presidency, there were 630 American military fatalities in Afghanistan. In the first five years of Obama's presidency, there were 1,671. In his acceptance speech at the 2012 Democratic National Convention, Obama dedicated a very short paragraph to Afghanistan. "We've blunted the Taliban's momentum in Afghanistan and in 2014, our longest war will be over," Obama said with uncanny prescience. He slammed Romney for not explaining "how he'll end the war in Afghanistan." He then concluded with the boast, "Well, I have, and I will." At the time, of course, only God knew how the war would end, and He had been very nearly banned from the convention. As to Obama, despite his blarney, he did not have a clue how he could successfully wrap up this war, or any war for that matter. His cluelessness in this regard became all too obvious when Iraq lapsed into chaos in the summer of 2014.

A few days before the convention, at a rally in Boulder, Colorado, Obama had been even more specific about the nation's exit strategy from Afghanistan. After blasting Romney for his lack of concrete plans, Obama said, "We are bringing our troops home from Afghanistan. And I've set a timetable. We will have them all out of there by 2014." This pledge lasted no more than two hours. On board Air Force One right after the speech, Press Secretary Jay Carney tried to unravel the tangle. "He never said that all the troops would be out," claimed Carney, who once again found himself lying to undo the lies his boss had already told. Carney blathered on about steps and milestones and transfers, knowing full well that multiple thousands of Americans would remain in Afghanistan through the end of Obama's presidency.

Six months after Obama's second inauguration, the administration signaled that American troops would remain in Afghanistan for at least another eight years beyond his presidency. A twenty-five-page "Security and Defense Cooperation Agreement between the United States of America and the Islamic Republic of Afghanistan" committed the United States to continue the fight against al-Qaeda "until the end of 2024 and beyond."

On Memorial Day 2014, at Arlington National Cemetery, Obama announced the war's conclusion. "Now, because of [the military personnel's] profound sacrifice, because of the progress they have made, we're at a pivotal moment," said Obama. "Our troops are coming home. By the end of this year, our war in Afghanistan will finally come to end [sic]." The president did not specify what "progress" had been made nor what the ten thousand to sixteen thousand troops left behind—as much as half the then-current contingent—would do to keep themselves busy. To protect his legacy, Obama will likely call them "advisers." Friendly historians will likely do so too.

OBAMA AND BIDEN WILL RESTORE RESPECT FOR THE RULE OF LAW AND AMERICA'S VALUES

At a press briefing in September 2009, Major Garrett of Fox News stumped White House press secretary Robert Gibbs with a simple question. Garrett wanted to know whether Vice President Biden had pressed for a strategy that emphasized drones and deemphasized ground forces. Visibly flustered, Gibbs replied, "I think you can understand why I'm not going to get into internal discussions." Garrett did not understand. Said he, "You can't say one way or the other whether that's true or not?" Replied Gibbs abruptly, "I'm not going to get into it." End of conversation.

More than three years later, no longer a press secretary, Gibbs explained to a startled MSNBC host, Chris Hayes, why he had been so evasive. "When I went through the process of becoming press secretary," said Gibbs, "one of the first things they told me was you're not even to acknowledge the drone program. You're not even to discuss that it exists." For the first time, a knowledgeable insider spoke to the illusory nature of Obama's promised transparency. Gibbs followed up by tracing Obama's famed Kansas roots back to a more meaningful source, Professor Marvel, a.k.a. the Wizard of Oz. "Here's what's inherently crazy about that proposition: you're being asked a question based on reporting of a program that exists," he continued. "So you're the official government spokesperson acting as if the entire program—pay no attention to the man behind the curtain."

When Gibbs made these remarks in February 2013, Obama had not yet officially acknowledged that there was a drone program. A week after Gibbs's interview, Attorney General Eric Holder addressed the drone issue and, in so doing, rattled the thinking members of his own party. In a letter to Republican senator Rand Paul, Holder said that, under the right circumstances, it would be legal and necessary "for the President to authorize the military to use lethal force within the territory of the United States." This was the same president who promised in his *Blueprint for Change*, "Obama and Biden will restore respect for the rule of law and America's values."

For that matter, this was the same attorney general who launched a three-year investigation to see if anyone could be prosecuted for torture during the Bush years. By Holder's lights, it would be legal to kill an American by drone to stop "a cata-strophic attack" but illegal to waterboard that same individual to prevent that same attack. It is hard to know the mind of a terrorist, but a good guess is that most would rather be dunked a few times than vaporized by a drone strike.

In May 2013, Obama tried to make some sense of his adminis-tration's drone policy in an address at the National Defense Uni-versity. He was feeling the heat, less from the right than from the members of his own base unnerved by Holder's position. To those who might not have heard him say this a thousand times before, Obama repeated that we Americans had "compromised our basic values—by using torture to interrogate our enemies and detain-ing individuals in a way that ran counter to the rule of law."

Of course, Obama preferred detention and prosecution to the use of drones, but sometimes, he insisted, terrorists operated in "the most distant and unforgiving places on Earth" where cap-ture was not feasible, militarily or diplomatically. Since no place in the United States is that distant or that unforgiving, Obama was tacitly reversing Holder's position. More directly, he said no president "should" deploy armed drones over "U.S. soil," but that seemed more of a caution about the practice than a condemnation of it.

Among the terrorists who met the criteria for a rubout was a Yemen-based American citizen, Anwar al-Awlaki. Although not specifically targeted, at least three other Americans were killed by drones. These included al-Awlaki's sixteen-year old son. "No words" could justify the loss of the dead Americans or other ci-vilians, Obama assured the surviving family members. If nothing else, they could take some comfort knowing Obama did not order the strikes casually. The deaths would "haunt" him for the rest of his life—or at least until his next *holoholo* walkabout in Hawaii.

This was one time Obama was more than happy to share the glory. On the subject of drone strikes, he made at least half a dozen references to Congress, stressing how his White House always consulted the appropriate congressional committees before acting. With each reference he implied that by consulting Congress he was doing something that Bush had not done. This was unfair. Bush did brief congressional leaders on his administration's extraordinary techniques, including waterboarding, but Democratic leaders were not at all eager to acknowledge the same.

"We were not—I repeat—were not told that waterboarding or any of these other enhanced interrogation methods were used," said Nancy Pelosi when this issue surfaced in 2009. By this time, Pelosi had become House speaker. As such, she represented a party that had come to think of waterboarding as fondly as Republicans did partial birth abortion. She could not let her base think she knew about its use, let alone endorsed it.

Although the Republicans who accompanied Pelosi to these security briefings insisted she knew what they knew, the media ignored the Republicans and allowed Pelosi to squirm out of her jam. With the 2012 release of his memoir, *Hard Measures*, the former CIA counterterrorism chief Jose Rodriguez showed just how endemic lying often is within Democratic ranks. Rodriguez called Pelosi's denial "untrue" and lent specifics to his charge. "We explained that as a result of the techniques, [al-Qaeda honcho] Abu Zubaydah was compliant and providing good intelligence. We made crystal clear that authorized techniques, including waterboarding, had by then been used on Zubaydah." In his briefing to Pelosi, then the ranking member of the House Intelligence Committee, Rodriguez insisted, "We held back nothing." Despite the gravity of the lie, Pelosi suffered nothing save some temporary loss of the little credibility she had.

Although Obama's supporters sloughed off the drone revelations, the serious left was losing faith. Amnesty International, the ACLU, and Human Rights Watch all protested. "The U.S. government's targeted killing program has been cloaked in secrecy,"

wrote Human Rights Watch's executive diretor, Kenneth Roth,
"making it difficult to determine under which legal framework
the government believes it operates." Roth could not identify a
framework that made sense. As he saw it, under international
human rights law, a drone strike would be legal "only if necessary to stop an imminent threat to life." As bad a guy as Anwar
al-Awlaki was, he posed no such threat. Nor, certainly, did his
sixteen-year-old son.

WE REVEALED TO THE AMERICAN PEOPLE EXACTLY WHAT WE UNDERSTOOD AT THE TIME

In his Super Bowl Sunday interview with Fox News's Bill O'Reilly,
Obama told a compound lie that was, on many levels, the boldest
in the history of the presidency. After a few moments of fencing
on the subject of the September 11, 2012, attack on the American
consulate in Benghazi, O'Reilly said to Obama, "Your detractors
believe that you did not tell the world it was a terror attack because
your campaign didn't want that out." The postmodern president
bounced back, saying, "And they believe it because folks like you
are telling them that."

From Obama's perspective, truth was what he said it was. The
reason he despised Fox News, the nation's highest-rated cable
news channel, was that Fox alone among the news networks eval-
uated the validity of the White House narrative. In fact, on more
than a few occasions, Benghazi included, Fox's reporting showed
the administration's account of events to be pure hogwash. That
rankled, and a wounded Obama struck back.

In June 2009, the president launched an unprecedented attack
on a TV network. He was subtle at first. "I've got one television
station that is entirely devoted to attacking my administration,"

Obama complained. He did not mention Fox by name. He did not have to. The subtlety did not last. In September 2010, in an interview with *Rolling Stone* magazine, Obama made his distaste clear. After pointing out that Fox had an "undeniable point of view," one with which the president did not agree, he said, "It's a point of view that I think is ultimately destructive for the long-term growth of a country that has a vibrant middle class and is competitive in the world." Those were strong words, ungrounded maybe, but strong.

Obama avoided major damage in the Super Bowl Sunday interview, but in his attempt to escape unscathed, he exaggerated his innocence beyond all recognition. When O'Reilly pressed Obama on Benghazi, he responded, "We revealed to the American people exactly what we understood at the time." He then explained to skeptical Fox viewers why they should believe him: "The notion that we would hide the ball for political purposes when a week later we all said, in fact, there was a terrorist attack taking place and the day after I said it was an act of terror, that wouldn't be a very good cover-up."

As far as cover-ups went, it was, by Obama's rhetorical standards, "good" enough. It helped get him reelected two months later. From a moral perspective, however, it was not good at all. A review of the facts from that evening and the weeks afterward shows just how cruelly indifferent to the truth Obama—and those in the media who enabled him—had become.

HERE'S WHAT HAPPENED. YOU HAD A VIDEO THAT WAS RELEASED BY SOMEBODY WHO LIVES HERE, SORT OF A SHADOWY CHARACTER.

American ambassador Christopher Stevens arrived in Benghazi on September 10, 2012, unaware that President Obama's counterterrorism adviser John Brennan had been "running his own private war," Oliver North–style, against Libyan jihadists and that they were preparing to strike back.

Stevens did know, however, that security in Benghazi had badly degraded since rebels had begun their assault on the Qaddafi government eighteen months prior. During that time, there had been at least twenty attacks against Western—including American—interests. The violence and consistency of the attacks prompted the British to close their Benghazi mission in June 2012. Despite the high-threat environment, a 2014 House Armed Service Committee (HASC) report noted, "Administration decision makers were apparently reluctant to discuss publicly the deteriorating security situation in Libya or make changes in the U.S. diplomatic presence or military force posture that might have mitigated the dangers there."

Although the authors of the HASC report did not say so directly, they implied that decision makers hesitated to reinforce security lest they call into question the "success" of the prior year's Libyan campaign. "The inaction in Libya is in stark contrast to security improvements instituted elsewhere in the region," wrote the authors.

Sean Smith, a Foreign Service IT professional who accompanied Stevens, apparently got a whiff of the danger ahead. Shortly after noon, September 11, Libyan time, he posted online: "Assuming we don't die tonight. We saw one of our 'police' that guard the compound taking pictures." Smith's concerns proved correct just after 9:00 p.m.—3:00 p.m. Washington time—when a rocket-propelled grenade smashed against the front gate of the makeshift State Department compound.

The locally hired security fled immediately. This left seven Americans in the compound: Stevens, Smith, and five Diplomatic Security Service (DSS) agents. One DSS agent secured Stevens and Smith in a protected room in the ambassador's villa, two manned the tactical operations center, and two others barricaded themselves in the DSS villa. Stevens and the others immediately alerted their chain of command that they were in jeopardy. At 3:40 p.m. (unless otherwise specified, all times cited will be EDT, six hours earlier than Libyan time) Stevens called his number two man in Tripoli, Greg Hicks, and told him, "Greg, we're under attack." At 4:05 p.m. the State Department Operations Center issued an alert to all relevant agencies, "U.S. Diplomatic Mission in Benghazi under Attack." There was no lack of communication to the outside world.

At the time of the incident, General Carter F. Ham, commander of US Africa Command, just happened to be visiting the Pentagon. "It became pretty apparent to me, and I think to most at Africa Command pretty shortly after this attack began, that this was an attack," said Ham. The fact that the attackers were using rocket-propelled grenades and well-aimed small arms fire made it clear to him that "this was certainly a terrorist attack and not just—not something sporadic." He personally shared the news with General Martin E. Dempsey, chairman of the Joint Chiefs of Staff, and both "immediately" briefed Secretary of Defense Leon Panetta.

Back in Benghazi, things were falling apart quickly. Attackers swarmed the villa where Stevens and Smith were concealed. Unable to penetrate their safe room, the attackers set the building on fire. The DSS agent broke out an opening, but Stevens and Smith got lost in the smoke and could not follow. They would both apparently die of smoke inhalation. A mile or so away, the staff at the fortified CIA annex got the call for help. Stationed there was Ty Woods, a twenty-year Navy SEAL veteran and a ten-year veteran of the CIA's paramilitary Global Response Staff (GRS). Woods overrode the objections of the CIA's chief of base and promptly organized a seven-man GRS rescue team. At 4:25 p.m. they loaded up two Toyota Land Cruisers and drove to the State Department compound, arriving within a half hour of the initial attack.

Instead of driving into the melee, Woods had his team park discreetly outside against the compound wall. . They then climbed up on the vehicles and set up an L-shaped ambush on the top of the wall. Unlike the DSS agents, Woods and his crew were prepared to "unleash hell" on the attackers, and they had the firepower to do it. It did not take them long to rout the enemy and establish enough temporary security to round up the DSS agents. They also located Smith, unconscious but not yet dead in the building still ablaze. As the enemy reorganized, Woods's crew came under withering fire and had to retreat before they could locate Stevens's body. They headed back to the CIA annex with all the living safe and accounted for.

At 5:00 p.m. Panetta and Dempsey met with President Obama in the White House for a prescheduled meeting. There they discussed the attack with the president, most likely including the fact that Smith and Stevens had been reported as missing. The president authorized the pair to take all necessary steps and left the specifics up to them. They had no further contact with the president that evening and none at all with Secretary of State Hillary Clinton.

Meanwhile, in Tripoli, thirteen hours away from Benghazi by car, Woods's old Navy SEAL friend Glen Doherty and six colleagues, most of them CIA, commandeered a jet to join the fray.

In Benghazi, the Libyan militiamen reorganized outside the CIA annex and launched still another attack there around midnight local time. Soon after that, it had become clear in Tripoli that Anshar al-Sharia was claiming credit for the attacks via Twitter. At about 8:00 p.m. in Washington, Secretary Clinton called Greg Hicks in Tripoli. They spoke mostly about the status of Stevens, now reported to be in a hospital controlled by Anshar al-Sharia. There was no talk of a video or a riot. At 9:00 p.m. the prime minister of Libya called Hicks to tell him that Stevens was dead. Hicks would later be "effectively demoted" for telling the truth about what happened that night.

All through that night and early morning in Benghazi, while the GRS and DSS agents, along with local security, were holding off the attackers at the CIA annex there, Obama was holed up in the White House, likely in the family quarters. To this day, little is known about how he spent the hours between 5:30 p.m. and midnight. Obama did speak for an hour by phone with Benjamin Netanyahu. Obama called not to discuss Benghazi, but rather to alleviate any tension over his perceived snub of the Israeli prime minister. This perception, reported Lynn Sweet of the *Chicago Sun-Times*, presented "a political problem to a president who is wooing the Jewish vote." The *Sun-Times* posted Sweet's story, based obviously on a self-serving White House release, at 9:18 that evening. Public relations was apparently on the president's mind.

About an hour later, Secretary Clinton released a memo titled "Statement on the Attack in Benghazi." This statement read like a classic exercise in moral equivocation, but the concocted premise on which it was based rendered it absurd. "Some have sought to justify this vicious behavior as a response to inflammatory material posted on the Internet," said Clinton. "The United States deplores any intentional effort to denigrate the religious beliefs of others. Our commitment to religious tolerance goes back to the very beginning of our nation. But let me be clear: There is never any justification for violent acts of this kind." Yes, murdering innocent Americans is bad, but then again so are blasphemous art forms (except maybe *Book of Mormon* on Broadway, which Clinton saw and applauded).

While the White House dithered, Doherty and his crew were scrambling to reach the CIA annex in Benghazi. Arriving about 5:00 a.m. Benghazi time, they quickly took up defensive positions and helped the agents in place fend off a new wave of attackers trying to scale the wall. When the heat subsided, Doherty sought out Woods, who was manning the MK46 machine gun on the rooftop of the annex building. There, they embraced like brothers and resumed the fight until a couple of well-aimed French 81-mm mortars killed them both.

One of the fighters who accompanied Doherty was communicating through a ROVER handheld device with an unarmed Predator overhead. The picture on the ROVER convinced the CIA chief that a large enemy element was assembling outside the annex, and if they did not evacuate immediately, they might never escape. Thanks in large part to the unprompted heroism of Woods and Doherty, the CIA was able to save the State Department personnel and its own staff, perhaps thirty Americans in all, and get them out of Benghazi alive.

The next morning in Washington, even before the families of Woods and Doherty had been notified, President Obama, packed and ready to leave for a Las Vegas fund-raiser, addressed the nation from the Rose Garden. "Since our founding, the United States has been a nation that respects all faiths," said Obama, echoing Clinton's assigned motive for the attack. "We reject all efforts to denigrate the religious beliefs of others. But there is absolutely no justification to this type of senseless violence. None. The world must stand together to unequivocally reject these brutal acts." In essence, he blamed the still-unknown videographer before blaming the murderers. Obama did not use the words "Islam," "Muslim," or "terrorist." Only toward the end of the speech, after mentioning Afghanistan and Iraq, did Obama make a perfunctory gesture about the enemy. Said Obama: "No acts of terror will ever shake the resolve of this great nation, alter that character, or eclipse the light of the values that we stand for."

On Sunday, September 16, UN ambassador Susan Rice appeared on *five* political talk shows and served America extra helpings of the BS it had already grown used to hearing. On *Meet the Press*, for instance, Rice told the host, David Gregory, that what happened initially in Benghazi was "a response to a hateful and offensive video that was widely disseminated throughout the Arab and Muslim world." She made the same claim on the other four shows as well.

Curiously, less attention was paid to what Barack Obama was saying. A week after the attack, on September 18, he took his first questions about Benghazi. Bizarrely, he chose a late-night comedy show, *The Late Show with David Letterman*, as the venue to introduce the subject. Had Bush ever done something this tasteless, every schoolchild in America would know about it. By this time, the president was aware that even while the attack was in progress, Anshar al-Sharia had claimed responsibility. The president also knew that on September 16, Libyan president Mohamed Magariaf insisted the attack was planned. Said Magariaf, the idea that the attack was a "spontaneous protest that just spun out of control is completely unfounded and preposterous." Obama's interview with David Letterman went as follows:

LETTERMAN: Now, I don't understand, um, the ambassador to Libya killed in an attack on the consulate in Benghazi. Is this an act of war? Are we at war now? What happens here?

OBAMA: Here's what happened. . . . You had a video

that was released by somebody who lives here,
sort of a shadowy character who—who made
an extremely offensive video directed at—at
Mohammed and Islam.

LETTERMAN: Making fun of the Prophet Mohammed.

OBAMA: Making fun of the Prophet Mohammed. And so,
this caused great offense in much of the Muslim
world. But what also happened, extremists and
terrorists used this as an excuse to attack a
variety of our embassies, including the one, the
consulate in Libya.

The usually irreverent Letterman seemed offended that someone would make fun of the "Prophet Mohammed." Obama repeated the title and shared his host's seeming indignation. Later
in the interview, Obama cited the video again, now mimicking
the nonsense that Clinton formally introduced on the night of
the attack. "As offensive as this video was—and obviously, we denounced it, the United States government had nothing to do with
it—that's never an excuse for violence," said Obama.

Two days later, at a Univision forum, Obama spoke again of
the video. This time, without intending to, he suggested why the
administration might have wanted to suppress news of the attack.
The Libyans, said Obama, "understand because of the incredible
work that our diplomats did as well as our men and women in
uniform, we liberated that country from a dictator who had terrorized them for forty years."

If these same Libyans planned an attack on the American
consulate, that suggested something other than a happily liberated people. For nearly ten years, Democrats had been mocking
vice president Dick Cheney's expressed belief that in Iraq Americans would "be greeted as liberators." Obama did not want that
same hulking albatross hanging around his neck. No, the Libyan

people were grateful. Unfortunately, there was this "offensive video or cartoon directed at the prophet Muhammad," which prompted "some to carry out inexcusable violent acts directed at Westerners or Americans." Here, Obama refused to identify who the "some" were and falsely broadened the victims to include "Westerners."

It was not until Obama appeared on *The View* on September 25 that he admitted at least part of the truth and even then he did so grudgingly. Joy Behar's question all but forced him to. "I heard Hillary Clinton say it was an act of terrorism," said Behar correctly. Clinton had conceded the same four days earlier. So had Jay Carney. "Is it? What do you say?" asked Behar.

"We're still doing an investigation," answered Obama. "There's no doubt that the kind of weapons that were used, the ongoing assault, that it wasn't just a mob action." Not "just" a mob action? This was the same Barack Obama who would shamelessly tell Bill O'Reilly more than a year later, "We revealed to the American people exactly what we understood at the time."

In truth, Obama would not even reveal what he had been doing on the night of the attack. Wanting answers, Senator Lindsay Graham held up the confirmation of defense secretary nominee Chuck Hagel until he got some. In mid-February 2013, apparently overlooking the call from Netanyahu, the White House sent a letter to the Senate claiming the president did not make any phone calls the night of September 11. "During the entire attack, the president of the United States never picked up the phone to put the weight of his office in the mix?" asked a disbelieving Graham.

A week later, Fred Lucas of CNSNews.com, doing the work the major media used to do, followed up on Obama's time line that evening and got an entirely different answer out of White House press secretary Jay Carney. "He was in regular communication with his national security team directly, through them," said Carney before adding the surprise jolt, "and spoke with the secretary of state at approximately 10:00 p.m. He called her to get an update on the situation."

CNSNews.com spent a week just trying to find out what time that evening Clinton had released her statement blaming the now imprisoned videographer for the attack. In still another show of transparency, the State Department refused to respond. In her tracking of the releases from other news sites, the earliest confirmed posting Lucas could find of the Clinton statement was 10:32 p.m. Washington time. As Lucas relates, MSNBC posted a Reuters story that cited the Clinton statement and traced the Benghazi attacks to "inflammatory material posted on the Internet." The timing suggests she and Obama coordinated this misdirection during their 10:00 p.m. phone call.

A question that remains unanswered is where Clinton got her information. It did not come from Greg Hicks. "The YouTube event was a non-event in Libya," he told Congress. It certainly did not come from the military. Colonel George Bristol of the US Marines, a regional commander who was in communication with the embassy in Tripoli throughout the night, told the House Armed Services Committee that he could remember no one suggesting the Benghazi affair was anything but a planned attack. To the specific question, "In any of the informal discussions that you were a part of or had the ability to hear about, did anyone call this a demonstration that got out of control?" Bristol answered, "No."

In his 2014 best seller, *Blood Feud*, Edward Klein traced the video excuse to Obama himself. According to Klein's source, a member of Clinton's team of legal advisers, "Obama wanted [Clinton] to say that the attack had been a spontaneous demonstration triggered by an obsure video on the Internet that demeaned Mohammed, the prophet and founder of Islam." This request was made during his 10 p.m. call. "Hillary," the president reportedly told Clinton, "I need you to put out a State Department release as soon as possible."

Klein's source claimed that Clinton was "sick about it" and called her husband, Bill Clinton, to get his advice before complying with Obama's directive. Bill reminded Hillary that Obama had an aversion to calling terrorism what it was, citing his description of the 2009 Fort Hood massacre as "workplace violence." In truth, Obama did not himself call the rampage by Major Nidal Malik Hasan "workplace violence" at least not publicly: US Army officials did the labeling despite Hasan's boast that he shot dozens of his fellow soldiers to protect Taliban leaders in Afghanistan. In the five subsequent years, however, White House officials, Obama included, never called the massacre an act of terror. There would be no terrorism on Obama's watch—or at least as little as the man who shot Osama bin Laden could get away with.

It was not until May 19, 2013, eight months after the Benghazi attack, that a newsman asked the obvious question of a White House spokesman, "What did the president do the rest of that night to pursue Benghazi?" The questioner was Chris Wallace of Fox News. The individual questioned was Dan Pfeiffer, a senior adviser to the president. Pfeiffer dodged this way and that to avoid answering the question, in the process all but accusing Wallace of being a conspiracy theorist. Wallace kept pressing. "The ambassador goes missing, ends up the first ambassador in more than thirty years is killed. Four Americans, including the ambassador, are killed. Dozens of Americans are in jeopardy," asked Wallace. "Where was he? What did he do? How did he respond?" Pfeiffer rebutted with various riffs on the Clintonian theme: "What difference does it make?" He would not even say whether Obama was in the situation room.

As Wallace knew, Obama and his advisers planned military strategy in the situation room. They planned political strategy upstairs in the family quarters. Pfeiffer was savvy enough to duck that question. After two years of administrative ducking, Americans know more about the movements of Woods and Doherty in

Benghazi than they knew about those of Obama and Clinton in Washington.

In a thoughtful piece in *National Review*, the former federal prosecutor Andy McCarthy reviewed the potential motives Obama and Clinton had to suggest some rationale for a September 11 attack other than the obvious. Given that a presidential election loomed less than two months into the future, McCarthy imagined several. For one, Obama and his campaign team had been making the case that al-Qaeda had been decimated and the Islamic threat had been neutralized. For another, they had been boasting how well the administration had handled the so-called Arab Spring, especially in Libya. For a third, they had been subtly creating the impression that America's real security problem stemmed from "Islamophobia" and the reaction it caused. "All of that being the case," wrote McCarthy, "I am puzzled why so little attention has been paid to the Obama-Clinton phone call at 10 p.m. on the night of September 11."

In April 2014, Judicial Watch secured, through a Freedom of Information Act suit, an e-mail that confirmed McCarthy's suspicions. On September 14, 2012, Benjamin Rhodes, the deputy national security adviser, had sent an e-mail titled "PREP CALL with Susan" to United Nations Ambassador Susan Rice. Rhodes was briefing Rice on how to handle the Benghazi questions when she appeared on the upcoming Sunday talk shows. Among the goals Rhodes cited was "to underscore that these protests are rooted in an Internet video, and not a broader failure of policy." This spurious talking point clarified why the Obama administration felt compelled to deceive: if the video did not cause the Benghazi assault, then a policy failure must have. Two months before the election, that was one truth no one in the White House was eager to share.

As usual, White House press secretary Jay Carney tried his demeaning best to make the president's untruths sound true. ABC's Jonathan Karl put Carney's talent to the test on the subject of the Rhodes e-mail.

KARL: Jay, I guess you're aware that Judicial Watch obtained an e-mail from Ben Rhodes to staff members about the Benghazi attack.

CARNEY: That's incorrect. But go ahead.

KARL: Oh, okay.

CARNEY: The e-mail and the talking points were not about Benghazi. They were about the general situation in the Muslim world where you saw, as you may recall.

KARL: It was an e-mail to prepare Susan Rice for those talk shows.

CARNEY: But you misstated it. In fact, this was not—it was explicitly not about Benghazi. It was about the overall situation in the region.

Carney's apparent strategy was to run out the clock on Karl's time. To exhaust Karl's patience and that of his colleagues, Carney kept repeating the canard that the talking points "were not about Benghazi." A second reporter almost got Carney off the hook when he switched the conversation to that week's empty diversion, the controversy surrounding the Los Angeles Clippers' owner, Donald Sterling, but a frustrated Karl jumped back in. "Why were you holding back this information? Why was this e-mail not turned over to the Congress?" he asked forcefully. "Why did it take a court case for you to release this e-mail? Why was it classified?" Karl got no help from his fellow reporters, and Carney, as usual, was allowed to squirm away.

THE SUGGESTION THAT ANYBODY IN MY TEAM . . . WOULD PLAY POLITICS OR MISLEAD WHEN WE'VE LOST FOUR OF OUR OWN, GOVERNOR, IS OFFENSIVE. THAT'S NOT WHAT WE DO.

On Tuesday night, October 16, 2012, members of the Obama team entered the debate hall at Hofstra University in a state of great unease. Much to the shock of the Obama faithful, Republican Mitt Romney had beaten their man in the first debate. Romney beat him so badly, in fact, that if it had been a Little League game the ump would have invoked the mercy rule by about the third inning. The campaign could not endure a repeat. The Town Hall–style format would help. So would a friendly moderator not above calling a fair ball foul when the situation demanded.

The evening's most notorious exchange began inauspiciously. The question from the audience that prompted it came from Long Islander Kerry Ladka. She asked in regard to the Benghazi consulate, "Who denied enhanced security and why?" The question went to President Obama, and he launched into a well-rehearsed set piece about how he was handling the issue. Romney responded much as one would expect him to respond, criticizing the White House's response to the attack, especially Obama's Las Vegas fund-raising trip a day afterward, and Obama's Mideast policy in general.

At this point, Crowley conceded a shortage of time and an excess of audience questions. Nevertheless, instead of moving on to that next question, she asked a question of her own. Even before she began to ask, however, Obama was strolling confidently toward Crowley as though he knew what was going to happen next. The question involved Secretary of State Clinton's taking responsibility for embassy security. Asked Crowley, "Does the buck stop with the secretary of state?"

Obama was more than ready for this one. "Secretary Clinton has done an extraordinary job, but she works for me," said he forcefully. "I'm the president, and I'm always responsible." From there Obama launched into a pitch-perfect, if thoroughly dishonest, defense of his own role in the affair: "The day after the attack, Governor, I stood in the Rose Garden, and I told the American people and the world that we were going to find out exactly what happened, that this was an act of terror, and I also said we are going to hunt down those who committed this crime."

Obama did not throw the "act of terror" line away. He said it clearly and defiantly as though he knew he could get away with it. Feigning outrage, Obama then told of how he manfully greeted the caskets as they arrived at Andrews Air Force Base and how he took offense at the very suggestion that anyone on his "team" would "play politics or mislead when we have lost four of our own."

Sensing an opening, Romney moved in for the coup de grâce over Crowley's protests that he respond "quickly." Romney looked straight at Obama, raised his eyebrows quizzically, and asked, "You said in the Rose Garden the day after the attack it was an act of terror? It was not a spontaneous demonstration, is that what you are saying."

Now back on his stool, Obama answered uncomfortably, "Please proceed. Please proceed, Governor." Romney turned back to Crowley and said that he just wanted to get Obama's response on record. With the camera still on Romney, the TV audience heard Obama say off-camera, "Get the transcript." The camera then moved to a wide shot and showed Crowley waving a piece of paper. Many viewers believed that to be the transcript and wondered how Crowley just happened to have it. "He did in fact, sir, call . . . ," said Crowley hesitantly to Romney, "so let me call it an act of terror."

"Can you say that a little louder, Candy," said a suddenly revived Obama while the Obama fans in the audience, Michelle included, cheered in violation of the rules. "He did call it an act of terror," said Crowley, consummating the most egregious act of real-time media malpractice in recent memory. She then stumbled through a temporizing bit of nonsense about the two weeks it took for the "whole idea" to be revealed.

When Romney then tried to discuss Ambassador Susan Rice's appearance on five Sunday talk shows, Obama walked into his space and started talking over him. At that point, Crowley said, "I want to move you on and people can go to the transcripts." She then turned quickly to an audience member who wanted to talk about AK-47s, "a question we hear a lot," said Crowley preposterously.

As to what Obama actually said in his September 12 Rose Garden speech, there is no mystery. He laid out the cause and effect of the Benghazi attack as he saw it one and a half minutes into the presentation: "While the United States rejects efforts to denigrate the religious beliefs of others, we must all unequivocally oppose the kind of senseless violence that took the lives of these public servants." It was hard to misinterpret his meaning. The effort "to denigrate the religious beliefs of others" clearly referred to the absurd trailer for the would-be film *The Innocence of Muslims*. The violence that followed, said Obama, was "senseless." Here, Obama strongly implied that four Americans were killed in a spontaneous outburst devoid of strategy and provoked by the offending video. There was no other way to read this.

Three minutes later near the end of a five-plus-minute speech, Obama added, "No acts of terror will ever shake the resolve of this great nation." This bit of generic tough talk was the rhetorical life raft to which Crowley, the president, and the true believers clung. Before the emergence of the Internet, they might have gotten away with it, but as the record unequivocally shows, Obama's "team," the president included, did play politics with the truth for as long as two weeks after the event and right up through the debate.

Obama was stalling for time. He could not afford a full-body Benghazi blow in this second debate. With Crowley's help, witting or otherwise, he hoped to reverse the momentum from the first debate and bury the Benghazi controversy under the media chatter about the new comeback kid. That did not exactly happen, but he escaped better than he might have. With respect to the promised hunt for those who killed the four Americans, for nearly two years that proved about as fruitful as OJ's hunt for the Colombian drug dealers who killed his ex-wife. Finally, in June 2014, authorities arrested Abu Khattala for his suspected role in the attack. The *New York Times* identified Khattala as a "a local, small-time Islamist militant," one with "no known connections to international terrorist groups." As many as twenty other suspects remain at large.

WE HAVE A BASIC PRINCIPLE: WE DO NOT LEAVE ANYBODY WEARING THE AMERICAN UNIFORM BEHIND

To defend their exchange of five high-level terrorists held at Guantánamo for the presumed deserter, Sergeant Bowe Bergdahl, Obama and his staffers shot off an extraordinary volley of assorted flak, little of which had anything to do with the truth. The sharp-eyed Joseph Miller, the pen name of a ranking Department of Defense official writing for the *Daily Caller*, labored to distinguish "The Top 8 Lies" among the many.

At the head of Miller's list was the notion that Bergdahl was "very sick." Said Obama at a press conference in Brussels responding to the stateside outcry, "We had a prisoner of war whose health had deteriorated and we were deeply concerned about [*sic*]." Secretary of Defense Chuck Hagel expressed even greater concern. "In particular his health was deteriorating," said Hagel. "It was our judgment that if we could find an opening and move very quickly, we needed to get him out of there, essentially to save his life." A few days after Hagel's comments, the Taliban released a video of a dazed, confused, but apparently healthy Bergdahl walking unaided to an American helicopter.

As Miller notes, Bergdahl's alleged death spiral was among the reasons the White House ignored the law requiring it to notify Congress thirty days prior to the release of any detainee from Guantánamo. Another reason cited by White House officials was that the Taliban threatened to kill Bergdahl if the details of the exchange were made known. Senate Intelligence chairwoman Dianne Feinstein, a California Democrat, wasn't buying her own party's wolf tickets. "I don't think there was a credible threat," she told *Politico*. "I have no information that there was."

The rationale for the White House end run around Congress took another hit when it was revealed just how many staffers knew about the prisoner exchange. "Probably the most distressing thing or the most disturbing thing I heard," said Representative Peter King after a White House meeting more than a week after the exchange, "was at least 80 to 90 people in the administration were aware of this proposed deal, and yet they couldn't notify anyone in Congress."

To quiet the furor over the one-sided exchange, the president's national security adviser Susan Rice stepped up to the plate once again and pinch-hit for her boss. When CNN's Candy Crowley asked her, "Point-blank, did the U.S. negotiate with terrorists?" Rice claimed that since the negotiations were filtered through the government of Qatar, the answer was "no." In fact, though, as Miller points out, Qatar wasn't holding Bergdahl captive. The Haqqani Network was, and in 2012 the White House had officially designated it a terrorist group.

That same Sunday morning, Rice made her way over to the ABC studios. There she earned a place in the Cooperstown of mendacity with her assertion that Bergdahl served with "honor and distinction." In the subsequent days, as more details about Bergdahl's desertion of his post emerged, observers left and right expressed shock at the seeming illogic of the White House spin. "I think what bothers people is having our commander-in-chief on television putting a glow of euphoria around this guy," said retired US Army general Barry McCaffrey. McCaffrey could not fathom why Rice claimed Bergdahl served with "honor and distinction" when she and the president "knew full well this wasn't the case."

The White House spun any number of other confections about the prisoner exchange, most notably the idea that the released terrorists posed no threat. One great deception, however, underscored the entire Bergdahl Kabuki. It was the same one that underscored Obama's role as commander in chief: he had to pretend that he cared. When Obama told the press in Brussels, "We have a basic principle: We do not leave anybody wearing the American uniform behind," it was for him just another talking point. When Rice spoke about America's "sacred obligation" to its soldiers, it was again just so much talk. Obama, in particular, saw nothing "sacred" about America's past or about its presence in the world. Indeed, if he felt any obligation at all to Americans in harm's way, he would not have spent the evening of September 11, 2012, plotting campaign strategy.

CHAPTER 12

THE TRANSFORMER

We are five days away from fundamentally transforming the United States of America," said Barack Obama in an unwittingly honest moment five days before the 2008 election. From Inauguration Day on, the president would transform America from a country whose White House respected the truth to one whose White House played with it. This was never more obvious than during the interview with O'Reilly at the Super Bowl, when Obama played with the very notion of transforming America. "Mr. President," asked O'Reilly, "why do you feel it's necessary to fundamentally transform the nation that has afforded you so much opportunity and success?"

Said Obama, "I don't think we have to fundamentally transform the nation." He then finessed, saying, "I think that what we have to do is make sure that here in America, if you work hard, you can get ahead." Despite this generic disclaimer, Obama had certainly tried to transform America. By the time of the interview, the great majority of Americans without Obamaphones knew that the transformation he promised was not exactly the one he delivered.

Among the millions who got to experience the transformation

firsthand was Edie Littlefield Sundby, a California woman suffering from stage 4 gallbladder cancer. Although this kind of cancer proves fatal to 98 percent of its victims within five years, Sundby had been fighting it and beating it for seven. The fight cost her insurer $1.2 million, but "never once," Sundby wrote in a *Wall Street Journal* op-ed, did UnitedHealthcare question any treatment or procedure recommended by her medical team. Sundby made the most of that investment. She put her faith in God and in medical science and helped her own cause with a vigorous embrace of life and nature. In October 2011, more than a year after Obamacare had been signed into law, she chronicled her experience for the *New York Times.* As a testament to her faith, she wrote her op-ed from a campsite "beside the Gilahina River in the wilds of Alaska." If she had any anxiety about how Obamacare would affect her health plan, it did not come through in the article.

In January 2013, Sundby received the most troubling news since her diagnosis. Owing to the provisions of the Affordable Care Act, UnitedHealthcare had to withdraw from the individual California market. The company was canceling her affordable and highly effective health insurance as of December 31, 2013. Sundby's attempt to duplicate the plan through a California health exchange just added headaches to her already fragile condition. "What happened to the president's promise, 'You can keep your health plan'? Or to the promise that 'You can keep your doctor'?" she wrote. "Take away people's ability to control their medical-coverage choices and they may die. I guess that's a highly effective way to control medical costs. Perhaps that's the point." Perhaps that was the point.

FOR MY MOTHER . . . TO SPEND THE LAST MONTHS OF HER LIFE IN THE HOSPITAL ROOM ARGUING WITH INSURANCE COMPANIES . . . THERE'S SOMETHING FUNDAMENTALLY WRONG ABOUT THAT

In his second debate with Senator John McCain, just before he said, "If you've got a health care plan that you like, you can keep it. All I'm going to do is help you to lower the premiums on it. You'll still have choice of doctor. There's no mandate involved," then-senator Obama said something even more deeply dishonest. Responding to a question by the moderator, Tom Brokaw, as to whether health care was a right or a responsibility, Obama answered, "For my mother to die of cancer at the age of fifty-three and have to spend the last months of her life in the hospital room arguing with insurance companies because they're saying that this may be a pre-existing condition and they don't have to pay [for] her treatment, there's something fundamentally wrong about that."

The temptation is to call the exploitation of a dying relative a new political low, but that would be unfair to Al Gore. As vice president, Gore pioneered that unhallowed ground at the 1996 Democratic National Convention. There Gore told a maudlin tale of how he knelt by the bedside of his nicotine-addicted sister Nancy, then dying of lung cancer, squeezed her hand, and said, "I love you." Gore suggested that the experience turned him into a crusader against tobacco: "That is why," he thundered, "until I draw my last breath, I will pour my heart and soul into the cause of protecting our children from the dangers of smoking."

This speech might have had a more lasting effect had it not been for a few veteran Tennessee reporters. They remembered the old Al Gore, the very same one who, in 1988, four years *after* his sister's death, campaigned for president as a friend of tobacco. "All of my life," he crowed, "I hoed it, chopped it, shredded it, put it in the barn and stripped it and sold it." The very year Nancy died, Gore helped Big Tobacco fight efforts to put the words "death" and "addiction" on cigarette warning labels. True, once he got beyond these minor detours, Gore hopped onto the road to reform in plenty of time for the convention.

In his second 2008 debate with McCain, Obama had a strategic advantage. Even a serious reporter would have had a hard time fact-checking the tale about his dying mother, and in 2008 there were damn few of those reporters in the major media. Obama got to skate on this claim for years. It was not until July 13, 2011, that those *New York Times* readers who found their way to page A16 learned that Obama had "mischaracterized a central anecdote about his mother's deathbed dispute with her insurance company." This revelation came from a new biography of Obama's mother written by the *Times'* own Janny Scott. Although largely flattering, Scott's bio revealed that Ann Dunham's employer-provided Cigna health policy paid her hospital bills directly. Dunham had "to pay only the deductible and any uncovered expenses, which, she said, came to several hundred dollars a month."

Scott based her reporting on letters between Cigna and Dunham. Reported the *Times*, "A White House spokesman chose not to dispute either Ms. Scott's account or Mr. Obama's memory, while arguing that Mr. Obama's broader point remained salient." Yes, the larger point, the *pravda*, always remains salient in Obamaland. To his credit, the *Times'* Kevin Sack challenged that contention. He quoted the Harvard health policy professor Robert J. Blendon to the effect that if these facts had been known in 2008, "People would have considered it a significant error." Blendon added: "I just took for granted that it was a pre-existing condition health insurance issue."

Had Obama let the story die at this point, it would have been easier to forgive him, but he did not. He and his campaign team knew how well the story worked in the 2008 campaign and they likely figured it would work again in 2012 with a little tweaking. The vehicle they used to revive the fraud was a documentary-style campaign video, *The Road We've Traveled*. The narration by lovable Hollywood everyman Tom Hanks lent the video added credibility, as did the supportive commentary by Michelle Obama. Covering the following audio sequence were heart-tugging images of Obama and his mom:

HANKS: He knew from experience the cost of waiting [on health care reform].

OBAMA: When my mom got cancer, she wasn't a wealthy woman and it pretty much drained all her resources.

MICHELLE: She developed ovarian cancer, never really had good, consistent insurance. That's a tough thing to deal with, watching your mother die of something that could have been prevented. I don't think he wants to see anyone go through that.

HANKS: And he remembered the millions of families like his who feel the pressure of rising costs and the fear of being denied or dropped from coverage.

"Something that could have been prevented"? Here, Michelle very nearly accused Cigna of killing her mother-in-law, but then again, this was not an unusual implication from the Obama camp. Later in 2012, a pro-Obama super PAC, Priorities USA Action, put out an ad claiming that Mitt Romney and his company, Bain Capital, had blood on their hands for a woman's death. That woman's husband, Joe Soptic, had worked for a steel plant in which Bain had taken an ownership position. "I lost my health care, and my family lost their health care. And, a short time after that, my wife became ill. I don't know how long she was sick and I think maybe she didn't say anything because she knew that we couldn't afford the insurance," said Soptic in the ad. "I do not think Mitt Romney realizes what he's done to anyone, and furthermore I do not think Mitt Romney is concerned."

The ad itself was flagrantly dishonest. For one, Soptic's wife was never covered under her husband's insurance plan. For another, Romney had little to do with the purchase of Soptic's company, took a leave of absence immediately afterward to run in Massachusetts against Ted Kennedy for the US Senate, and left Bain Capital altogether two years before the bankruptcy of Soptic's company to rescue the Salt Lake City Olympics. In fact, had Bain not been involved, the plant would likely have closed sooner.

Worse than the crime, as they say, was the cover-up. When the ad backfired, Obama's people claimed no connection to it. Said White House press secretary Robert Gibbs on Air Force One, "We don't have any knowledge of the story of the family." This claim quickly fell apart when it was revealed that Soptic's story had already been used in a campaign slide show earlier in 2012 and featured in a campaign ad. In fact, Soptic himself had starred on a conference call hosted by Obama's deputy campaign manager, Stephanie Cutter. "Thank you, Joe," Cutter said at the call's end. "We really appreciate you . . . sharing your experiences."

For the most part, though, this was all inside baseball. The truth about Obama's mother and Soptic's wife reached few Obama supporters, and it persuaded fewer still. Millions of them voted for Obama in 2012 not particularly caring whether his health care pitch was valid or not. They assumed the changes would not affect them much in any case. They were wrong. "I was really shocked," said a Coloradan, Cathy Wagner, once an avid Obamacare supporter, upon receiving her cancellation notice. "All of my hopes were sort of dashed. Oh my gosh, President Obama, this is not what we hoped for, it's not what we were told." Wagner, unfortunately, was in good company.

THERE'S NO MANDATE INVOLVED

In late November 2007, Senator Barack Obama got clever. He knew that the only way he could hope to win the Democratic nomination was by beating John Edwards and Hillary Clinton in the upcoming Iowa caucuses. If Clinton won, given her organizational strength in the early primary states, she could all but bank the nomination.

By this point, the Edwards and Clinton campaigns had each released their candidate's health care reform plans. They were very nearly identical and shared one distinctive feature: each mandated coverage. In introducing his own plan in Council Bluffs on November 24, Obama flanked his opponents on the side they were least expecting, the right. He rejected mandated health coverage for adults. A disgusted Paul Krugman wrote in the *New York Times* that Obama was simply "echoing right-wing talking points." For Obama what was true was that which worked. His goal at the time was to win Iowa. Transforming America would come later. Obama reduced his opponents' "essential argument" to one point: "the only way to get everybody covered is if the government forces you to buy health insurance." Obama dismissed that argument. He would stick to his anti-mandate philosophy all the way through the general election campaign.

Krugman could barely contain his frustration. "What seems to have happened," said the Nobel Prize–winning economist, "is that Mr. Obama's caution, his reluctance to stake out a clearly partisan position, led him to propose a relatively weak, incomplete health care plan." Krugman had yet to understand something about Obama: he had no great passion for or against mandates. In truth, he had no great passion at all. By the time of his September 2009 health care speech, the one that prompted Joe Wilson's plaintive wail, Obama had fully reversed himself on mandates. Now echoing left-wing talking points, he denounced those individuals who failed to sign up for health care as "irresponsible." He even accused them of trying to "game the system." Lest he provide a target for his critics, Obama avoided all variations of the word "mandate" in his 2009 speech. Under his plan, no one would be "forced" or "mandated" to get health insurance; people would merely be "required."

In that same 2007 Iowa speech, one that proved how spectacularly empty were his promises, Obama suggested a few other flaws in Clinton's proposed plan. "What I am convinced of is, if we actually hope to pass universal health care this time around, we have to bring Republicans and Democrats together," said Obama. "We have to have an open and transparent process so that the American people participate in the debate and see exactly what we're doing."

I WILL SIGN A UNIVERSAL HEALTH CARE BILL INTO LAW BY THE END OF MY FIRST TERM AS PRESIDENT THAT WILL COVER EVERY AMERICAN

As early as June 2007, Senator Barack Obama was promising the sun and the stars. In a way, he had to. Senator Hillary Clinton and Senator John Edwards had already promised the moon. All of this astral-promising led to some fairly comical debates, one of the more amusing of which took place, appropriately enough, in Las Vegas.

Something about the dry desert air—or perhaps Obama's surge in the polls—made Ms. Clinton just a little bit testy. "I have a universal health care plan that covers everyone," she told the moderator, Wolf Blitzer of CNN. "I've been fighting this battle against the special interests for more than fifteen years, and I am proud to fight this battle." As Clinton saw it, Obama was all helmet and no bicycle. "He talks a lot about stepping up and taking responsibility and taking strong positions," she said. "But when it came time to step up and decide whether or not he would support universal health care coverage, he chose not to do that." By Clinton's accounting, Obama's plan would have left fifteen million uninsured, about the population, she assessed, of all the upcoming primary states—Iowa, South Carolina, New Hampshire, and Nevada.

Obama fired back with a comment that pushed the hubrometer into the red zone. "The fact of the matter is that I do provide universal health care," said Obama. If ever a statement cried out for parsing, it was this one. Clinton had a "plan" that covered everyone. She questioned whether Obama "supported" a comparable plan. Obama, by his lights, did not need to bother with a *plan*. No, said Obama, "I do provide universal health care." The same royal "I" who would cause the planet to heal and the oceans to subside was prepared to provide health care for three hundred million people.

Although he had not quite yet put a plan together, Obama had been on record promising universal health care coverage as early as June 2007. In a speech grandly titled "A Politics of Conscience" and delivered at a United Church of Christ synod in Hartford, Connecticut, Obama lamented the fate of the forty-five million Americans said to lack health insurance. This was a problem he was prepared to solve. In his most preacherly cadence, Obama made "a solemn pledge" that he would "sign a universal health care bill into law" by the end of his first term as president. This plan would not just "cover every American" but simultaneously "cut the cost of a typical family's premiums by up to $2,500 a year." Given the audience for his speech, Obama assured the congregants that this promise was not just a matter of policy or ideology. It was "a moral commitment."

There was a recklessness about many of Obama's promises, and this was one of them—two of them, actually. According to the most recent projections of the Congressional Budget Office, the number of uninsured Americans will remain above thirty million through the year 2024. This was fifteen million more people than even Hillary accused Obama of abandoning and thirty million or so more than he promised to cover himself.

As to the savings of $2,500 a year per family, that was a dog that could never bark. Obamacare had too many cost enhancers hardwired into it. Insurers could no longer set the ratio of what older customers paid compared with the young. They could not charge different premiums based on a person's health at the time of enrollment. They could not refuse individuals with preexisting conditions. They would have to pay various taxes and fees. They would have to include ten "essential health benefits" in the package of every insured person whether that person wanted those benefits or not, and when all the calculating was over, they would have to pass the added costs along to the insured. Some might benefit, but an awful lot would get hurt.

By 2014, the "$2,500 per family" pledge had become a punch line, even for Democrats. In February of that year, Senator Amy Klobuchar, Representative Tim Walz, and Representative Collin Peterson, all Minnesota Democrats, addressed a town hall meeting at South Central College in Mankato. When they offered to take questions from the floor, one gentleman asked, "I thought the Affordable Care Act would save $2,500 per family. What happened?" Klobuchar and Walz looked at each other quizzically, and the crowd broke out laughing. Said Peterson, sitting in the middle of the panel, "I voted 'no.' So I'll let these guys handle that." At this point the crowd applauded. Lawmakers may not have had cost figures handy, but everyone in the room knew how they were trending. In the three years after Obamacare was signed into law in 2010, the costs did not go down $2,500 per family as promised. They went up $2,581 a family. Yes, inflation would have pushed the costs of insurance coverage up regardless of Obamacare, but not that much, nor that quickly.

WE'LL HAVE THE NEGOTIATIONS TELEVISED ON C-SPAN

As she approached the presidential primaries in 2008, Hillary Clinton had at least two obvious weak points on the health care front. One she could turn to her advantage: yes, she failed to reform health care during her husband's first term, but, by golly, she at least she made the effort. "On balance I think we made the right decision to try to reform the whole system," wrote Clinton in her tedious, self-serving memoir *Living History*. "Someday we will fix the system. When we do it, it will be the result of more than fifty years of efforts by Harry Truman, Richard Nixon, Jimmy Carter and Bill and me. Yes, I'm still glad we tried."

The second point of vulnerability offered no easy defense. Various groups had successfully sued Clinton's health care task force over its composition, including the awkward fact that the very chair of the task force was not a government employee. As Clinton herself conceded, this strategy fostered "an impression with the public and the media that we were conducting secret meetings." Throughout the primary season, candidate Obama zeroed in on this soft spot in the Clinton carapace, her "one really big mistake." This was a mistake he would not repeat. Starting in November

2007, and no fewer than seven times thereafter, Obama promised not only to make health care negotiations public, but also to air them on the public policy cable channel C-SPAN.

The C-SPAN riff tested sufficiently well that Obama continued to use it even after he forced Clinton out of the campaign. At a Town Hall meeting in Chester, Virginia, in August 2008, he waxed particularly rhapsodic on the larger subject of health care transparency. "I'm going to have all the negotiations around a big table," he told those gathered. "We'll have doctors and nurses and hospital administrators. Insurance companies, drug companies—they'll get a seat at the table. They just won't be able to buy every chair." This would be a big table indeed, and that was just for starters. "We'll have the negotiations televised on C-SPAN," Obama continued, "so that people can see who is making arguments on behalf of their constituents, and who are making arguments on behalf of the drug companies or the insurance companies." This way, he insisted, citizens could "stay involved in this process."

As with many of the health care promises Obama made during the campaign, he made this one because it tested well and sounded good. To do as he promised would take some extra effort, but that effort was the only real obstacle. Apparently, it was obstacle enough. Obama didn't bother trying. By July 2009, even the media had begun to notice. The routinely obeisant McClatchy news service lamented in a headline "Obama Campaign Vow of Public Debate on Health Care Fading." As the McClatchy reporters acknowledged, "The two biggest deals so far—industry agreements to cut drug and hospital costs—were reached in secret." Yes, in March 2009 C-SPAN did carry a White House forum on health reform at which the president spoke, but this was a kickoff event, not a negotiation.

McClatchy gave the Obama people a generous opportunity to defend Obama's shift in priorities, but the administration's responses showed only how shallow his promises were. "I don't think the president intimated that every decision putting together a health care bill would be on public TV," said White House press secretary Robert Gibbs. "It's unrealistic to think every aspect of the negotiations is going to be public," said Senate majority whip Dick Durbin, a Democrat from Illinois. "Sometimes for people to say what's really on their mind, it helps to do it outside the public eye," said Democratic senator Thomas Carper of Delaware—a slice of the obvious that Obama should have absorbed long before he littered the landscape with his promises.

All of these reservations notwithstanding, Gibbs assured the McClatchy reporters that Obama had "demonstrated more transparency than any president." To the knowing, this translated as "more than the Clintons did when they tried to hijack the health care system, but just barely." Like so many of Obama's promises, the promise to air negotiations on C-SPAN had turned into something of an inside joke. No one took it seriously, not even Obama's grassroots group Organizing for America (OFA). OFA's leaders actually boasted in their e-mail blasts of the "behind-the-scenes committee negotiations." Being pros, they understood why Obama promised what he did. The promise worked. It helped get him elected. The public forgot. Time to move on.

WE ARE NOT GOING TO PASS UNIVERSAL HEALTH CARE WITH A FIFTY-PLUS-ONE STRATEGY

In speaking to the *Concord Monitor* editorial board in November 2007, Senator Obama promised, "We are not going to pass universal health care with a fifty-plus-one strategy." On the audio recording of this meeting, Obama actually sounded as though he meant what he was saying, and there was good reason to say it. To be accepted by the public, transformative legislation—Social

Security, the Civil Rights Act, Medicare—needed at least some level of bipartisan congressional support.

With comfortable majorities in both chambers when elected, Obama did not bother to secure that support. In fact, he seemed to take delight in taunting the opposition. Just three days into the presidency, Obama invited top House and Senate Republicans to the White House to discuss the stimulus bill. When they raised objections to some of its features, Obama curtly reminded them, "I won." Not "We won," but "I won." Although both the House and the Senate had increased their Democratic majorities in the 2008 election, Obama did a one-man end zone dance in front of the humiliated Republicans.

When the debate switched to health care, Obama amped up the insults. On the occasion of his health care speech in September 2009, he dressed down congressional Republicans in front of the nation. "Instead of honest debate, we have seen scare tactics," Obama scolded. "Some have dug into unyielding ideological camps that offer no hope of compromise. Too many have used this as an opportunity to score short-term political points, even if it robs the country of our opportunity to solve a long-term challenge."

If Obama did not need Republican votes—and he would get none in either House or Senate—he did need the votes of all sixty senators who caucused with the Democrats. So he and his allies set about whipping them into line. Had C-SPAN televised the squalid negotiations that resulted, Netflix could have halted production on *House of Cards* and shown the highlights. President Underwood had nothing on President Obama or Senate majority leader Reid when it came to dirty dealing.

Reid offered Senator Ben Nelson a unique and permanent exemption from the state share of Medicaid expansion for Nebraska. This "Cornhusker Kickback" would have added millions to the federal tax burden had not the naked extortion of it all alarmed America. Undismayed, Reid pulled off his own "Louisiana Purchase," offering a $300 million increase for Medicaid in Louisiana to secure the vote of Democratic senator Mary Landrieu. Among other sweetheart deals, ample new funding for community health centers won the heart and the vote of Vermont socialist Bernie Sanders. "You'll find a number of states that are treated differently than other states," said Reid without apology. "That's what legislating is all about. It's compromise."

To make sure that the senators stayed bought, Reid brought the Affordable Care Act to the Senate floor in December 2009 before the surprise winner of the special election in Massachusetts, Republican Scott Brown, could take his seat in January. The bill passed the Senate on Christmas Eve 2009 by a 60–39 vote. One Republican was absent. This wasn't exactly a fifty-plus-one strategy. It was sixty-plus-zero.

UNDER OUR PLAN, NO FEDERAL DOLLARS WILL BE USED TO FUND ABORTIONS, AND FEDERAL CONSCIENCE LAWS WILL REMAIN IN PLACE

In March 2010, Representative Bart Stupak, an otherwise obscure Michigan Democrat, found himself someplace he never expected to be—at the center of a political maelstrom. As the leader of a small group of nominally pro-life House Democrats, he controlled the votes the president needed to pass the Affordable Care Bill into law. To the surprise of the president, those votes were not immediately forthcoming. Stupak and his colleagues had good reason to resist. The bill that the Senate sent to the House included no language to prevent the funding of abortion or to protect the conscience of believers. To this point, the words in Obama's September 2009 health care speech—"no federal dollars will be used to fund abortions"—remained just words.

Those words would have quickly passed into history had not Team Stupak insisted they be inserted into the bill. And that was a problem for two reasons. One was that the Senate had no great passion to insert them. Its members did not bother to include an antiabortion amendment when they had the chance. The second and more intractable problem was that Republican Scott Brown had taken his seat. The Republicans in the Senate could now kill the whole bill if it came back their way.

As a solution, Obama proposed an executive order. Although wary, Stupak at the time did not yet recognize how little a promise from Obama meant. So he took a big bite of the apple and handed it to his colleagues, and they bit as well. His fellow congressmen applauded, as did the media and Democrats everywhere. For a moment at least, Stupak had to feel like a hero, but then again maybe not. Shortly after the vote, he announced that after nine terms in Congress, he would not run again.

Among those celebrating Stupak's surrender were Obama's solicitor general, Elana Kagan, and her pal the Harvard Law luminary Laurence Tribe. "I hear they have the votes, Larry!! Simply amazing," Kagan wrote to Tribe in one of her e-mails. Tribe responded, "So health care is basically done! Remarkable. And with the Stupak group accepting the magic of what amounts to a signing statement on steroids." However cynical his response, Tribe saw Obama's conjuring trick for what it was. The executive order was scarcely worth more than a signing statement, which was worth close to nothing. Obama would soon enough appoint Kagan to the Supreme Court and, despite her partisan interest in the bill's passage, she would choose not to recuse herself when Obamacare came before the Court.

Whatever hopes Stupak may have entertained about canonization were dashed on January 20, 2012. That was the day on which Secretary Kathleen Sebelius's Department of Health and Human Services (HHS) introduced the "HHS Mandate." This executive fiat required virtually all private health insurance plans to include coverage for contraceptive drugs and devices, surgical sterilizations, and abortion-inducing drugs.

In mandating this coverage, Obama spit in the eye of the Catholic Stupak and his church. Said Stupak at an entirely irrelevant Democrats for Life panel at the 2012 convention, "I am perplexed and disappointed that, having negotiated the executive order with the president, not only does the HHS mandate violate the executive order but it also violates statutory law." With his leverage gone, so was the attention. Stupak had no further value to a party that never took him seriously in the first place.

The betrayal was worse than Stupak knew. In early 2014, Representative Chris Smith, a Republican from New Jersey and a veteran pro-lifer, showed just how thoroughly Obama had gone back on his word. In signing the Stupak executive order, Obama had promised to maintain Hyde Amendment restrictions governing abortion policy and to extend those restrictions to the new exchanges. The Hyde Amendment had two parts. One prohibited direct funding for abortion. The second banned funding for any health insurance that covered abortion except in cases of rape or incest, or to save the life of the mother. Under the Affordable Care Act, Smith pointed out, "massive amounts of public funds" in the forms of tax credits would underwrite insurance plans that covered abortions. This included every single Obamacare plan in Connecticut and Rhode Island and 103 of the 112 plans available to congressional staff in the Washington, DC, area. After selling his vote for an executive order, Stupak was able to convince himself that Obama's promise would "protect the sanctity of life in health care reform." He should have known better. This was after all the guy who voted against the Born-Alive Infants Protection Act—twice.

Happily for Obama, his supporters had long since forgotten about Stupak, the conscience clause, and the executive order

Obama wrote on Stupak's behalf when the Supreme Court
ruled in favor of Hobby Lobby's religious freedom suit. In a narrowly written decision, the Supreme Court ruled that a closely
held company like Hobby Lobby could not be forced to provide
abortion-inducing drugs to its employees. Democrats went ber-
serk, and Obama egged them on. "President Obama believes that
women should make personal health care decisions for themselves rather than their bosses deciding for them," read the official
White House statement. "Today's decision jeopardizes the health
of women who are employed by these companies." It did no such
thing, and the president knew it.

I WANT TO THANK ALL OF YOU FOR . . . PROVIDING QUALITY HEALTH CARE TO WOMEN ALL ACROSS AMERICA

At the April 2013 Planned Parenthood event in Washington, DC,
Obama did something exceptionally evasive even by his own
loose standards. He gave a seventeen-hundred-word speech to
America's leading provider of abortions—327,166 in the previous
calendar year, more than the population of Tampa—without mentioning the word "abortion." This would be like giving a speech at
Cooperstown without mentioning baseball.

Like many abortion supporters, Obama preferred "right to
choose," a phrase he used four times, although he never specified
what the choices were. And for good reason. Planned Parenthood
is not particularly keen on letting pregnant women know their
options. In 2012, for every adoption referral, Planned Parenthood
doctors performed 149 abortions. Avoiding the word "abortion,"
Obama stuck to the conceit that many women saw Planned Parenthood as "their primary source of health care—not just for contraceptive care." Given the audience, he knew enough not to repeat

the falsehood he uttered in the second presidential debate against Mitt Romney, namely that women "rely on [Planned Parenthood] for mammograms." At an October 18 rally in New Hampshire, Obama was even more specific, claiming Planned Parenthood did, in fact, "provide women with mammograms."

This was not true. Planned Parenthood clinics do not "provide" mammograms. At best, they provide referrals for mammograms. Under "health info and services," the website of a typical clinic lists "abortion" on top and then "birth control, morning-after pill, STDs, women's health." As a "primary source" of health care, the neighborhood CVS MinuteClinic serves women better than Planned Parenthood.

In promoting any product one is schooled to sell the benefits more than the features. In promoting Planned Parenthood, Obama refused to mention the product, let alone the features, and couched the benefits in the Orwellian language of abortion-speak. "Somewhere there's a woman who's breathing easier today," said Obama, "because of the support and counseling she got at her local Planned Parenthood health clinic." As the multiracial child of a single mother, Obama should be breathing easier that he was born before *Roe v. Wade* put Planned Parenthood in the abortion business.

NO ONE WILL TAKE IT AWAY. NO MATTER WHAT.

If past presidents could boast of signature achievements, Obama could boast of a signature lie. It took him a while to formulate it. On the campaign trail, he shamelessly told America, "I do provide universal health care," but he was always a little fuzzy on the details. By the time of the Democratic National Convention in August 2008, he had had a few months as the designated nominee to pull some specifics together—but if he'd done so, he chose not to share them at the Denver convention.

"If you have health care, my plan will lower your premiums," he told the enthralled audience. "If you don't, you'll be able to get the same kind of coverage that members of Congress give themselves." He then repeated the nonsense about his dying mother haggling with insurance companies and promised to force these companies to "stop discriminating against those who are sick and need care the most." And that was pretty much it for health care, a pastiche of old lies and unattainable new promises. Vintage Obama.

On June 15, 2009, Obama rolled out some of the details of Obamacare, then still in its embryonic stage, with a much tougher audience, the gathered physicians of the American Medical Association. There was nothing casual about what he was about to say. In a speech as significant as this one, at least a dozen sets of knowing eyes would have reviewed every word, every phrase, including the passage that follows:

> I know that there are millions of Americans who are content with their health care coverage—they like their plan and they value their relationship with their doctor. And that means that no matter how we reform health care, we will keep this promise: If you like your doctor, you will be able to keep your doctor. Period. If you like your health care plan, you will be able to keep your health care plan. Period. No one will take it away. No matter what. My view is that health care reform should be guided by a simple principle: Fix what's broken and build on what works.

Obama would repeat variations of this pledge thirty or forty more times, but there is no denying the fastness of the promise in this, its declaratory phase. "No matter how we reform health care" this pledge would hold. "No one will take it away," said Obama with certainty. "No matter what." Obama would build his presidency on this promise. He would pass the Affordable Care Act on this promise. He would get reelected on this promise. It would prove to be the most consequential lie in domestic political history.

At the time, though, it was not a lie, not technically anyhow. Obama may very well have believed what he said. That belief could not have lasted long. Four days after the speech, the Associated Press ran an unusually perceptive analysis, explaining in some detail how millions of Americans would be forced to change their health care coverage if the plans, then being formulated by senatorial committees, were enacted. Dallas Salisbury, head of a nonpartisan information clearinghouse on health and pension benefits, told the AP what was obvious to everyone in his industry: "If [Obama] was a king, he would deliver that, but he's not king." He called Obama's promise "an aspirational statement."

Curiously, the White House seemed to agree. Wrote the AP, "White House officials suggest the president's rhetoric shouldn't be taken literally: What Obama really means is that government isn't about to barge in and force people to change insurance." The Republican health policy expert Gail Wilensky, a former Medicare director, laid out the eventual outcome with some accuracy: "They may not force you to leave in any direct sense, but they could put rules and procedures in place that make it impossible to continue what you have now." Undeterred by objective analysis, including that from the Congressional Budget Office, which projected ten million Americans losing their plan, Obama kept on making the same flawed promise.

On April Fools' Day 2010, Obama spoke to a giddy crowd in Portland, Maine, about the Affordable Care Act that he had just signed into law. For nearly a year, experts had been warning the White House about the hazards of promising more than he could deliver. But with the crowd chanting, "Yes we can," Obama could hardly refrain from reading the scripted punch line: "if Americans like their doctor, they will keep their doctor. And if you like your insurance plan, you will keep it. No one will be able to take that away from you. It hasn't happened yet. It won't happen in the future."

Egging on the Portland crowd, Obama mocked his Republican opposition and their "foxes guarding the chicken coop" health reform plan, one that, he claimed, would "completely deregulate the insurance industry." This was, of course, an absurd charge. Had George Bush ever said anything this hyperbolic about the Democrats in Congress, it would have been on a bumper sticker within a week. Later, as Obamacare unraveled, a bitter Obama reversed his claim. Now, the Republicans did not even have a plan. "There's not even a pretense now that they're going to replace it with something better," said Obama at an August 2013 press conference, ignoring the multiple plans Republicans had already proposed.

There was no excuse for not seeing the unraveling coming.

In August 2012, Glenn Kessler, the author of the Fact Check column for the *Washington Post*, did a comprehensive report on Obama's claim that the premiums "will go down." As Kessler reported, under Obamacare insurers had to offer an "essential health benefits" package that included coverage in ten categories, among them some vote-tempting goodies like maternity and newborn care, substance-use-disorder services, and pediatric services.

According to HHS's own numbers, 62 percent of those enrolled in private insurance plans as of December 2011 did not have coverage for maternity services, which made perfect sense for those not willing or able to have children. Another 34 percent lacked coverage for substance-abuse services, again not an issue for the chronically sober. Indifferent to what customers wanted or needed, the department's report crowed that 8.7 million Americans would gain maternity coverage under the "essential health benefits" clause, an empty boast given that single men and middle-aged single women were the most likely cohorts to lack insurance.

Kessler also cited a recent report in *Health Affairs* showing that more than half of the individual insurance plans Americans held in 2010 would not qualify under Obamacare rules in 2014. The change in rules would not only raise prices on new plans, but also ensure that millions of Americans could not keep their old plans, no matter how much they liked them.

August 2012 was not a good time for Obama to face the obvious, let alone acknowledge it publicly. In his first debate against Mitt Romney, on October 3 of that year, Obama mentioned "You keep your own insurance. You keep your own doctor" quickly and in passing. He knew enough not to advance this promise in a venue where he could be challenged, even if Romney was handicapped by his own past. As governor of Massachusetts, Romney had implemented a plan with many of Obamacare's features. The best case he could make against Obamacare was an anodyne states-as-laboratory appeal to the Tenth Amendment, one of the twenty-seven amendments about which low-information voters neither knew or cared. In the second and third debates, Obama stayed away from his "you can keep your plan" vow altogether. So, unfortunately, did Romney. And so, not surprisingly, did Candy Crowley. The rest, as they say, is history.

NOW, IF YOU HAD ONE OF THESE SUBSTANDARD PLANS BEFORE THE AFFORDABLE CARE ACT BECAME LAW AND YOU REALLY LIKED THAT PLAN, YOU WERE ABLE TO KEEP IT

President Obama arrived in Boston for a speech in late October 2013, arguably the worst month of his presidency to that point.

The healthcare.gov website had flopped on its opening at the beginning of the month, and its performance had yet to improve.
That disaster Obama could explain away—"We are working over-
time to improve it" (*cheers, applause*)—and he certainly tried to
do just that. More difficult to dismiss were the millions of cancellation letters insurance companies were sending to their customers across America.

Obama likely chose Massachusetts to make this speech because it gave him the opportunity to compare the inept launch of
Obamacare with the rocky start of Romneycare, now assumed to
be a great success. No matter where he made this speech, however,
Obama faced a task that would have given Sisyphus a new appre-
ciation for his rock. He had to untell the epic lie that he had been
telling for the last four or five years. Unable to stick this one on the
Republicans, he found a new target, "bad apple insurers."

In Obama's retelling, these bad apples had "free rein" to sell
their customers "substandard plans" that promised much and
delivered little. "Now if you had one of these substandard plans
before the Affordable Care Act became law and you really liked
that plan, you were able to keep it," said Obama. "That was part
of the promise." The subtle part of the promise, Obama implied,
was that if these bad apples decided to cancel or downgrade
these plans, they had to replace them with a plan that covered
the "essential health benefits" mandated by Obamacare. He then
gave examples of the wonders thereof and concluded this breath-
takingly dishonest appeal by saying, "So if you're getting one of
these letters, just shop around in the new marketplace. That's
what it's for."

The administration so feared Edie Sundby because she cut
through this Gordian knot of lies with one swift stroke. Sundby
had essentially the same plan before Obamacare was passed. It
had not been changed substantially or downgraded. There was no
reason under Obama's logic that she should have had to change

it except, of course, that the changes mandated by Obamacare forced her company out of the market. Even for those companies that remained in the market, HHS administrators wrote the "grandfather" regulations tightly, in no small part to force insurance companies to alter their plans. This being the age of transparency, HHS announced this game-changer in the *footnote* of a February 2013 report: "We note that, as the Affordable Care Act is implemented, we expect grandfathered coverage to diminish, particularly in the individual market."

When Megyn Kelly of Fox News asked Sundby whether her plan was "substandard" as Obama suggested, she replied, "That's absurd and frankly it's condescending because it's not true." Sundby described her plan as "fabulous" and "fantastic, giving me total freedom to choose." That freedom allowed her to receive care at Memorial Sloan Kettering in New York and M. D. Anderson in Houston, the two best cancer hospitals in the world. "I am alive today because of my medical insurance and because of my doctors," she said.

Not content to let Sundby have her say, the always classy White House struck back. Dan Pfeiffer, the senior adviser last seen stonewalling Chris Wallace on Benghazi, promptly tweeted, "The Real Reason That the Cancer Patient Writing in Today's Wall Street Journal Lost Her Insurance," and supplied a link to an article in a leftist blog blaming UnitedHealthcare for her problems. Said Sundby in response, "I don't understand why they felt that was necessary." Apolitical and a registered independent, Sundby did not yet understand the priorities of the Obama White House. As each year passed, fewer and fewer Americans understood them.

CHAPTER 13

CONSEQUENCES

I n the first six years of his presidency, Obama and his people would dishonor one vow after another, not just about health care reform, but about guns, about marriage, about taxes, about war, about peace, about jobs, about abortion, about campaign reform, about race, about transparency, about the rule of law, about very nearly everything. "He made so many promises," said the deeply disappointed Obama acolyte Barbara Walters five years into the presidency. "We thought that he was going to be . . . the next messiah." The messiah he was clearly not. He was not even an honest man. Lamented Walters, "People feel very disappointed because they expected more."

Obama has told so many indisputable lies in his first six years that it is hard to cull out a top twenty-five. The ranking that follows evaluates the false statements that Obama has intentionally made and incorporates the variables of flagrancy, shamelessness, and consequence. Nothing that George Bush ever said would have cracked this list.

25. *Over the next two years, this plan will save or create 3.5 million jobs.* The original miscalculation was forgivable. The

subsequent juggling of the books to finesse the miscalculation was not.

24.   *If I am the Democratic nominee, I will aggressively pursue an agreement with the Republican nominee to preserve a publicly financed general election.* A bad start, this introductory move showed Obama early on just what the media would let him get away with.

23.   *So don't tell me I don't have a claim on Selma, Alabama.* If both of Obama's parents had been white, this bit of progressive blasphemy would have ended Obama's campaign before the sun set on Alabama.

22.   *We'll have the negotiations televised on C-SPAN.* To see all that double-dealing, we had to wait for *House of Cards.*

21.   *Qaddafi threatens a bloodbath that could destabilize an entire region.* An oldie but goldie; the left has been selling "bloodbaths" successfully since the Spanish civil war.

20.   *I intend to close Guantánamo, and I will follow through on that.* If Obama had passed the jihadists off as Dreamers and hired them out to his Hollywood pals as pool boys, congressional Dems might have played along.

19.   *But the debate is settled. Climate change is a fact.* Now if Obama could just convince those thirty thousand or so dissenting scientists to get on board, he might have a better case.

18.   *This administration has done more for the security of the state of Israel than any previous administration.* Barbra Streisand may have bought this nonsense, but Benjamin Netanyahu has proved a tougher sell.

17.   *For my mother . . . to spend the last months of her life in the hospital room arguing with insurance companies . . . there's*

something fundamentally wrong about that. There is something fundamentally even more wrong about lying on a mother's grave. Al Gore only exploited his dead sister.

16.   *I've written two books. I actually wrote them myself.* Obama is that rare literary genius who cannot get his subjects and verbs to match.

15.   *The person I saw yesterday was not the person that I met twenty years ago.* If the media had discovered Jeremiah Wright before Iowa, Obama would still be writing columns for the *Hyde Park Herald.*

14.   *My father left my family when I was two years old.* The "two years" created the illusion of a blessed multicultural union, but Mr. and Mrs. Obama may not have spent a single night under the same roof.

13.   *We need to close the revolving door that lets lobbyists come into government freely.* Having lobbyists come in the servants' entrance made this no less a lie.

12.   *I believe that marriage is the union between a man and a woman. . . . God's in the mix.* The polls proved a more authoritative source than God on this one.

11.   *Under our plan, no federal dollars will be used to fund abortions, and federal conscience laws will remain in place.* Jane Roe admittedly lied. The industry was built on lies. What's one more lie among friends?

10.   *We've got shovel-ready projects all across the country.* Most of that shoveling was going on in Oval Office, but, hey, Obama sold nearly a trillion dollars worth of pork on the back of this bad boy.

9.   *I didn't set a red line.* This double-talk had the Norwegians looking up the number of the local repo man.

8.   *Not even a smidgen of corruption.* Obama shocked even O'Reilly with the sheer effrontery of this nonsense about the IRS scandal.

7.   *The Fast and Furious program was a field-initiated program begun under the previous administration.* The president told this whopper *after* Jay Carney got his knuckles rapped for telling the same whopper.

6.   *No more secrecy.* Edward Snowden would seem to have a different take on this.

5.   *Here's what happened. You had a video that was released by somebody who lives here, sort of a shadowy character.* Although the DOJ is still looking for the killers of the four valiant Americans, it did succeed in bringing the video maker to "justice" mere weeks after the attack on Benghazi.

4.   *We revealed to the American people exactly what we understood at the time.* Lying about the original Benghazi lie only compounded the shame.

3.   *If you like your doctor, you will be able to keep your doctor. Period. If you like your health care plan, you will be able to keep your health care plan. Period. No one will take it away. No matter what.* This is the compound lie that got Obama reelected and sent us so far down the road to serfdom we may not be able to turn back.

2.   *Transparency and the rule of law will be the touchstones of this presidency.* This two-headed promise has been violated more wantonly than a goat at a Taliban bachelor party.

1.   *I, Barack Hussein Obama, do solemnly swear that I will execute the Office of President of the United States faithfully, and will to the best of my ability, preserve, protect, and defend the Constitution of the United States. So help me God.* Obama had his hand on the Bible when he stumbled through this one in January 2009. He had better hope God is merciful.

NOTES

Chapter 1: The Postmodernist

1   "what you have": "Health Care Speech to Congress," *New York Times*, September 9, 2009, www.nytimes.com/2009/09/10/us/politics/10obama.text .html.

2   drowned him out: "In Full: Obama Health Care Address," YouTube video, posted by "CBS," September 9, 2009, www.youtube.com/watch?v=U1YN F9I25yU.

2   "lack of civility": Kevin Hechtkopf, "Rep. Wilson Apologizes for Obama Speech Outburst," CBSNews.com, September 10, 2009, www.cbsnews.com/ news/rep-wilson-apologizes-for-obama-speech-outburst/.

2   at least once: "Reid Calls Bush a Liar," YouTube video, from the *Charlie Rose Show*, posted by "Reidisms," February 23, 2010, www.youtube.com/ watch?v=sMhhEZ_okc0.

2   the state's congressional delegation: Molly Hooper "'You Lie': Rep. Wilson Apologizes for Yell," *The Hill*, September 10, 2009, http://thehill.com/ homenews/house/58035-you-lie-mccain-calls-on-wilson-to-apologize.

3   "dishonest presidency": Marc Thiessen, "Obama's Dishonest Presidency," *Washington Post*, November 4, 2013, www.washingtonpost.com/opinions/ marc-thiessen-obamas-dishonest-presidency/2013/11/04/841947c6-4561-11e3 -b6f8-3782ff6cb769_story.html.

3   "whatever he wants": Garth Kant, "Liberal Icon Urges Obama Impeachment," *WND*, January 20, 2014, www.wnd.com/2014/01/liberal-icon-urges -obama-impeachment/.

4   prettier over time: Barack Obama, *Dreams from My Father: A Story of Race and Inheritance* (New York: Random House, 2007), 43.

4   "witness for secular humanism": Ibid.

4   "explain their frustrations": Saira Anees, "Obama Explains Why Some Small Town Pennsylvanians Are 'Bitter,'" ABC News, Political Punch, April 11, 2008, http://abcnews.go.com/blogs/politics/2008/04/obama-explains-2/.

4 "from my mother": Obama, *Dreams*, 63.

5 "in the narrative": Ibid., xvi.

5 "stitched-together": Ibid., 308.

5 "artful shaping": David Remnick, *The Bridge: The Life and Rise of Barack Obama* (New York: Random House, 2010), 231.

5 "character creations and rearrangements": David Maraniss, *Barack Obama: The Story* (New York: Simon & Schuster, 2012), Nook Edition, 25.

5 "politically calculating chameleon nature": Remnick, *Bridge*, 516.

5 "A lie told often": Lenin quotes, Goodreads, www.goodreads.com/author/quotes/104630.Vladimir_Lenin.

6 "articulate and bright and clean": Jason Horowitz, "Biden Unbound: Lays into Clinton, Obama, Edwards," *New York Observer*, February 5, 2007, http://observer.com/2007/02/biden-unbound-lays-into-clinton-obama-edwards/.

6 "no Negro dialect": Mark Preston, "Reid Apologizes for Racial Remarks about Obama During Campaign," CNN.com, January 9, 2010, http://www.cnn.com/2010/POLITICS/01/09/obama.reid/. John Heilemann and Mark Halperin, *Game Change* (New York: HarperCollins, 2010), 36.

6 shown a leftward skew: "Media Bias Basics: Journalists' Political Views," report by Media Research Center, undated, http://archive.mrc.org/biasbasics/biasbasics.asp.

6 "He went to Harvard": David Remnick, "The Joshua Generation," *The New Yorker*, November 17, 2008, www.newyorker.com/reporting/2008/11/17/081117fa_fact_remnick.

6 "Barack is viewed in part": Ibid.

7 "Family Duties Took Precedence": Barack Obama, "Family Duties Took Precedence," *Hyde Park Herald*, January 12, 2000.

8 "I was completely mortified": Remnick, "The Joshua Generation."

9 "If I am the Democratic nominee": "Reform Groups Urge Obama to Reaffirm Pledge to Presidential Public Financing System," open letter from Campaign Legal Center, League of Women Voters, Common Cause, Public Citizen, Democracy 21, U.S. PIRG, February 15, 2008, available at www.campaignlegalcenter.org/index.php?option=com_content&view=article&id=816%3Apr3082&catid=36&Itemid=60.

9 "groundbreaking success in raising money": Shailagh Murray and Perry Bacon Jr., "Obama to Reject Public Funds for Election," *Washington Post*, June 20, 2008, www.washingtonpost.com/wp-dyn/content/article/2008/06/19/AR2008061900914.html.

10 "The Congress will push me": "1988 George H. W. Bush Speech," August 18, 1988, C-SPAN, www.c-span.org/video/?3848-2/1988-george-hw-bush-speech.

11 In a desperate attempt to save: "Clinton on Flowers '92," YouTube video, from *60 Minutes*, televised January 26, 1992, posted by "Jim Heath," November 20, 2011, www.youtube.com/watch?v=lwXE52e9JFg.

12 "Blizzard of Lies": William Safire, "Blizzard of Lies," *New York Times*, January 8, 1996, www.nytimes.com/1996/01/08/opinion/essay-blizzard-of-lies .html.

12 protect his presidency: "Vast Right Wing Conspiracy," YouTube video, posted by "Who2TV," January 27, 2010, www.youtube.com/watch?v=Ewt korQKGFE.

13 "demagogic improvisations": Christopher Hitchens, *No One Left to Lie To* (Toronto: McClelland & Stewart, 1999), Google Edition, chapter 7.

13 "The president, then": Peter Baker and Juliet Eilperin, "Debate on Impeachment Opens," *Washington Post*, December 11, 1998, www.washington post.com/wp-srv/politics/special/clinton/stories/impeach121198.htm.

13 strategy played out: Jerry White, "White House Lied about Threat to Air Force One," *World Socialist* website, September 28, 2001, http://www.wsws.org/ en/articles/2001/09/bush-s28.html.

14 "an intentionally deceptive message": David Corn, *The Lies of George W. Bush: Mastering the Politics of Deception* (New York: Random House, 2004), Nook Edition, 10.

15 "The 935 Lies": Mark Morford, "The 935 Lies of George W. Bush: Yes, you already knew. But now they're actually quantifiable. Like, say, stab wounds," *SFGate*, January 30, 2008, www.sfgate.com/entertainment/morford/article/ The-935-lies-of-George-W-Bush-Yes-you-already-3296633.php.

15 $25,000 fine: Associated Press, "Clinton Disbarred from Practice Before Supreme Court," *New York Times*, October 1, 2001, www.nytimes .com/2001/10/01/national/01WIRE-CLIN.html.

15 "Bush is a liar": Corn, *Lies*, 6.

16 "who soils the Oval Office": Ibid., 15.

16 "the acute onset of paranoia": Charles Krauthammer, "The Delusional Dean," *Washington Post*, December 5, 2003, A31, available at http://townhall .com/columnists/charleskrauthammer/2003/12/05/bush_derangement_syndrome/ page/full.

16 "I'm a uniter": Corn, *Lies*, 37.

16 "the unlikely trio": "Remarks by the President on Immigration," The White House, Office of the Press Secretary, June 15, 2012, http://www.white house.gov/the-press-office/2012/06/15/remarks-president-immigration.

17 "crafty and disinguous": Corn, *Lies*, 200–1.

17 "the blackest lie," Richard Butler, *The Greatest Threat: Iraq, Weapons of Mass Destruction, and the Growing Crisis of Global Security* (New York: Public Affairs, 2001), 170.

17 "In the four years": Robert Moon, "Democrats on Saddam's WMD," Examiner.com, January 20, 2010, www.examiner.com/article/democrats-on -saddam-s-wmd.

17 "somewhat likely": Ben Smith, "More Than Half of Democrats Believed Bush Knew," *Politico*, April 22, 2011, www.politico.com/blogs/bensmith/0411/ More_than_half_of_Democrats_believed_Bush_knew.html.

18 the so-called whistle-blower spouse: Wilson gave this speech in July 2003 at EPIC, the Education for Peace in Iraq Center. Although the original audio file has been pulled, excerpts from the speech can be found at Clarice Feldman, "Joe Wilson's Speech," *American Thinker*, October 10, 2005, www.americanthinker .com/blog/2005/10/joe_wilsons_speech.html.

18 "We know that he has stored": "Text of Gore's Speech," *USA Today*, un-dated, http://usatoday30.usatoday.com/news/nation/2002-09-23-gore-text_x .htm.

18 "He betrayed this country!": Katherine Seelye, "Gore Says Bush Betrayed the U.S. by Using 9/11 as a Reason for War in Iraq," *New York Times*, February 9, 2004, www.nytimes.com/2004/02/09/politics/campaign/09GORE.html.

18 "I will be voting": "John Kerry on War & Peace," OnTheIssues.org, un-dated, www.ontheissues.org/celeb/John_Kerry_War_+_Peace.htm.

18 "This is at least the second": Glenn Kessler, "Kerry's Claim That He Op-posed Bush's Invasion of Iraq," *Washington Post*, Fact Checker, September 10, 2013, www.washingtonpost.com/blogs/fact-checker/wp/2013/09/10/kerrys-claim -that-he-opposed-bushs-invasion-of-iraq/.

Chapter 2: The African American

21 the tone was much softer: "Transcript of Uncirculated Interview of Illi-nois State Senator Barack Obama," February 16, 2001, http://www.barronsawyer .com/obama2001transcript.pdf.

21 "novelistic contrivances": Remnick, *Bridge*, 238.

21 "blacker and more disaffected": Maraniss, *Barack Obama*, 345.

22 "heightens whatever opportunity arises": Remnick, *Bridge*, 239.

22 "I met Obama sometime in the 1990s": Walter Shapiro, "Bill Ayers Talks Back," *Salon*, November 17, 2008, www.salon.com/2008/11/17/ayers/.

22 "He wanted to be mayor": David Mendell, *Obama: From Promise to Power* (New York: HarperCollins, 2007), 92.

23 "counted 38 instances": Ben Smith, "The Real Story of Barack Obama," *BuzzFeed*, June 17, 2012, www.buzzfeed.com/bensmith/the-real-story-of -barack-obama.

23 "a big, dark woman": Obama, *Dreams*, 103.

23 "harbinger" of Michelle: Remnick, *Bridge*, 241.

23   the Swiss grandmother: Maraniss, *Barack Obama*, 415.

24   "Do you mind if I call you": Obama, *Dreams*, 103.

24   birthplace as "Kenya": Ben Shapiro, "Obama's Lit Agency Used 'Born in Kenya' Bio until 2007," *Big Government* (blog), Breitbart.com, May 17, 2012, http://www.breitbart.com/Big-Government/2012/05/17/Obama-pamphlet-in-use-2007.

24   "I would imagine myself": Obama, *Dreams*, 136.

25   As early as July 2005: Dan Armstrong, "Barack Obama Embellishes His Resume," *Analyze This* (blog), July 9, 2005, www.analyzethis.net/2005/07/09/barack-obama-embellishes-his-resume/.

25   all too often fictionalized: Shelby Steele, *The Bound Man: Why We Are Excited about Obama and Why He Can't Win* (New York: Simon & Schuster, 2008), 25–32.

25   "Does WaPo Know": John Nolte, "Does WaPo Know Obama Shoved a Little Girl?" *Big Journalism* (blog), Breitbart.com, May 10, 2012, www.breitbart.com/Big-Journalism/2012/05/10/Does-WaPo-Know-Obama-Shoved-a-Little-Girl.

26   "had been tested": Obama, *Dreams*, 60–61.

26   "He was my knight": Remnick, *Bridge*, 73.

26   "matters to people here": Ibid., 502.

26   "I don't think Obama could have been": Ibid., 505.

26   "Like many characters in the memoir": Maraniss, *Barack Obama*, 517.

27   "We had a big fight": Obama, *Dreams*, 211.

27   "with white girlfriends": Maraniss, *Barack Obama*, 538.

27   "A memoir literally means": "Winfrey Stands behind 'Pieces' Author," CNN.com, January 12, 2006, www.cnn.com/2006/SHOWBIZ/books/01/11/frey.lkl/index.html?section=cnn_latest.

27   "There are several black ladies": Obama, *Dreams*, 211.

27   "In her eminent practicality": Ibid., 439.

28   "I met Michelle": Barack Obama, *The Audacity of Hope* (New York: Crown/Three Rivers Press, 2006), 327.

28   "Like I did": Text of Obama's speech at the New Economic School, *New York Times*, July 7, 2009, www.nytimes.com/2009/07/07/world/europe/07prexy.text.html.

28   "[in] a slightly different": Gwen Ifill, "Gwen Ifill Reviews David Remnick's Biography of Barack Obama, 'The Bridge,'" *Washington Post*, April 4, 2010, www.washingtonpost.com/wp-dyn/content/article/2010/04/02/AR2010040201516.html.

28   "My very existence": "Barack Obama in Selma," YouTube video, posted by "obloga," March 5, 2007, www.youtube.com/watch?v=95KC7CF5B9E.

30   "A reader, Gregory": Michael Dobbs, "Obama's 'Camelot Connection,'" *Washington Post*, Fact Checker, March 31, 2008, http://voices.washingtonpost .com/fact-checker/2008/03/obamas_camelot_connection.html.

30   "have abandoned their responsibilities": Julie Bosman, "Obama Sharply Assails Absent Black Fathers," *New York Times*, June 16, 2008, www.nytimes .com/2008/06/16/us/politics/15cnd-obama.html.

30 "to cut [Obama's] nuts": "Jackson Apologizes for 'Crude' Obama Remarks," CNNPolitics.com, July 9, 2008, http://www.cnn.com/2008/POLITICS/07/09/ jesse.jackson.comment/.

31   racial scapegoat Zimmerman: Jack Cashill, *"If I Had a Son": Race, Guns, and the Railroading of George Zimmerman* (Washington, DC: WND Books, 2013).

31   "seeks to lead," Steele, *Bound Man*, 71.

31   In the month of his inauguration: Neil Munro, "Poll: Race Relations Have Plummeted since Obama Took Office," *Daily Caller*, July 25, 2013, http:// dailycaller.com/2013/07/25/race-relations-have-plummeted-since-obama-took -office-according-to-poll/.

Chapter 3: The All-American

33   "generally adoring press coverage": Remnick, *Bridge*, 443.

34   "My parents shared": "Text of Obama's Speech at the 2004 Democratic National Convention," *Washington Post*, July 27, 2004.

34   Obama's "signature appeal": Remnick, *Bridge*, 360.

34   "son with him": Maraniss, *Barack Obama*, 204–7.

35   "of the marriage": Jack Cashill, "The Obama Lie That Drove the Birther Movement," *American Thinker*, April 29, 2011, www.americanthinker .com/2011/04/the_obama_lie_that_drove_the_b.html.

35   "courage to explore": Obama, *Dreams*, 22.

35   "hole in a life": Maraniss, *Barack Obama*, 460.

36   "two years old": "Prepared Remarks of President Barack Obama: Back to School Event," September 8, 2009, whitehouse.gov, http://www.whitehouse.gov/ MediaResources/PreparedSchoolRemarks.

36   "lived at [6085 Kalanianole]": Maraniss, *Barack Obama*, 200.

36   "gone from Honolulu": Ibid., 209.

36   each contorted the time line: For confirming detail, see Jack Cashill, "Obama Sr. Bio Reworks Nativity Fraud," WND.com, July 11, 2011, www.wnd .com/2011/07/320833/.

37   "to lead the effort": John Drew, "Meeting Young Obama," *American Thinker*, February 24, 2011, www.americanthinker.com/2011/02/meeting_ young_obama.html.

37   "these two topics": Ibid.

38   "Eurocentrism, and patriarchy": Obama, *Dreams*, 100.

38   historic American evils: Obama, *Audacity*, 21.

38   attended in New York: Stanley Kurtz, *Radical-in-Chief: Barack Obama and the Untold Story of American Socialism* (New York: Simon & Schuster, 2010), 25.

39   "number was 47544": Paul Kengor, *The Communist—Frank Marshall Davis: The Untold Story of Barack Obama's Mentor* (New York: Mercury Radio Arts Publishing, 2012), 4.

39   "1980s to the 1990s": Ibid., 15.

39   "teenage poetry": Maraniss, *Barack Obama*, 310.

39   "about my grandfather": Todd Purdum, "Raising Obama," *Vanity Fair*, March 2008, www.vanityfair.com/politics/features/2008/03/obama200803.

39   "a single mention of Davis": Kengor, *Communist*, 276.

40   "right-wing blogosphere," Remnick, *Bridge*, 71.

40   "as surrogate grandfather": Ibid., 94.

40   "a moderate Republican": Jordan Fabian, "Obama: More Moderate Republican Than Socialist," Fusion.net, October 14, 2013, http://fusion.net/leadership/story/obama-considered-moderate-republican-1980s-12240.

40   red state and blue: *Newsweek*, December 27/January 3, 2005.

41   "obsessive-compulsive tic": Joe Klein, "The Fresh Face," *Time*, October 15, 2006, http://content.time.com/time/magazine/article/0,9171,1546362,00.html.

41   "good for everybody": Natalie Gewargis, ABC News, October 14, 2008, http://abcnews.go.com/blogs/politics/2008/10/spread-the-weal/.

42   "to disadvantaged students": Frank Miele, "Does 1979 Newspaper Column Shed Light on 2008 Campaign Story?" *Daily Inter Lake*, September 28, 2012, www.dailyinterlake.com/opinion/columns/frank/article_7924e4f0 -0468-11e2-8da2-0019bb2963f4.html.

42   Davis and Jarrett worked together: Kengor, *Communist*, 15.

42   called *Inside City Hall*: "Percy Sutton (Malcom X's Lawyer) Says Barack Obama Knows and Was Financed by the Racist Radical Muslim and Saudi Advisor Dr. Khalid Al-Mansour, Part II," YouTube video, posted by "harvard lawgrad," October 5, 2008, www.youtube.com/watch?v=MIVO8MZYXo8.

43   "the Indians in America": Khalid al Mansour, "A Little on History of Jews," YouTube, January 21, 2007, https://www.youtube.com/watch?v=AIrW rxuR_GM.

43   "Barack Obama's campaign is": Ben Smith, "Obama Camp Denies Sutton Story," *Politico*, September 4, 2008, www.politico.com/blogs/bensmith/0908/ Obama_camp_denies_Sutton_story.html.

44   "in that television interview": Ibid.

44   "to put the story to rest": Ibid.

44   kept digging: Kenneth Timmerman, "Obama's Harvard Years: Questions Swirl," *NewsMax*, September 23, 2008, www.newsmax.com/KenTimmerman/ obama-harvard-/2009/12/14/id/342454/.

44   "on behalf of the family": Ibid.

45   "an enormous loss": Marcus Franklin, "Percy Sutton Laid to Rest," *BET*, January 7, 2010, http://www.bet.com/news/news/2010/01/07/ peoplepercysuttonlaidtorest.html.

45   "woman from Kansas": "Text of Obama's Race Speech," *Huffington Post*, November 17, 2008, www.huffingtonpost.com/2008/03/18/obama-race-speech -read-th_n_92077.html.

45   "given in this country": All previous quotes are cited in Robert Denton Jr., *Studies of Identity in the 2008 Presidential Campaign*, (Lanham, MD: Lexington Books, 2010), 47.

46   "capable of doing anything": Transcript of Jeremiah Wright's speech at the National Press Club, April 28, 2008, http://press.org/sites/default/ files/20080428_wright.pdf.

46   "twenty years ago": "Obama Finally Distances Himself from Reverend Wright," *New York Daily Intelligencer*, April 29, 2008, http://nymag.com/daily/ intelligencer/2008/04/obama_finally_distances_himsel.html.

46   quoted in *Dreams*: Obama, *Dreams*, 293.

47   "won't be a problem?": "Transcript of Obama and Clinton Debate," ABC News, April 16, 2008, http://abcnews.go.com/Politics/DemocraticDebate/story ?id=4670271.

47   "attend the same school": Ben Smith, "Ax on Ayers," *Politico*, February 26, 2008, www.politico.com/blogs/bensmith/0208/Ax_on_Ayers.html.

47   "a garden variety Marxist-Leninist": Drew, "Meeting Young Obama."

48   "boards together. So?": Bill Ayers, *Public Enemy: Confessions of an American Dissident* (Boston: Beacon Press, 2013), Nook Edition, 9.

48   "recruitment to the Board,": Stanley Kurtz, "Obama's Challenge," *National Review Online*, September 23, 2008, www.nationalreview.com/articles /225752/obamas-challenge/stanley-kurtz.

48   shredded that lie,: Ibid.

48   "onto the Annenberg board": Remnick, *Bridge*, 280.

49   "That was not the bill": Josh Hicks, "Did Obama Vote to Deny Rights to Infant Abortion Survivors?" *Washington Post*, Fact Checker, September 10, 2012, www.washingtonpost.com/blogs/fact-checker/post/did-obama-vote -to-deny-rights-to-infant-abortion-survivors/2012/09/07/9852895a-f87d-11e1 -8398-0327ab83ab91_blog.html.

49   "word for word": Ibid.

49   "betrayal of God's will": Penny Starr, "Obama at Prayer Breakfast: 'Killing the Innocent' Is 'Ultimate Betrayal of God's Will,'" CNSNews.com, February 6, 2014, http://cnsnews.com/news/article/penny-starr/obama-prayer-breakfast-killing-innocent-ultimate-betrayal-god-s-will.

49   affection for moderate nominees: Obama, *Audacity*, 82.

50   "notable blemish": Eric Lichtblau and Mark Johnston, "Pardon Is Back in Focus for the Justice Nominee," December 1, 2008, *New York Times*, www.nytimes.com/2008/12/02/us/politics/02holder.html.

50   "vastly different way": Holder was addressing the Women's National Democratic Club, and his speech was broadcast by CSPAN-2. Video available through Breitbart.com, www.breitbart.com/Big-Government/2012/03/18/Holder-Fight-Guns-Like-Cigarettes.

50   the same Sharpton: Jake Tapper, "The Skeletons and Suits in Sharpton's Closet," *Salon*, June 21, 2003, www.salon.com/2003/06/21/sharpton_7/.

51   "that kind of treatment?": Mike Levine, "Fed-Up Eric Holder Rips Congress: 'Unprecedented, Unwarranted, Ugly, and Divisive,'" ABCNews.com, The Note, April 10, 2014, http://abcnews.go.com/blogs/politics/2014/04/a-fed-up-eric-holder-goes-after-congress-unprecedented-unwarranted-ugly-and-divisive/.

51   his forced resignation: Scott Wilson and Garance Franke-Ruta, "White House Adviser Van Jones Resigns amid Controversy over Past Activism," *Washington Post*, September 6, 2009, http://voices.washingtonpost.com/44/2009/09/06/van_jones_resigns.html.

51   "to be a revolutionary": Kathy Shaidle, "Van Jones, 'Green Jobs Czar,' a Self-Described 'Communist,' Arrested during Rodney King Riots," Examiner.com, July 17, 2009, www.examiner.com/article/van-jones-green-jobs-czar-a-self-described-communist-arrested-during-rodney-king-riots.

51   "attacks to occur": "Respected Leaders and Families Launch 9/11 Truth Statement Demanding Deeper Investigation into the Events of 9/11," 911Truth.org, October 26, 2004, www.911truth.org/911-truth-statement/.

Chapter 4: The Genius

53   "genius of Barack Obama": Jack Cashill, *Deconstructing Obama: The Lives, Loves, and Letters of America's First Postmodern President* (New York: Simon & Schuster, 2011), 3 (original source no longer accessible).

53   "ever to become president": *Don Imus Show*, November 10, 2008, transcript available at http://freedomswings.wordpress.com/2008/11/11/obama-is-our-smartest-president/.

53   "personal charisma": Laurence H. Tribe, "Morning-After Pride," *Forbes*, November 5, 2008, www.forbes.com/2008/11/05/obama-victory-race-oped-cx_lt_1105tribe.html.

53   "by an American politician": Klein, "Fresh Face."

54   convention speech "brilliant": Charles Krauthammer, "Obama's Altitude Sickness," *Washington Post*, September 12, 2008, www.washingtonpost.com/wp-dyn/content/article/2008/09/11/AR2008091102840.html.

54   biographer David Remnick: Remnick, *Bridge*, 444.

54   "they defy expectations": Steele, *Bound Man*, 14.

54   "I think Barack knew": Remnick, *Bridge*, 274.

54   refused Trump's request: Beth Fouhy, "Donald Trump: Obama Wasn't Qualified for Ivy League," *Huffington Post*, April 25, 2011, www.huffingtonpost.com/2011/04/25/donald-trump-obama-ivy-league_n_853525.html.

55   "from those years": Janny Scott, "Obama's Account of New York Years Often Differs from What Others Say," *New York Times*, October 30, 2007, www.nytimes.com/2007/10/30/us/politics/30obama.html.

55   "genius of George Bush": "Bush/Gore Grades and SAT Scores," Inside Politics.org, June 17,2005, www.insidepolitics.org/heard/heard32300.html.

55   B+ average at Occidental: Maraniss, *Barack Obama*, 460.

56   back to grade school: Remnick, *Bridge*, 116.

56   "too well in college": Ibid., 56.

56   honors of any sort: The author has a photocopy of the actual program.

56   "affirmative action policy": Barack Obama, "Letter to the Editor," *Harvard Law Record*, November 16, 1990, available at http://thesophic.wordpress.com/2011/08/29/obamas-1990-note-to-the-harvard-law-record-as-someone-who-has-undoubtedly-benefited-from-affirmative-action-programs-during-my-academic-career/.

56   "steeped in honesty": Oona King, "Book Review: Obama's Dreams from My Father," Oonaking.com, June 15, 2012, www.oonaking.com/in-the-press/item/214-book-review-obama-s-dreams-from-my-father.html.

57   Obama's literary baseline: Barack Obama, "Breaking the War Mentality," *Sundial* 7, no. 12, March 10, 1983, www.columbia.edu/cu/computinghistory/obama-sundial.pdf.

57   1988 essay, "Why Organize": Barack Obama, "Why Organize," *Illinois Issues*, 1990, http://illinoisissues.uis.edu/archives/2008/09/whyorg.html.

57   "the *states* of war": Maraniss, *Barack Obama*, 504.

57   "the *taste* of war": Obama, "Breaking the War Mentality."

57   "made of whole cloth": Dave Weigel, "Meet the Obama Love Letter Truthers," *Slate*, May 18, 2012, www.slate.com/blogs/weigel/2012/05/18/meet_the_obama_love_letter_truthers.html.

58   "wrote them myself": "Obama Speaks about Writing," YouTube video, posted by "mmteacher1," July 11, 2008, www.youtube.com/watch?v=On1CPd1OcPs.

58   mentor Bill Ayers: Cashill, *Deconstructing Obama.*

58   his postpresidential memoir: David Remnick, "Going the Distance," *The New Yorker*, January 27, 2014, www.newyorker.com/reporting/2014/01/27/140127fa_fact_remnick.

58   Ayers helped Obama with *Dreams*: Remnick, *Bridge*, 254.

59   "endless series of meetings": Obama, *Audacity.*

59   "nearly a chapter a week": Remnick, *Bridge*, 444.

59   "what I'd written": Daphne Dunham, "20 Second Interview: A Few Words with Barack Obama," Amazon.com, http://www.amazon.com/gp/feature.html?ie=UTF8&docId=1000327751.

59   "to write the book": Remnick, *Bridge*, 444.

59   "outtakes from a stump speech": Michiko Kakutani, "Obama's Foursquare Politics, with a Dab of Dijon," *New York Times*, October 17, 2006, www.nytimes.com/2006/10/17/books/17kaku.html.

60   "attention they need to learn": Barack Obama, "Teaching Our Kids in a 21st Century Economy," remarks prepared for delivery at the[UNKNOWN FONT:MS Mincho]{dec63}[END FONT]Center for American Progress,[UNKNOWN FONT:MS Mincho]{dec63}[END FONT]Washington, DC, October 25, 2005, available at www.motherjones.com/politics/2005/11/teaching-our-kids-21st-century-economy.

60   "sustained attention they need to learn": Obama, *Audacity*, 97.

60   "White House since Lincoln,": Jonathan Raban, "The Golden Trumpet," *The Guardian*, January 23, 2009, http://www.theguardian.com/world/2009/jan/24/barack-obama-inauguration-speech-presidency-president-review-jonathan-raban.

60   his 2009 inaugural address: Ibid.

61   "Did you know I wrote it?": "Terrorist Ayers Confesses Sharing Obama's 'Dreams,'" Investors.com, November 26, 2013, http://news.investors.com/ibd-editorials-obama-care/112613-680812-bill-ayers-claims-authorship-of-obama-dreams-memoir.htm?ntt=ayers%20wrote%20obama.

61   Rove showed him: Sean Hannity, "Cable Exclusive with 'Courage and Consequence' Author Karl Rove," FoxNews.com, March 10, 2010, www.foxnews.com/story/2010/03/10/cable-exclusive-with-courage-and-consequence-author-karl-rove/.

61   "respect the Constitution": Joe Miller, "Obama a Constitutional Law Professor?" FactCheck.org, March 28, 2008, www.factcheck.org/2008/03/obama-a-constitutional-law-professor/.

62   designation passed unnoticed: Daryl Owen, "Obama Sends Lobbyists into the Wilderness," *Washington Post*, April 3, 2009, www.washingtonpost.com/wp-dyn/content/article/2009/04/02/AR2009040203099.html.

62   "location on the South Side": Jodi Kantor, "Teaching Law, Testing Ideas, Obama Stood Slightly Apart," *New York Times*, July 7, 2008, www.nytimes.com/2008/07/30/us/politics/30law.html.

63   "best hope on earth": "Obama Speech: Oceans Receding, Planet Healing," YouTube video, posted by "Ed Morrissey," March 2, 2010, www.youtube .com/watch?v=u2pZSvq9bto.

63   "Is Barack Obama the Messiah?": Dotcomabc, "Is Barack Obama the Messiah?" ABCNews.com, Political Punch, February 10, 2008, http://abcnews .go.com/blogs/politics/2008/02/is-barack-obama/.

63   any higher than the vice presidency: Jerzy Kosinski, *Being There* (New York: Harcourt, 1970).

64   "plagued the region for centuries": "Obama: 'Middle East Is Obviously an Issue That Has Plagued the Region for Centuries,'" *Real Clear Politics*, Real Clear Politics Video, January 29, 2010, www.realclearpolitics.com/video/2010/01/29/ obama_middle_east_is_obviously_an_issue_that_has_plagued_the_region_ for_centuries.html.

64   the day's loudest cheers: Alexander Mooney, CNN, Political Ticker, May 28, 2009, http://politicalticker.blogs.cnn.com/2009/05/28/biden-takes -dig-at-obama-over-teleprompter-use-2/.

65   in the last forty-eight hours: "Obama Asthma Teleprompter Gaffe," You-Tube video, posted by "Garrett Smith," September 7, 2008, www.youtube.com/ watch?v=cxxxGUeZtno.

65   politely, if uncomfortably: "Obama Botches Spelling of 'Respect' While Lauding Aretha Franklin," CBSNews.com, March 7, 2014, www.cbsnews.com/ news/obama-botches-spelling-of-respect-while-lauding-aretha-franklin/.

65   "One left to go": "Obama Claims He's Visited 57 States," YouTube video, posted by "Obamagaffe," May 9, 2008, www.youtube.com/watch?v=EpGH02D tIws.

65   "wheeling and dealing": "News Conference by President Obama," The White House, Office of the Press Secretary, April 4, 2009, www.whitehouse.gov/ the-press-office/news-conference-president-obama-4042009.

66   "or here in Asia": "News Conference by President Obama," The White House, Office of the Press Secretary, November 14, 2011, www.whitehouse.gov/ the-press-office/2011/11/14/news-conference-president-obama.

66   2010 National Prayer Breakfast: "Obama Can't Pronounce 'Corpsman,'" YouTube video, posted by "theblogprof," February 4, 2010, www.youtube.com/ watch?v=dlkK65y_-T4.

66   "in the audience here today": Ed Morrissey, "Obama Confuses Veterans Day and Memorial Day Again," FoxNews.com, February 21, 2012, http:// nation.foxnews.com/president-obama/2012/02/21/obama-confuses-veterans -day-and-memorial-day-again.

66   "Special Olympics or something": Jake Tapper and Huma Khan, "Obama Apologizes for Calling His Bad Bowling 'Like the Special Olympics,'" ABC News, March 20, 2009, http://abcnews.go.com/Politics/story?id=7129997.

66   "Don't call my bluff": Russell Berman and Sam Youngman, "Obama Warns Cantor: 'Don't Call my Bluff,'" *The Hill*, July 13, 2011, http://thehill.com/ homenews/administration/171403-obama-warns-cantor-dont-call-my-bluff -in-debt-talks.

67   her Democratic National Committee–bred accusations: Jennifer Loven, "Administration, Sebelius Back Off Argument over National Guard," *Lawrence Journal-World*, May 9, 2007, http://www2.ljworld.com/news/2007/may/09/ administration_sebelius_back_argument_over_nationa/.

67   "an entire town destroyed": "Obama Misstates Toll from Tornado," *Chicago Tribune*, May 9, 2007, http://articles.chicagotribune.com/2007-05-09/ news/0705090164_1_death-toll-tornado-sen-barack-obama.

68   "Auschwitz and Treblinka": "Transcript of Obama's Speech against the Iraq War," NPR.org, January 20, 2009, www.npr.org/templates/story/story .php?storyId=99591469.

68   "that kind of pain": Jonathan Weisman, "Obama's Uncle and the Liberation of Auschwitz," *Washington Post*, May 27, 2008, http://voices.washington post.com/44/2008/05/27/obamas_uncle_and_the_liberatio.html.

69   to merit a "Mostly True": Robert Farley, "Obama's Auschwitz Error," *PolitiFact*, May 28, 2008, http://www.politifact.com/truth-o-meter/article/ 2008/may/28/right-soldier-wrong-camp/.

69   "What man could speak": "Obama Politicizes the Holocaust," *TwoConservatives* (blog), May 27, 2008, http://twoconservatives.blogspot.com/2008/05/ obama-politicizes-holocaust.html.

69   "talked about that before": "Spiegel Interview with Obama's Great-Uncle: 'I Was Horrified by Lengths Men Will Go to Mistreat Other Men,'" *Spiegel Online International*, May 26, 2009, http://www.spiegel.de/international/ germany/spiegel-interview-with-obama-s-great-uncle-i-was-horrified-by -lengths-men-will-go-to-mistreat-other-men-a-626703.html.

69   "and recruit and retain": "Fulfilling a Sacred Trust with Our Veterans," campaign document produced by Obama for America, archived at www.doc-umentcloud.org/documents/550009-barack-obama-2008-fulfilling-a-sacred -trust-with.html.

70   "My father served": "Fortunate Grandson," Snopes.com, September 26, 2010, http://www.snopes.com/politics/obama/service.asp.

70   "to punish" them by voting: Dan Farber, "Obama Explains His Remark about Punishing 'Enemies,'" CBSNews.com, November 1, 2010, www.cbsnews .com/news/obama-explains-his-remark-about-punishing-enemies/.

70   "we bring a gun": Ben Smith, "Obama Brings a Gun to a Knife Fight," *Politico*, June 14, 2008, www.politico.com/blogs/bensmith/0608/Obama_ brings_a_gun_to_a_knife_fight.html.

71   "make with our veterans": Sara Kugler, "Barack Obama Quietly Visits Wounded War Veterans," Associated Press, June 28, 2008, available at www

.washingtonpost.com/wp-dyn/content/article/2007/05/28/AR2007052801022_
pf.html.

71   "in his or her head": Nancy Friedman, "Word of the Week: Kinsley
Gaffe," *Fritinancy* (blog), August 22, 2011, http://nancyfriedman.typepad.com/
away_with_words/2011/08/word-of-the-week-kinsley-gaffe.html.

71   Organization of the Islamic Conference (OIC): Pamela Geller, "57 Islamic States of Obama," *Atlas Shrugs*, May 11, 2008, http://pamelageller
.com/2008/05/57-islamic-stat.html/.

71   "remain a dominant military superpower": "Obama: America a Superpower 'Whether We Like It or Not,'" FoxNews.com, April 15, 2010, www.fox
news.com/politics/2010/04/15/obama-america-superpower-like/.

72   "Somebody else made that happen": "Obama 7.13.2012: If you've got a
business—you didn't build that. Somebody else made that happen," YouTube
video, posted by "tokm908," July 13, 2012, www.youtube.com/watch?v=C
ZO7XOpwa8.

72   "you've made enough money": "Remarks by the President on Wall Street
Reform in Quincy, Illinois," The White House, Office of the Press Secretary,
April 28, 2010, www.whitehouse.gov/the-press-office/remarks-president-wall
-street-reform-quincy-illinois.

72   roughly $5.5 million: Mark Landler and Jim Rutenberg, "Obamas and
Bidens to Release Tax Returns," *New York Times*, April 13, 2012, www.nytimes
.com/2012/04/13/us/politics/obamas-and-bidens-to-release-tax-returns.html.

73   "punished with a baby": Transcript of "Ballot Bowl 2008," CNN.com,
March 29, 2008, http://transcripts.cnn.com/TRANSCRIPTS/0803/29/bb.01
.html.

73   went with the correction: "Obama's Muslim Faith," YouTube video,
posted by "Nobamamania," October 24, 2008, www.youtube.com/watch?v=IG
wzRdTJipo.

73   interests at heart: "Text of Obama's Race Speech," *Huffington Post*.

Chapter 5: The Economist

75 "parts of the real economy": Jonathan Alter, *The Promise: President Obama,
Year One* (New York: Simon & Schuster, 2010), 64.

75   *Dreams* went gold in 2004: Christopher Andersen, *Barack and Michelle:
Portrait of an American Marriage* (New York: William Morrow, 2009), 162.

76   "and think like Mencken": Fred Seigel, *The Revolt against the Masses: How
Liberalism Has Undermined the Middle Class* (New York: Encounter Books,
2013), Nook Edition, 64.

76   quintessential "bobos in Paradise": David Brooks, *Bobos in Paradise: The
New Upper Class and How They Got There* (New York: Simon & Schuster, 2000).

76   "going to be created": Transcript of *Anderson Cooper 360 Degrees*, December 18, 2008, http://transcripts.cnn.com/TRANSCRIPTS/0812/18/acd.02.html.

77   "make them work": Politico staff, "Transcript from 'Meet the Press,'" *Politico*, December 7, 2008, www.politico.com/news/stories/1208/16278.html.

77   using the phrase "shovel ready": "Text of Obama's speech to Congress and the Nation," *Los Angeles Times*, February 24, 2009, http://latimesblogs.latimes.com/washington/2009/02/obama-text-spee.html.

77   had been paid out: Brooks Jackson, with Joe Miller and Jess Henig, "Obama's Economic Speech," FactCheck.org, December 11, 2009, www.factcheck.org/2009/12/obamas-economic-speech/.

77   "live up to its billing": Alec MacGillis, "Obama Skeptical about 'Shovel-Ready' Projects' Long-Term Impact," *Washington Post*, December 3, 2009, www.washingtonpost.com/wp-dyn/content/article/2009/12/03/AR2009120303632.html.

78   "the execution efficient": "Text: Obama's Speech on Jobs," CBSNews.com, December 8, 2009, www.cbsnews.com/news/text-obamas-speech-on-jobs/.

78   "J-O-B-S, jobs": Michelle Malkin, "The Increasingly Erratic, Super-Gaffetastic Joe Biden," *National Review Online*, October 22, 2008, http://nationalreview.com/articles/226060/increasingly-erratic-super-gaffetastic-joe-biden/michelle-malkin.

78   "create jobs for burly men": "Video: Christina Romer Explains a New Report about Job Creation," Change.gov, January 11, 2009, http://change.gov/newsroom/entry/video_christna_romer_explains_a_new_report_about_job_creation/.

78   "thing as shovel-ready projects": Peter Baker, "Education of a President," *New York Times Magazine*, October 17, 2010, http://www.nytimes.com/2010/10/17/magazine/17obama-t.html.

79   "shovel-ready as we expected": "Obama Jokes at Job Council: 'Shovel Ready' Jobs Were Not as Shovel-Ready as We Expected," undated, http://nation.foxnews.com/president-obama/2011/06/13/obama-jokes-jobs-council-shovel-ready-was-not-shovel-ready-we-expected.

79   over the subsequent two years: "Text of Obama's Speech to Congress and the nation," *Los Angeles Times*.

79   to a perfect 3.5 million total: "The Recovery Act—Year One," Whitehouse.gov, February 17, 2010, www.whitehouse.gov/photos-and-video/video/recovery-act-year-one.

80   in that same period: "Employment Level," Bureau of Labor Statistics, http://www.bls.gov/webapps/legacy/cpsatab1.htm.

80   his claim to be "half true": Louis Jacobson, "Obama Says Stimulus Is Responsible for 2 Million Jobs Saved or Created," *PolitiFact*, www.politifact.com/truth-o-meter/statements/2010/feb/17/barack-obama/obama-says-stimulus-responsible-millions-jobs-save/.

80   cowritten by Romer: Christina Romer and Jared Bernstein, *The Job Impact of the American Recovery and Reinvestment Act*, January 9, 2009, http:// otrans.3cdn.net/ee40602f9a7d8172b8_ozm6bt5oi.pdf.

80   unemployment below 8 percent "mostly false": Molly Moorhead, "Mitt Romney Says President Promised Peak of 8 Percent Unemployment," *PolitiFact*, February 8, 2012, www.politifact.com/truth-o-meter/statements/2012/feb/08/ mitt-romney/mitt-romney-says-president-promised-peak-8-percent/.

81   more than three million jobs: "Video: Christina Romer Explains," Change.gov.

81   "of 7.2 percent is terrible": Ibid.

81   below Romer's "terrible" 7.2 percent: "Databases, Tables & Calculators by Subject," Bureau of Labor Statistics, http://data.bls.gov/timeseries/ LNS14000000.

81   slightly upward in early 2014: Ibid.

81   Reagan's last month in office: Ibid.

82   "What about Republicans": "Obama: 'The Private Sector Is Doing Fine,' " *Real Clear Politics*, June 8, 2012, www.realclearpolitics.com/video/2012/06/08/ obama_the_private_sector_is_doing_fine.html.

82   stood at nearly 24 percent: "Employment Level," Bureau of Labor Statistics, http://www.bls.gov/webapps/legacy/cpsatab1.htm.

82   "those days are over": "Transcript from 'Meet the Press,'" *Politico*.

83   "kept clear of pet projects": Dan Eggen and Ellen Nakashima, "Despite Pledges, Stimulus Has Some Pork," *Washington Post*, February 13, 2009.

83   "most outrageous" stimulus projects: Elizabeth Harrington, "The 10 Most Outrageous Stimulus Projects," *Washington Free Beacon*, February 17, 2014, http://freebeacon.com/issues/the-10-most-outrageous-stimulus-projects/.

83   "100 Stimulus Projects: A Second Opinion": Tom Coburn, *100 Stimulus Projects: A Second Opinion*, June 2009, www.coburn.senate.gov/public/index .cfm?a=Files.Serve&File_id=59af3ebd-7bf9-4933-8279-8091b533464f.

84   "even to worthy projects": Jonathan Martin, "Obama Team Wants Earmarks Out of Stimulus," *Politico*, January 27, 2009, www.politico.com/news/ stories/0109/18013.html.

84   "near zero-emissions power plant(s)": Kimberly Kindy, "With Help of Stimulus, FutureGen 'Clean Coal' Plant May Be Revived," *Washington Post*, March 6, 2009, www.washingtonpost.com/wp-dyn/content/article/2009/03/05/ AR2009030502138.html?sid=ST2009030600119.

85   "our most important national priorities": "Barack Obama Speech— Address to Joint Session of Congress," Chicago.about.com, February 24, 2009, http://chicago.about.com/od/chicagopeople/a/ObamaSpeech209.htm.

85   "president of the United States of America": Barack Obama, "Remarks in Green Bay, Wisconsin," September 22, 2008, The American Presidency Project, www.presidency.ucsb.edu/ws/index.php?pid=84331.

85 "not spending money unwisely": "The First McCain-Obama Presidential Debate," September 26, 2008, Commission on Presidential Debates, www.debates.org/index.php?page=2008-debate-transcript.

85 reflected "Democratic priorities": Robert Pear, "House Passes Spending Bill, and Critics Are Quick to Point Out Pork," *New York Times*, February 25, 2009, www.nytimes.com/2009/02/26/us/politics/26spend.html.

86 political donations and earmarks: Michael Bernard, "Obama's 'No Earmarks' Promise Broken," Yahoo! Voices, March 4, 2009, http://voices.yahoo.com/obamas-no-earmarks-promise-broken-2788698.html?cat=75.

86 said Obama a bit prematurely: "Obama Calls Fremont Company 'Testament to American Ingenuity,'" *Pleasanton Weekly*, May 27, 2010, http://pleasanton weekly.com/square/index.php?i=3&d=1&t=5093.

87 "oil is a finite resource": "Remarks by the President to the Nation on the BP Oil Spill," The White House, Office of the Press Secretary, June 15, 2010, www.whitehouse.gov/the-press-office/remarks-president-nation-bp-oil-spill.

87 moderated by CNN's Candy Crowley: "October 16, 2012, Debate Transcript," Commission on Presidential Debates, www.debates.org/index.php?page=october-1-2012-the-second-obama-romney-presidential-debate.

88 "percentages as Romney said": Ben Finley with Lucas Isakowitz, "Obama's Drilling Denials," October 19, 2012, *FactCheck*, www.factcheck.org/2012/10/obamas-drilling-denials/.

89 gas production were "booming": "Full Transcript: Obama's 2014 State of the Union Address," *Washington Post*, January 28, 2014, www.washingtonpost.com/politics/full-text-of-obamas-2014-state-of-the-union-address/2014/01/28/e0c93358-887f-11e3-a5bd-844629433ba3_story.html.

Chapter 6: The Sunshine President

91 "open and accessible government": Lisa Ellman and Melanie Ann Pustay, "Sunshine Week: In Celebration of Open Government," *The White House Blog*, March 11, 2103, www.whitehouse.gov/blog/2013/03/11/sunshine-week-celebration-open-government.

91 "spending taxpayer dollars": Andrew Kaczynski, "Obama's 2008 Campaign Booklet Promises Transparency and Accountability," *BuzzFeed*, August 2, 2012, www.buzzfeed.com/andrewkaczynski/obamas-2008-campaign-booklet-promises-transparenc.

92 "secretive, opaque, and closed": "Transparency in Government," YouTube.com, December 8, 2009, https://www.youtube.com/watch?v=pXp3yumdGhU.

92 "touchstones of this presidency": "Remarks by the President in Welcoming Senior Staff and Cabinet Secretaries to the White House," The White House, Office of the Press Secretary, January 21, 2009, www.whitehouse.gov/the-press-office/remarks-president-welcoming-senior-staff-and-cabinet-secretaries-white-house.

92   promise proved to be: Leonard Downie Jr., *The Obama Administration and the Press: Leak Investigations and Surveillance in Post-9/11 America*, Committee to Protect Journalists, October 10, 2013, http://cpj.org/reports/2013/10/obama-and-the-press-us-leaks-surveillance-post-911.php.

93   who did the silencing: John Hughes, "Club Hails Signing of Press Freedom Law," National Press Club, May 17, 2010, http://press.org/news-multimedia/news/club-hails-signing-press-freedom-law.

94   "Signing of Press Freedom Law": Ibid.

94   "we're going after you": Downie, *The Obama Administration and the Press*.

95   "fair administration of justice": Ibid.

95   Washington correspondent James Rosen: Ibid.

95   "dangerous road to go down": Ann Marimow, "A Rare Peek into a Justice Department Leak Probe," *Washington Post*, May 19, 2013, www.washingtonpost.com/local/a-rare-peek-into-a-justice-department-leak-probe/2013/05/19/0bc473de-be5e-11e2-97d4-a479289a31f9_story.html.

95   Obama said defiantly: Andrew Johnson, "Obama: I Have Complete Confidence in Eric Holder," *National Review Online*, May 16, 2013, www.nationalreview.com/corner/348531/obama-has-'complete-confidence-eric-holder'-andrew-johnson.

96   "any lack of self-reporting": Marisa Taylor and Jonathan Landay, "Obama's Crackdown Views Leaks as Aiding Enemies of U.S.," McClatchyDC, June 20, 2013, http://www.mcclatchydc.com/2013/06/20/194513/obamas-crackdown-views-leaks-as.html.

96   "dangerous for national security": Ibid.

96   opined the *Wall Street Journal*: "A Journalist 'Co-Conspirator,'" *Wall Street Journal*, May 20, 2013, http://online.wsj.com/news/articles/SB10001424127887324102604578495253824175498.

96   "national security and press freedom": James Goodale, "Only Nixon Harmed a Free Press More," *New York Times*, May 21, 2013, www.nytimes.com/roomfordebate/2013/05/21/obama-the-media-and-national-security/only-nixon-harmed-a-free-press-more.

97   "across-the-board hostility": Katrina Trinko, "NYT Reporter: Obama Administration 'Most Closed, Control Freak Administration I've Ever Covered,'" *National Review Online*, October 10, 2013, www.nationalreview.com/corner/360895/nyt-reporter-obama-administration-most-closed-control-freak-administration-ive-ever.

97   "affirmation of press freedom": Mark Landler, "Obama, in Nod to Press, Orders Review of Inquiries," *New York Times*, May 23, 2013, www.nytimes.com/2013/05/24/us/politics/obama-offering-support-for-press-freedom-orders-review-of-leak-investigations.html.

97   "rare thing in an administration": Paul Bremmer, "On PBS, David Remnick Praises Obama Administration as Scandal-Free, Pro-Science,"

Newsbusters (blog), January 21, 2014, http://newsbusters.org/blogs/paul
-bremmer/2014/01/21/pbs-david-remnick-praises-obama-administration
-scandal-free-pro-scienc.

98   would blow their cover: Downie, *The Obama Administration and the Press.*

98   "photographs of the president": Ibid.

99   "accountable administration in *history*": "Press Release—Obama Pledges
Most Transparent and Accountable Administration in History," The American Presidency Project, August 15, 2007, http://www.presidency.ucsb.edu/
ws/?pid=93244.

99   first chief technology officer (CTO): "Barack Obama on Government
Transparency," YouTube video, posted by "GLASSBOOTHdotORG," November 3, 2008, www.youtube.com/watch?v=CU0m6Rxm9vU.

99   "before I sign it": Obama, "Remarks in Green Bay, Wisconsin."

99   less than male ones: Caroline May, "Analysis: Men Still Make a Lot More
Than Women in Obama's White House," *Daily Caller,* January 16, 2014, http://
dailycaller.com/2014/01/16/analysis-men-still-make-a-lot-more-than-women
-in-obamas-white-house/.

100   "We asked the White House": Angie Holan, "Obama Signs First Law
without Web Comment," *PolitiFact,* January 29, 2009, www.politifact.com/
truth-o-meter/promises/obameter/promise/234/allow-five-days-of-public
-comment-before-signing-b/.

100   "We will be implementing": Angie Holan, "Still No 'Sunlight before
Signing,'" *PolitiFact,* February 4, 2009, www.politifact.com/truth-o-meter/
promises/obameter/promise/234/allow-five-days-of-public-comment-before
-signing-b/.

100   "When we finally discovered": Angie Holan, "Credit Card Bill of Rights
Passed without Five-Day Break," *PolitiFact,* May 26, 2009, www.politifact.com/
truth-o-meter/promises/obameter/promise/234/allow-five-days-of-public
-comment-before-signing-b/.

100   and, yes, "transparent": "President Obama Discusses Efforts to Reform
Spending, Government Waste; Names Chief Performance Officer and Chief
Technology Officer," The White House, Office of the Press Secretary, April 18,
2009, www.whitehouse.gov/the-press-office/weekly-address-president-obama
-discusses-efforts-reform-spending-government-waste-n.

101   directive on open government: "Transparency in Government," YouTube.
com, December 8, 2009, https://www.youtube.com/watch?v=pXp3yumdGhU.

101   as only Jon Stewart can: Doug Beizer, "'Daily Show' Chides Kundra,
Chopra, and Burns TSA," *FCW* (blog), December 10, 2009, http://fcw.com/
blogs/insider/2009/12/kundra-chopra-jon-stewart.aspx.

101   was helping shape them: Downie, *The Obama Administration and the
Press.*

102   "he does his daily business": Ibid.

102 "I've ever covered": Ibid.

102 "find out what's in it": "We Have to Pass the Bill So You Can Find Out What's in It," FoxNews.com, March 9, 2010, http://nation.foxnews.com/nancy -pelosi/2010/03/09/we-have-pass-bill-so-you-can-find-out-what-it.

103 before Congress: Obama, "Remarks in Green Bay, Wisconsin."

103 the fate of the stimulus funds: James Gimpel, Frances Lee, and Rebecca Thorpe, "Geographic Distribution of the Federal Stimulus of 2009," *Political Science Quarterly* 127, no. 4 (Winter 2012–2013), 567–95, www.psqonline.org/ article.cfm?IDArticle=19006.

104 "when I am president": Barack Obama, "Agenda: Ethics," Change.gov, http://change.gov/agenda/ethics_agenda.

104 "work in" or "get a job in": Jake Tapper, "Obama Ad Omits Lobbyist Reference," *ABC News*, December 29, 2007, http://abcnews.go.com/Politics/ Vote2008/story?id=4064444.

104 "No political appointees": "Obama Ethics Plan," Organizing for America, http://l.barackobama.com/issues/ethics/.

105 lobbyist community as well: David Kirkpatrick, "In Transition, Ties to Lobbying," *New York Times*, November 14, 2008, www.nytimes .com/2008/11/15/us/politics/15transition.html.

106 "the nation's national security": Howard Kurtz, "Socking It to Him," *Washington Post*, July 22, 2004, www.washingtonpost.com/wp-dyn/articles/ A5267-2004Jul22.html.

106 "speaks the language of government": "Strategies for Growth," Albright Stonebridge Group, http://www.albrightstonebridge.com/capabilities.

106 "become the most controversial": Angie Holan, "Obama's Lobbyist Rule: Promise Broken," *PolitiFact*, March 17, 2009, www.politifact.com/truth-o -meter/article/2009/mar/17/obamas-lobbyist-rules-promise-broken/.

106 "the city's revolving door": Mark Leibovich, *This Town: Two Parties and a Funeral—Plus, Plenty of Valet Parking!—in America's Gilded Capital* (New York: Penguin Group, 2013), Nook Edition, 152.

107 who dared speak out: Obama for America, "The Change We Need in Washington," http://obama.3cdn.net/0080cc578614b42284_2a0mvyxpz.pdf.

107 see working in government: David Wise, "Leaks and the Law: The Story of Thomas Drake," *Smithsonian Magazine*, August 2011, http://www .smithsonianmag.com/history/leaks-and-the-law-the-story-of-thomas-drake -14796786/?no-ist=&page=1.

107 this $1.2 billion boondoggle: Ibid.

108 an op-ed a few years later: Thomas Drake and Jesselyn Radack, "A Sur- prising War on Leaks under Obama," August 1, 2011, Philly.com, http://articles .philly.com/2011-08-01/news/29838846_1_whistle-blowers-jesselyn-radack -obama.

109 "under its own weight": Downie, *The Obama Administration and the Press*.

109 asked Bennett rhetorically: *United States of America v. Thomas Drake*, "Transcript of Proceedings," July 15, 2011, http://www.fas.org/sgp/jud/drake/071511-transcript.pdf.

109 "deserves better than this": Ibid.

Chapter 7: The Constitutionalist

111 "Help the Poor, or I Will": Lesley Clark and Anita Kumar, "Obama to Congress: Help the Poor, or I Will," McClatchy DC, January 28, 2014, http://www.mcclatchydc.com/2014/01/28/216132/obama-to-tell-congress-help-the.html.

111 "going to do": "Full Transcript: Obama's 2014 State of the Union Address," *Washington Post*.

111 "So I Act Alone": "Obama: Congress Obstructs, So I Act Alone," *Washington Post*, June 28, 2014, http://www.washingtonpost.com/politics/congress/obama-congress-obstructs-so-i-act-alone/2014/06/28/90183f38-feab-11e3-b57b-a7a0ebc8dd2d_story.html?tid=pm_pop.

112 presidents who overreached: Garry Wills, "A Pattern of Rising Power," *New York Times*, November 18, 1973, http://www.nytimes.com/books/00/11/26/specials/schlesinger-imperial.html.

112 "heights under George W. Bush": John Conyers Jr., "Learning the Lessons of the Bush Imperial Presidency," *Washington Post*, January 16, 2009, www.washingtonpost.com/wp-dyn/content/article/2009/01/15/AR2009011503152.html.

112 In 2005, Andrew Rudalevige: Andrew Rudalevige, *The New Imperial Presidency: Renewing Presidential Power after Watergate* (Ann Arbor: University of Michigan Press, 2005).

112 "America has ever known": Jim Hightower, "Bush's Imperial Presidency," *Truthout*, April 30, 2006, www.truth-out.org/archive/item/62466:jimhightower—bushs-imperial-presidency.

112 "beyond all legal justification": Adam Cohen, "Just What the Founders Feared: An Imperial President Goes to War," *New York Times*, July 23, 2007, www.nytimes.com/2007/07/23/opinion/23mon4.html.

112 "The biggest problem": Barack Obama, speech at Thaddeus Stevens College, March 31, 2008, video available at http://lancasteronline.com/news/local/is-barack-obama-breaking-a-campaign-promise-he-made-in/article_f4e03fae-9828-11e3-8200-0017a43b2370.html.

113 "transparancy and the rule": "Remarks by the President," January 21, 2009.

113 "for most of our history": Obama, *Audacity*, 95.

114   back some "five years": "Obama: Seen Unprecedented Pattern of Obstruction," Bloomberg.com, November 21, 2013, http://www.bloomberg.com/video/obama -seen-unprecedented-pattern-of-obstruction-kgr7VxQ5SkGmHPm9i37oKQ .html.

114   "to work for it": Justin Sink, "Obama: 'I'll Act on My Own' Agenda," *The Hill*, January 18, 2014, http://thehill.com/blogs/blog-briefing-room/news/195869 -obama-ill-act-on-my-own.

114   "on my own": Ben Wolfgang, "Obama Ignores Boehner's Lawsuit Threat: 'I'll Keep Taking Actions on My Own,'" *Washington Times*, June 28, 2014, http://www.washingtontimes.com/news/2014/jun/28/obama-ignores-boehners -lawsuit-threat-ill-keep-tak/.

114   "his agenda": Philip Rucker, "Obama's 7 State of the Union Talking Points. No. 6: 'The Pen and Phone' Strategy," *Washington Post*, January 27, 2014, http:// www.washingtonpost.com/blogs/the-fix/wp/2014/01/27/obamas-7-state-of- the-union-talking-points-no-6-the-pen-and-phone-strategy/.

115   "Yes! Nullify it!": Remnick, "Going the Distance."

115   "Apparently he doesn't give": Nat Hentoff, "Liberal Icon Urges Obama Impeachment," *WND*, January 20, 2014, www.wnd.com/2014/01/liberal-icon -urges-obama-impeachment/.

115   Ignorance was no excuse: "Testimony of Professor Nicholas Rosenkranz before the House Judiciary Committee," December 3, 2009, http://gretawire. foxnewsinsider.com/2013/12/03/has-president-obama-overstepped-his-constit utional-authority-here-is-what-a-georgetown-law-professor-testified-to-earlier -today-click-to-read/.

116   yelled at a white voter. John Fund, "Holder's Black Panther Stonewall," *Wall Street Journal*, August 20, 2009, http://online.wsj.com/news/articles/SB10 001424052970203550604574361071968458430.

116   "in my Justice Department career": J. Christian Adams, "Inside the Black Panther Case," *Washington Times*, June 25, 2010, www.washingtontimes.com/ news/2010/jun/25/inside-the-black-panther-case-anger-ignorance-and-/.

117   "to imagine what would": Ibid.

117   "career attorneys in the department": "Holder Hearing Transcript," March 1, 2011, http://www.scribd.com/doc/102353998/Holder-Hearing-Transcript.

117   "not involved in that decision": *"Judicial Watch v. United States De-partment of Justice,"* July 23, 2012, https://ecf.dcd.uscourts.gov/cgi-bin/show _public_doc?2010cv0851-32.

118   civil rights of white voters: Ryan J. Reilly, "The Black Panther Case: A Legacy of Politicized Hiring," *Main Justice*, December 23, 2009, www.main justice.com/2009/12/23/the-black-panther-case-a-legacy-of-politicized-hiring/.

118   "to dilute their votes": "Summary of the Noxubee, Mississippi, Voting Rights Case," Adversity.net, July 4, 2007, http://www.adversity.net/noxubee/.

118 "discriminating against whites": Andrew Cohen, "On Voting Rights, Discouraging Signs from the Hill," *Atlantic*, July 18, 2013, www.theatlantic .com/national/archive/2013/07/on-voting-rights-discouraging-signs-from-the -hill/277894/.

118 "pedigree different": Jerry Markon and Krissah Thompson, "Bias Led to 'Gutting' of New Black Panthers Case, Justice Official Says," *Washington Post*, September 25, 2010, www.washingtonpost.com/wp-dyn/content/article/ 2010/09/24/AR2010092403873.html

119 "law in this case": Ibid.

119 "should be beyond that": Seth Stern, "Obama-Schumer Bill Proposal Would Criminalize Voter Intimidation," *New York Times*, January 31, 2007, www.nytimes.com/cq/2007/01/31/cq_2213.html.

119 "Would Criminalize Voter Intimidation": Ibid.

119 "intimidation I've ever seen": Fund, "Holder's Black Panther Stonewall."

119 Bull insulted "my people": "Holder Hearing Transcript," March 1, 2011.

119 "everyone's right to vote": "Full Transcript: Obama's 2014 State of the Union Address," *Washington Post*.

120 "God's in the mix": Monica Nista, "For Obama at Saddleback, a Tough Crowd on Some Issues," ABC News, August 16, 2008, http://abcnews.go.com/ blogs/politics/2008/08/for-obama-at-sa/.

120 Mendell about either: Mendell, *Obama*, 77.

121 "defend the law of the land": Charlie Savage and Sheryly Gay Stolberg, "In Shift, U.S. Says Marriage Act Blocks Gay Rights," *New York Times*, February 23, 2011, www.nytimes.com/2011/02/24/us/24marriage.html.

121 "his views were 'evolving'": Ibid.

121 In 1996, less than a decade: MacKenzie Weinger, "Evolve: Obama Gay Marriage Quotes," *Politico*, May 9, 2012, www.politico.com/news/stories /0512/76109.html.

122 "attributed them to God": Obama, *Audacity*, 223.

122 day as Rosenkrantz: Jonathan Turley, "The President's Constitutional Duty to Faithfully Execute the Laws," testimony before the House Judiciary Committee, December 3, 2013.

123 "position on gay rights": Matt Apuzzo, "Holder Sees Way to Curb Bans on Gay Marriage," *New York Times*, February 24, 2014, www.nytimes .com/2014/02/25/us/holder-says-state-attorneys-general-dont-have-to-defend -gay-marriage-bans.html.

123 "ignoring the rule of law": Neil Munro, "GOP Attorneys General UNLOAD on Holder After AG Says to Ignore Law," *Daily Caller*, February 25, 2014, http:// dailycaller.com/2014/02/25/lawyers-slams-holders-legal-attack-on-marriage/.

123 "as he's going along": Barack Obama, speech in Billings, Montana, May 19, 2008, video available at http://rncresearch.tumblr.com/post/39656542347/ msnbc-profiles-obamas-flip-flop-on-signing-statements.

124 "end run around Congress": Ibid.

124 *New York Times* took notice: Charlie Savage, "Obama Challenges Provisions in Budget Bill," *New York Times*, December 23, 2011, www.nytimes.com/2011 /12/24/us/politics/obama-issues-signing-statement-on-budget-bill.html.

125 *"repeated* several objections": Ibid.

125 "previous administration": Susan Crabtree, "White House: Obama's Signing Statements Are Legit—Unlike Bush's," *TPM*, April 18, 2011, http:// talkingpointsmemo.com/dc/white-house-obama-s-signing-statements-are -legit-unlike-bush-s.

125 held at Guantánamo: Eric Schmitt, Helene Cooper, and Charlie Savage, "Bowe Bergdahl's Vanishing Before Capture Angered His Unit," *New York Times*, June 2, 2014, www.nytimes.com/2014/06/03/us/us-soldier-srgt-bowe -bergdahl-of-idaho-pow-vanished-angered-his-unit.html.

125 One problem beyond the obvious: Noah Rothman, "Jeffrey Toobin: Obama 'Clearly Broke the Law' on Bergdahl," *Mediaite*, June 2, 2014, www .mediaite.com/tv/jeffrey-toobin-obama-clearly-broke-the-law-on-bergdahl/.

126 "Nixon always wanted to be": "Turley: Obama the President That Richard Nixon Always Wanted to Be," *Real Clear Politics*, June 3, 2014, www.realclear politics.com/video/2014/06/03/turley_obama_the_president_that_richard_ nixon_always_wanted_to_be.html.

127 "information gathering, analysis, and argument": Obama, *Audacity*, 95.

127 "400 years": Erika Johnsen, "Sheila Jackson Lee: We've Lasted Some 400 Years Operating under the Constitution," *Hot Air*, March 12, 2014, http:// hotair.com/archives/2014/03/12/sheila-jackson-lee-weve-lasted-some-400 -years-operating-under-the-constitution/.

127 "passed when it did not": Rosenkrantz, testimony.

127 "that Congress has passed": Daniel Halper, "Obama: I Can't Just Suspend Deportations through Executive Order, There Are Laws on the Books," *Weekly Standard*, June 15, 2012, http://www.weeklystandard.com/blogs/obama-i-cant -just-suspend-deportations-through-executive-order-there-are-laws-books_ 647283.html.

128 "immigration action from Congress": "Remarks by the President on Im- migration," The White House, Office of the Press Secretary, June 15, 2012, www .whitehouse.gov/the-press-office/2012/06/15/remarks-president-immigration.

128 let alone his seat: Ibid.

128 "job and construction markets": Jeffrey Passel, D'Vera Cohn, and Ann Gonzalez-Barrera, "Net Migration from Mexico Falls to Zero—and Perhaps Less," Pew Research Hispanic Trends Project, April 23, 2012, www.pewhispanic. org/2012/04/23/net-migration-from-mexico-falls-to-zero-and-perhaps-less/.

129   "President Obama has once again": Stephen Dinan, "Obama Adds to List of Illegal Immigrants Not to Deport: Parents," *Washington Times*, August 23, 2013, www.washingtontimes.com/news/2013/aug/23/new-obama-policy-warns -agents-not-detain-illegal-i/.

129   "conception of prosecutorial discretion": Rosenkrantz, testimony.

129   "serve the cause of justice": Daniel Strauss, "DREAM Act Author Praises Obama's Immigration Announcement," *The Hill*, June 15, 2012, http://the-hill.com/blogs/floor-action/senate/232949-dream-act-author-praises-obama -deportation-policy-change.

129   "implementing this action": Julian Pecquet, "Mexican President Thanks Obama for 'Valor and Courage' in Immigration Order," *The Hill*, June 18, 2012, http://thehill.com/video/administration/233259-mexican-president-thanks -obama-for-valor-and-courage-in-immigration-order.

129   Blitzer and Calderón in 2010: Wolf Blitzer, CNN, May 19, 2010, transcript available at http://www.city-data.com/forum/illegal-immigration/982928-blitzer -calderon-discuss-illegal-immigration-mx.html.

130   "power is not enough?": Barbara Hollingsworth, "Rep. Gowdy Uses Obama's Own Words against Him in Response to Veto Threat," Cnsnews.com, March 13, 2014, http://cnsnews.com/news/article/barbara-hollingsworth/rep -gowdy-uses-obama-s-own-words-against-him-response-veto-threat.

130   three years prior: "Waves of Immigrant Minors Present Crisis for Obama, Congress," Reuters, May 28, 2014, http://www.reuters.com/article/2014/05/28/ us-usa-immigration-children-idUSKBN0E814T20140528.

130   "apiece per day": John Hayward, "Tidal Wave of 'Dreamers' Surges Across the Border, Looking for Amnesty," *Human Events*, May 29, 2014, http:// www.humanevents.com/2014/05/29/tidal-wave-of-dreamers-surges-across -the-border-looking-for-amnesty/.

Chapter 8: The Regulator

132   "favored a ban on handguns": "Gunning for Obama," FactCheck, May 6, 2008, www.factcheck.org/2008/05/gunning-for-obama/.

132   "small part of the document": Ibid.

133   "who Barack Obama is talking to": Tahman Bradley, "Clinton Attacks Obama on Guns," ABC News, May 4, 2008, http://abcnews.go.com/blogs/politics/ 2008/05/clinton-attacks/.

133   "lay in our shared border": "Text: Obama and Calderon in Mexico City," CBSNews.com, April 17, 2009, www.cbsnews.com/news/text-obama-and -calderon-in-mexico-city/.

133   purchases and gun sales: Scott Stewart, "Mexico's Gun Supply and the 90 Percent Myth," *Stratfor*, February 11, 2011, www.stratfor.com/weekly/20110209 -mexicos-gun-supply-and-90-percent-myth.

134   "this assertion as unreliable": "Firearms Trafficking: U.S. Efforts to Combat Arms Trafficking to Mexico Face Planning and Coordination Challenges," US Government Accountability Office, June 18, 2009, http://www.gao .gov/assets/300/291231.html.

135   added McDonough, clarifying nothing: Major Garrett, "Obama Repeats '90 Percent' Stat for U.S. Guns Recovered in Mexico," FoxNews.com, April 19, 2009, www.foxnews.com/politics/2009/04/19/obama-repeats-percent-stat -guns-recovered-mexico/.

135   "used in major crimes": "Text: Obama and Calderon in Mexico City," CBSNews.com.

135   "directed at the most important targets": Pete Yost, "Justice Dept: Fast and Furious Report Distorted," Associated Press, July 31, 2012, available at http:// cnsnews.com/news/article/justice-dept-fast-and-furious-report-distorted.

136   "their second amendment rights": Katie Pavlich, *Fast and Furious: Barack Obama's Bloodiest Scandal and Its Shameless Cover-Up* (Washington: Regnery, 2012), Nook Edition, 31.

137   "perfect storm of idiocy": Sharyl Atkisson, "Gunwalker Scandal Called 'Perfect Storm of Idiocy,'" CBSNews.com, July 27, 2011, www.cbsnews.com/ news/gunwalker-scandal-called-perfect-storm-of-idiocy/.

137   "locker of the Mexican drug cartels": J. J. Hensley, "Feds Link Arizona Buyers to Drug Cartels' Guns," *AZ Central*, September 18, 2010, www.azcentral .com/news/articles/2010/09/18/20100918gunbust0918.html.

137   "purchased at a Phoenix gun store": Pavlich, *Fast and Furious*, 51.

138   attention to the operation: Ibid.

138   "transported them into Mexico—is false": Letter, U.S. Department of Justice Office of Legislative Affairs, February 4, 2011, available at https://www .deseretnews.com/media/pdf/544034.pdf.

138   inspector general would confirm: John Dodson, *The Unarmed Truth: My Fight to Blow the Whistle and Expose Fast and Furious* (New York: Pocket Books, 2013).

138   "had been withheld from Congress": Carrie Johnson, "ATF Whistleblower Case Triggers Retaliation Inquiry," NPR.org, July 21, 2011, www.npr .org/2011/07/21/138574291/watchdogs-examine-smear-against-atf-agent.

139   "lot of moving parts": "Obama on 'Gunwalking'—'Serious Mistakes' May Have Been Made," CBSNews.com, March 23, 2011, www.cbsnews.com/videos/ obama-on-gunwalking-serious-mistakes-may-have-been-made/.

140   "Mr. Breuer authorized it": "Issa Grills Attorney General Holder on Operation Fast and Furious," YouTube.com, May 3, 2011, https://www.youtube .com/watch?v=4NqH88cSBqI.

140   "knew otherwise and said nothing": Pavlich, *Fast and Furious*, 96.

140   "the February 4 letter": Letter, Office of the Deputy Attorney General, December 2, 2011, http://oversight.house.gov/wp-content/uploads/2012/06/Feb-4-Dec-2-letters.pdf.

140   cabinet member ever cited: Sari Horwitz and Ed O'Keefe, "Fast and Furious Scandal: House Panel Recommends Contempt Vote on Eric Holder," *Washington Post*, June 20, 2012, www.washingtonpost.com/politics/fast-and-furious-scandal-obama-exerts-executive-privilege-house-panel-moves-forward-with-contempt-vote/2012/06/20/gJQAGImIqV_story.html.

141   "begun under the previous administration": "At Univision Forum, Obama Grilled on Fast and Furious & Lies Predictably," Liveleak.com, www.liveleak.com/view?i=d67_1348248145.

141   Furious had no precedent: Jake Tapper, "Fast and Furious—Today's Q's for O's WH," ABC News, June 21, 2012, http://abcnews.go.com/blogs/politics/2012/06/fast-and-furious-todays-qs-for-os-wh/.

141   "were held accountable": "At Univision Forum," Liveleak.

141   first full day in office: Huma Khan, "President Obama Sets Rules on Ethics and Transparency," ABC News, January 21, 2009, http://abcnews.go.com/blogs/politics/2009/01/president-oba-3-5/.

142   much as publicly reprimanded: Pavlich, *Fast and Furious*, 93.

142   hosted by CNN's Candy Crowley: "Transcript and Audio: Second Presidential Debate," NPR.org, October 16, 2012, www.npr.org/2012/10/16/163050988/transcript-obama-romney-2nd-presidential-debate.

143   "And we also recognize": Dan Merica and Catherine E. Shoichet, "'A New Mexico Is Emerging,' Obama Says; Speech Addresses Immigration, Education," CNN.com, May 4, 2013, www.cnn.com/2013/05/03/world/americas/mexico-obama-visit/.

144   "not otherwise pass Congress?": Pavlich, *Fast and Furious*, 108.

145   was a curious thing: "Obama in Tucson: Full Text of Prepared Remarks," *Washington Post*, January 12, 2011, http://voices.washingtonpost.com/44/2011/01/obama-in-tucson-full-text-of-p.html?wprss=44.

145   "Putting Cross Hair over District": Michael Daly, "Rep. Gabrielle Giffords' Blood Is on Sarah Palin's Hands after Putting Cross Hair over District," *Daily News*, January 9, 2011, www.nydailynews.com/news/national/rep-gabrielle-giffords-blood-sarah-palin-hands-putting-cross-hair-district-article-1.149099.

146   "a potentially dangerous mix": Felicia Sonmez and Rachel Weiner, "Sarah Palin crosshairs 'Never Intended to Be Gun Sights,' Says Aide," *Washington Post*, January 9, 2011, http://voices.washingtonpost.com/44/2011/01/palin-staffer-nothing-irrespon.html.

146   even "radical": James King, "Jared Loughner, Alleged Shooter in Gabrielle Giffords Attack, Described by Classmate as 'Left-Wing Pothead,'" *Phoe-*

nix New Times, January 8, 2011, http://blogs.phoenixnewtimes.com/valley fever/2011/01/jared_loughner_alleged_shooter.php.

146 "well up" in anger: Dan Barry, "Looking behind the Mug-Shot Grin," *New York Times*, January 15, 2011, www.nytimes.com/2011/01/16/us/16loughner .html.

147 "that agreed with it": " 'This Week' Transcript: President Barack Obama," ABC News, September 15, 2013, http://abcnews.go.com/ThisWeek/week -transcript-president-barack-obama/story?id=20253577&page=8.

148 "a fully automatic weapon": "Remarks by the President at a DCCC Event— San Francisco, CA," The White House, Office of the Press Secretary, April 4, 2013, www.whitehouse.gov/the-press-office/2013/04/04/remarks-president-dccc -event-san-francisco-ca.

148 the numbers on gun control: "Gun Control: Key Data Points from Pew Research," Pew Research Center, July 27, 2013, www.pewresearch.org/key-data -points/gun-control-key-data-points-from-pew-research/.

Chapter 9: The Statesman

151 pale of his local brief: "Transcript of Obama's Speech against the Iraq War," NPR.org, January 20, 2009, www.npr.org/templates/story/story.php?storyId=99591469.

151 "sovereign, stable and self-reliant Iraq": "Remarks by the President and First Lady on the End of the War in Iraq," whitehouse.gov, December 14, 2011, http://www.whitehouse.gov/the-press-office/2011/12/14/remarks-president -and-first-lady-end-war-iraq.

152 another fun-draiser in San Francisco: Larry Rohter, "Obama Says Real-Life Experience Trumps Rivals' Foreign Policy Credits," *New York Times*, April 10, 2008, www.nytimes.com/2008/04/10/us/politics/10obama.html.

152 "during this campaign": "Obama's College Trip to Pakistan," ABC News, April 8, 2008, http://abcnews.go.com/blogs/politics/2008/04/obamas-college/.

152 strength on foreign affairs: Jake Tapper, "Obama Delivers Bold Speech about War on Terror," ABC News, Aug. 1, 2007, http://abcnews.go.com/Politics/ Story?id=3434573.

153 "on Obama, Clinton, McCain": Glenn Kessler, "Rice Apologizes for Breach of Passport Data; Employees Looked at Files on Obama, Clinton, McCain," *Washington Post*, March 22, 2008, www.washingtonpost.com/wp -dyn/content/article/2008/03/21/AR2008032100377.html.

154 "policy and intelligence issues": Kate Bolduan, "Chief of Firm Involved in Breach Is Obama Adviser," March 22, 2008, CNN Politics.com, www.cnn .com/2008/POLITICS/03/22/passport.files/index.html.

154 thirteen-hundred-word front-page: R. Jeffery Smith, "Obama Taps CIA Veteran Brennan as Counterterror Adviser," *Washington Post*, Janu-

ary 9, 2009, www.washingtonpost.com/wp-dyn/content/article/2009/01/08/
AR2009010804108.

155   "cooperation between peoples": "The Nobel Peace Prize for 2009," Nobel-
prize.org, October 9, 2009, www.nobelprize.org/nobel_prizes/peace/laureates/
2009/press.html.

155   "majority of the world's population": Ibid.

156   "Obama over the edge": All three jokes listed in Jacqueline Klingbiel,
"Best Obama-Nobel Jokes," ABC News, http://abcnews.go.com/blogs/politics/
2009/10/best-obamanobel-jokes/.

156   "My accomplishments are slight": "Remarks by the President at the
Acceptance of the Nobel Peace Prize," The White House, Office of the Press
Secretary, December 10, 2009, www.whitehouse.gov/the-press-office/remarks
-president-acceptance-nobel-peace-prize.

157   "not going to change": Kelly Moeller, "Obama Wants to Be Absolutely
Clear on Who Is Israel's Friend," ABC News, July 22, 2008, http://abcnews.go
.com/blogs/politics/2008/07/obama-wants-to-2/.

157   "I have Israel's back": Oliver Knox, "AIPAC 2012: 'I Have Israel's Back,'
Obama Insists," Yahoo News, March 4, 2012, http://news.yahoo.com/blogs/
ticket/chips-down-israel-back-says-obama-while-reiterating-184525416.html.

157   "we care about it": "Press Conference by the President," The White House,
Office of the Press Secretary, March 6, 2012, www.whitehouse.gov/the-press
-office/2012/03/06/press-conference-president.

157   "achieve through honest means": Caroline Glick, "Obamacare Victims
and Israel," *Jerusalem Post*, Column One, October 31, 2013, www.jpost.com/
Opinion/Columnists/Column-One-Obamacare-victims-and-Israel-330307.

158   "any previous administration": Daniel Halper, "Obama: 'This
Administration Has Done More in Terms of the Security of the State of Israel
Than Any Previous Administration,'" *Weekly Standard*, December 1, 2011,
www.weeklystandard.com/blogs/obama-administration-has-done-more
-terms-security-state-israel-any-previous-administration_610835.html.

158   "Israel from Muslim aggression": Mark Tapson, "Obama: I've Done More
for Israel's Security Than Any President," *FrontPage*, December 7, 2011, www
.frontpagemag.com/2011/mark-tapson/obama-i've-done-more-for-israel's
-security-than-any-president/.

158   "to get to the damned table": "Panetta Scolds Israel on Peace Talks,"
Associated Press, December 3, 2011, available at www.foxnews.com/politics/
2011/12/02/panetta-laments-growing-israeli-isolation-in-region/.

159   "Obama's smug self-congratulation": Tapson, "Obama: I've Done More."

159   "deal with him every day!": Jake Tapper, "Hot Mic Catches Obama, Sarko,
Griping about Netanyahu," ABC News, November 8, 2011, http://abcnews.go
.com/blogs/politics/2011/11/hot-mic-catches-obama-sarko-griping-about
-netanyahu/.

159 "that has consequences": Jeffrey Goldberg, "Obama to Israel—Time Is Running Out," *Bloomberg View*, www.bloombergview.com/articles/2014-03 -02/obama-to-israel-time-is-running-out.

159 becoming an "apartheid state": Edward-Isaac Dovere, "John Kerry Back-pedals on Israel 'Apartheid State' Comment," *Politico*, April 28, 2014, www .politico.com/story/2014/04/john-kerry-apartheid-state-israel-106127.html.

160 "want any amendment whatsoever": "Sen. Robert Menendez (D-NJ) Rips Obama Administration for Opposing Iran Sanctions," YouTube video, posted by "EmergCmteForIsrael," December 1, 2011, www.youtube.com/watch?v=G 46Fnc_gVx4.

160 "any senator in recent memory": Jennifer Rubin, "Senate Passes Iran Sanc-tions 100–0; Obama Objects (Really)," *Washington Post*, December 2, 2011, www .washingtonpost.com/blogs/right-turn/post/senate-passes-iran-sanctions-100 -0-obama-objects-really/2011/12/02/gIQA7yELKO_blog.html.

161 "crippling sanctions on Iran": Joby Warrick, "U.S. Imposes New Sanctions on Iran," *Washington Post*, July 31, 2012, www.washingtonpost.com/world/ national-security/us-imposes-new-sanctions-on-iran/2012/07/31/gJQAQnx lNX_story.html.

161 "the language of Israel's leaders": Jodi Rudoren and Ashley Parker, "Romney Backs Israeli Stance on Threat of Nuclear Iran," *New York Times*, July 29, 2012, www.nytimes.com/2012/07/30/us/politics/romney-in-israel-hints-at -harder-line-toward-iran.html.

161 economic sanctions on Iran: Warrick, "U.S. Imposes New Sanctions."

161 "Step over Iran Sanctions": Mark Landler and Steven Lee Myers, "White House and Congress Are in Step over Iran Sanctions," *New York Times*, July 31, 2012, www.nytimes.com/2012/08/01/world/middleeast/obama-and-congress -in-step-over-iran-sanctions.html.

161 "damage to its strategic viability": Glick, "Obamacare Victims and Israel."

162 "government-to-government level: no": Major Garrett, "The Obama Admin-istration's Useful Lie about Iran Talks," CBSNews.com, December 4, 2013, www .cbsnews.com/news/the-obama-administrations-useful-lie-about-iran-talks/.

162 "good example of that": Josh Gerstein, "Fox Reporter Confronts State Department on Iran Denial," *Politico*, December 2, 2013, www.politico.com/ blogs/under-the-radar/2013/12/fox-reporter-confronts-state-department-on -iran-denial-178651.html.

163 "Useful Lie about Iran Talks": Garrett, "Useful Lie."

163 "are going to be eased": David Simpson and Josh Levs, "Israeli PM Net-anyahu: Iran Nuclear Deal 'Historic Mistake,'" CNN World, November 25, 2013, www.cnn.com/2013/11/24/world/meast/iran-israel/index.html.

163 "was signed this morning": Ibid.

163 "I will veto it": "Full Transcript: Obama's 2014 State of the Union Ad-dress," *Washington Post*.

164   "never do so in future": "Iran Dismisses Barack Obama's Claim That Sanctions Prompted Nuclear Talks," Agence France-Press, January 30, 2014, available at www.theguardian.com/world/2014/jan/30/iran-dismisses-barack -obama-nuclear-sanctions.

164   "cloak-and-dagger diplomacy": Garrett, "Useful Lie."

164   "health insurance Obama canceled": Glick, "Obamacare Victims and Israel."

164   including Prime Minister Netanyahu: "Full Transcript of Netanyahu Speech for Holocaust Remembrance Day," *Times of Israel*, June 29, 2014, http:// www.timesofisrael.com/full-transcript-of-netanyahu-speech-for-holocaust -remembrance-day.

164   "caused by this delusion": Elliot Abrams, "Getting Ready for a Bad Deal," *Weekly Standard*, May 12, 2014, www.weeklystandard.com/articles/getting -ready-bad-deal_788986.html.

165   during a debate: "Transcript and Audio: Third Presidential Debate," NPR.org, October 22, 2012, www.npr.org/2012/10/22/163436694/transcript -3rd-obama-romney-presidential-debate.

166   called this a "cheap trick": Dave Weigel, "Why Obama Got Russia Wrong (and Romney Got It Right)," *Slate*, March 3, 2014, www.slate.com/blogs/weigel/ 2014/03/03/why_obama_got_russia_wrong_and_romney_got_it_right.html.

166   picked up by a live microphone: J. David Goodman, "Microphone Catches a Candid Obama," *New York Times*, March 26, 2012, www.nytimes .com/2012/03/27/us/politics/obama-caught-on-microphone-telling-medvedev -of-flexibility.html.

167   "safekeeping of the chemical weapons": "Remarks by the President to the White House Press Corps" whitehouse.gov, August 20, 2012, http://www .whitehouse.gov/the-press-office/2012/08/20/remarks-president-white-house -press-corps.

167   "change my equation": Ibid.

167   "threat of force against Syria": Mark Landler, "Obama Threatens Force against Syria," *New York Times*, August 20, 2012, www.nytimes.com/2012/08/21/ world/middleeast/obama-threatens-force-against-syria.html.

168   "any predetermined action": Ibid.

168   "would be a grave mistake": Glenn Kessler, "President Obama and the 'Red Line' on Syria's Chemical Weapons," *Washington Post*, Fact Checker, September 6, 2013, www.washingtonpost.com/blogs/fact-checker/wp/2013/09/06/ president-obama-and-the-red-line-on-syrias-chemical-weapons/.

168   "weapons use within Syria": Ibid.

169   "Congress's own red line": Ibid.

169   "The world set a red line": "Remarks by President Obama and Prime Minister Reinfeldt of Sweden in Joint Press Conference," The White House, Office of the Press Secretary, September 4, 2013, www.whitehouse.gov/the-press

-office/2013/09/04/remarks-president-obama-and-prime-minister-reinfeldt
-sweden-joint-press-.

169   performance look like a strategy: "Remarks by the President in Address
to the Nation on Syria," The White House, Office of the Press Sectretary,
September 10, 2013, www.whitehouse.gov/the-press-office/2013/09/10/remarks
-president-address-nation-syria.

170   "strongly implicated the Syrian government": Rick Gladstone and C. J.
Chivers, "Forensic Details in U.N. Report Point to Assad's Use of Gas," *New
York Times*, September 16, 2013, www.nytimes.com/2013/09/17/world/europe/
syria-united-nations.html.

170   administration had been telling: Seymour M. Hersh, "Whose Sarin?"
London Review of Books, December 19, 2013, www.lrb.co.uk/v35/n24/seymour
-m-hersh/whose-sarin.

171   "assessments by Syrian officials": Joby Warrick, "More Than 1,400 Killed
in Syrian Chemical Weapons Attack, U.S. Says," *Washington Post*, August 30,
2013,   www.washingtonpost.com/world/national-security/nearly-1500-killed-in
-syrian-chemical-weapons-attack-us-says/2013/08/30/b2864662-1196-11e3
-85b6-d27422650fd5_story.html.

171   "horrible attack took place": Hersh, "Whose Sarin?"

171   "going to do about it": Gus Taylor and Stephen Dinan, "John Kerry:
Syrian Regime Killed 1,429 People in Chemical Attack," *Washington Times*,
August 30, 2013, www.washingtontimes.com/news/2013/aug/30/john-kerry
-syrian-regime-killed-1429-people-chemic/.

172   "great climactic challenges": "The Nobel Peace Prize for 2009," Nobel-
prize.org, October 9, 2009, www.nobelprize.org/nobel_prizes/peace/laureates/
2009/press.html.

173   "and sheer cloudy vagueness": George Orwell, "Politics and the English
Language," 1946, available at https://www.mtholyoke.edu/acad/intrel/orwell46
.htm.

173   "would necessarily skyrocket": Dan Spencer, "Obama on Cap and Trade:
'Electricity Rates Would Necessarily Skyrocket,'" Examiner.com, June 26,
2009,   www.examiner.com/article/obama-on-cap-and-trade-electricity-rates
-would-necessarily-skyrocket.

174   killed it in legislative utero: Evan Lehmann, "Senate Abandons Climate
Effort, Dealing Blow to President," *New York Times*, July 23, 2010, www.ny
times.com/cwire/2010/07/23/23climatewire-senate-abandons-climate-effort
-dealing-blow-88864.html.

174   "the year, and so on": Ethan Epstein, "What Catastrophe?" *Weekly Standard*, January 13, 2014, www.weeklystandard.com/articles/what-catastrophe
_773268.html.

174   evidence for global warming: Global Warming Petition Project, www
.petitionproject.org/index.php.

174 "Climate change is a fact": "Full Transcript: Obama's 2014 State of the Union Address," *Washington Post.*

174 His definitive speech on climate: "Remarks by the President on Climate Change," The White House, Office of the Press Secretary, June 25, 2013, www .whitehouse.gov/the-press-office/2013/06/25/remarks-president-climate-change.

175 "ultimately have political and economic causes": Orwell, "Politics and the English Language."

175 previous sixteen years: Jeff Tollefson, "Climate Change: The Case of the Missing Heat," *Nature*, January 15, 2014, http://www.nature.com/news/ climate-change-the-case-of-the-missing-heat-1.14525.

175 in thirty-five years: "Latest Data Shows Arctic Sea Ice Has Increased," reporting climatescience.com, February 2, 2014, http://www.reportingclimate science.com/news-stories/article/latest-data-shows-arctic-ice-volume-has -increased.html.

Chapter 10: The Revenuer

177 "for purposes of fairness": "Obama: Raise Taxes, Capital Gains—For Purposes of Fairness, 2008," Dailymotion video, posted by "Nick Furry," October 22, 2011, www.dailymotion.com/video/xlv7yv_obama-raise-taxes-capital-gains -for-purposes-of-fairness-2008_news.

178 "lower tax rate than his secretary": "Remarks by the President in State of the Union Address," The White House, Office of the Press Secretary, January 24, 2012, www.whitehouse.gov/the-press-office/2012/01/24/remarks-president -state-union-address.

178 ran the numbers: Paul Roderick Gregory, "Warren Buffett's Secretary Likely Makes between $200,000 and $500,000/Year," *Forbes*, January 25, 2012, www.forbes.com/sites/paulroderickgregory/2012/01/25/warren-buffetts- secretary-likely-makes-between-200000-and-500000year/.

179 "move together": Thomas Sowell, "Perpetuating Obama's Tax-Cut Lies," *National Review Online*, July 13, 2012, www.nationalreview.com/articles/ 309247/perpetuating-obama-s-tax-cut-lies-thomas-sowell.

179 "lagged by 7 percentage points": Susan Page, "McCain Leads Democrat Barack Obama by 50%–46% among Registered Voters," *USA Today*, September 8, 2008, http://usatoday30.usatoday.com/news/politics/election2008/2008-09 -07-poll_N.htm.

180 "those people aren't listening": "Transcript: Gov. Sarah Palin at the RNC," NPR.org, September 03, 2008, www.npr.org/templates/story/story.php?story Id=94258995.

180 "not any of your taxes": Angie Drobnic Holan, "Smokers, Tanning Afi- cionados, the Happily Uninsured: More Taxes Coming at Ya!" *PolitiFact*, April 8, 2010, www.politifact.com/truth-o-meter/promises/obameter/promise/515/ no-family-making-less-250000-will-see-any-form-tax/.

180 "investment tax, any tax": "Transcript of Palin, Biden Debate," CNNPolitics .com, October 3, 2008, www.cnn.com/2008/POLITICS/10/02/debate.transcript/.

180 "not one single dime": "Remarks of President Barack Obama—As Prepared for Delivery Address to Joint Session of Congress," The White House, Office of the Press Secretary, February 24th, 2009, www.whitehouse.gov/the_ press_office/Remarks-of-President-Barack-Obama-Address-to-Joint-Session -of-Congress.

181 bitter clinger crowd: Peter Roff, "Obama's Cigarette Tax Puts the Lie to His No New Taxes Pledge," *US News & World Report*, April 2, 2009, www .usnews.com/opinion/blogs/peter-roff/2009/04/02/obamas-cigarette-tax-puts -the-lie-to-his-no-new-taxes-pledge.

181 "did that intentionally for us": R. M. Schneiderman, "Jersey Shore's Snooki Bashes Obama's Tanning Tax," *Wall Street Journal*, June 10, 2010, http:// blogs.wsj.com/metropolis/2010/06/10/jersey-shores-snooki-bashes-obamas -tanning-tax/.

181 Roberts ruled a "tax": Matt Vespa, "Obamacare Shatters Obama's Promise on Fifth Anniversary of No-Tax-Hike Pledge," CNSNews.com, September 12, 2013, http://cnsnews.com/mrctv-blog/matt-vespa/obamacare-shatters -obamas-promise-fifth-anniversary-no-tax-hike-pledge.

181 middle and working classes: "Obama Backs Marketplace Fairness Bill," icsc.org, www.icsc.org/press/obama-backs-marketplace-fairness-bill.

181 interviewed President Obama live on the air: "Transcript: Bill O'Reilly Interviews President Obama," FoxNews.com, February 2, 2014, www.foxnews .com/politics/2014/02/02/transcript-bill-oreilly-interviews-president-obama/.

182 "into all of our lives": Beth Reinhard, "You Want Angry? I'll Show You Angry, Obama Says on the IRS Scandal," *National Journal*, May 15, 2013, www .nationaljournal.com/politics/you-want-angry-i-ll-show-you-angry-obama -says-on-irs-scandal-20130515.

182 Engelbrecht, remembered all too well: "Catherine Engelbrecht Congressional Testimony Transcript: IRS Targeting of True the Vote, King Street Patriots & Personally," *Before It's News*, February 7, 2014, http://beforeitsnews.com/ opinion-conservative/2014/02/catherine-engelbrecht-congressional-testimony -transcript-irs-targeting-of-true-the-vote-king-street-patriots-personally-2803 204.html.

182 "through the looking glass": Ibid.

183 "in the coming year": Ibid.

183 "little Mickey Mouse stuff": Ibid.

184 ethics complaint against Cummings: Ibid.

184 "potential political campaign intervention": "Inappropriate Criteria Were Used to Identify Tax-Exempt Applications for Review," Treasury Inspector General for Tax Administration Office of Audit, May 14, 2013, available at http://online.wsj .com/public/resources/documents/tigta-201310053_oa_highlights.pdf.

184 "not targeted because of it": "Engelbrecht Congressional Testimony," *Before It's News.*

185 "tea party" and "patriot": Josh Hicks, "IRS Chief Counsel's Office Involved in Targeting Controversy," *Washington Post*, July 17, 2013, www.washington post.com/blogs/federal-eye/wp/2013/07/17/irs-chief-counsel-involved-in -targeting-controversy/.

185 unnamed "local office": "O'Reilly Interviews President Obama," FoxNews .com.

185 "these applications," said Hofacre: "Written Testimony of Elizabeth Hofacre before the House Oversight and Government Reform Committee," US House of Representatives, House Committee on Oversight and Government Reform, July 18, 2013, http://oversight.house.gov/wp-content/uploads/2013/07/ Hofacre-Testimony-Final.pdf.

185 not the norm either: Hicks, "IRS Chief Counsel's Office."

185 "I don't recall" eighty times: Eliana Johnson, "William Wilkins, IRS Chief Counsel, Testifies on Targeting of Tea-Party Groups," *National Review Online*, November 27, 2013, www.nationalreview.com/corner/365080/william-wilkins -irs-chief-counsel-testifies-targeting-tea-party-groups-eliana-johnson.

186 restore that confidence: Rachel Bade, "Darrell Issa, Lois Lerner Lawyer Escalate IRS Conflict," *Politico*, June 20, 2014, http://www.politico.com/ story/2014/06/lois-lerner-irs-scandal-108399.html.

186 to a Texas schoolteacher: Emily Smith, "Presiden Admits ObamaCare Not the 'Smart Political Thing' in Letter," *New York Post*, Page Six, November 27, 2013, http://pagesix.com/2013/11/27/president-admits-obamacare-not-the -smart-political-thing-in-letter/.

186 agency's DC headquarters: David Martosko, "IRS Tea-Party Noose Tightens," *Daily Mail*, May 14, 2014, www.dailymail.co.uk/news/article-2628347/ IRSs-tea-party-noose-tightens-Documents-partisan-targeting-campaign -directed-headquarters-Washington.html.

186 "name of their common father": Ibid.

187 "shut the whole thing down": Frank Beckmann, "IRS Scandal Could Entangle Sen. Carl Levin," *Detroit Free Press*, May 16, 2014, www.detroitnews .com/article/20140516/OPINION01/305160001.

187 100 percent were: John D. McKinnon, "Camp: IRS Targeted Established Conservative Groups for Audits, Too," *Wall Street Journal*, February 11, 2014, http://blogs.wsj.com/washwire/2014/02/11/camp-irs-targeted-conservative -groups-for-audits/.

187 "tax-exempt, nonprofit groups": "Senate Democrats Urge IRS to Impose Strict Cap on Political Spending by Nonprofit Groups—Vow Legislation If Agency Doesn't Act," press release, Senators Charles E. Schumer, Michael Bennet, Sheldon Whitehouse, et al., March 12, 2012, www.schumer.senate.gov/ Newsroom/record.cfm?id=336270.

187   "Tea Party elites" for abuse: Becket Adams, "Chuck Schumer Call on IRS to Crack Down on Tea Party Funding: 'Redouble Those Efforts Immediately,'" *The Blaze*, January 24, 2014, www.theblaze.com/stories/2014/01/24/chuck -schumer-calls-for-irs-to-crack-down-on-tea-party-funding/.

187   were clearly conservative: Beckmann, "IRS scandal could entangle."

188   "what the president said": "Press Briefing by Press Secretary Jay Carney, 2/3/14," whitehouse.gov, February 3, 2014, http://www.whitehouse.gov/the -press-office/2014/02/03/press-briefing-press-secretary-jay-carney-2314.

Chapter 11: The Commander in Chief

189   bunch of old hippies: Mendell, *Obama*, 172–74.

189   have given his blessing: "Obama's Speech against the Iraq War," NPR.org.

190   "will do the reverse": Natalie Gewargis, "From the Fact Check Desk: Did Obama Say during the Debate over the Surge That 'There's No Doubt That Additional U.S. Troops Could Temporarily Quell the Violence'?" ABC News, July 29, 2008, http://abcnews.go.com/blogs/politics/2008/07/from-the-fact-c/.

190   "seen in the last year": Ibid.

191   "surprising as it was dismaying": Robert Gates, *Duty: Memoirs of a Secretary at War* (New York: Random House, 2014), 376.

191   "will follow through on that": "Obama on Economic Crisis, Transition," CBSNews.com, November 16, 2008, http://www.cbsnews.com/news/obama-on -economic-crisis-transition/.

192   "when it's hard": Dan Froomkin, "And Then, on the Second Day," *Washington Post*, January 22, 2009, http://voices.washingtonpost.com/white-house -watch/bush-rollback/and-then-on-the-second-day.html.

192   their air-conditioned gulag: Andrew Malcolm, "Obama and Guantanamo: A Chronology of His Broken Promise," *Los Angeles Times*, July 2, 2010, http://latimesblogs.latimes.com/washington/2010/07/obama-guantanamo .html.

192   administration official told Savage: Charlie Savage, "Closing Guantanamo Fades as a Priority," *New York Times*, June 25, 2010, www.nytimes .com/2010/06/26/us/politics/26gitmo.html.

193   "the prison at Guantánamo Bay": "Full Transcript: Obama's 2014 State of the Union Address," *Washington Post*.

193   "Close Guantánamo Prison": Carol Rosenberg, "Obama to Congress: Close Guantánamo Prison," *Miami Herald* January 30, 2014, www.miami herald.com/2014/01/29/3900143/obama-to-congress-we-need-to-close.html.

193   "It's Anti-American": Michael Shammas, "Obama Is Right: Close Guantanamo—It's Anti-American," *Huffington Post*, February 3, 2014, www .huffingtonpost.com/mike-shammas/close-guantanamoits-antia_b_4589960 .html.

193   "Keeping Prisoners at Guantanamo": Kevin Gosztola, "Obama's Deluded Remarks Ignore His Role in Keeping Prisoners at Guantanamo," *Firedoglake*, Dissenter, April 30, 2013, http://dissenter.firedoglake.com/2013/04/30/obamas -deluded-remarks-on-guantanamo-ignore-his-role-in-keeping-prisoners -detained/.

193   "conscience of the world": "Remarks by the President in Address to the Nation on Libya," The White House, Office of the Press Secretary, March 28, 2011, www.whitehouse.gov/the-press-office/2011/03/28/remarks-president-address -nation-libya.

193   the word "bloodbath": "The President's Weekly Address," March 26, 2011, The American Presidency Project, http://www.presidency.ucsb.edu/ws/index .php?pid=90184

194   Security Council Resolution 1973: "Remarks by the President in Address to the Nation on Libya," The White House, Office of the Press Secretary.

194   "in the war on terrorism": "Codel McCain Meets Muammar and Muatassim Al-Qadhafi," *Telegraph*, January 31, 2011, passed to the *Telegraph* by WikiLeaks, http://www.telegraph.co.uk/news/wikileaks-files/ libya-wikileaks/8294621/CODEL-MCCAIN-MEETS-MUAMMAR-AND -MUATASSIM-AL-QADHAFI.html.

195   "upwards of about 100,000": "Europe Fears Grow over Kosovo 'Disappeared,'" BBC News, April 19, 1999, http://news.bbc.co.uk/2/hi/europe/322817 .stm.

195   missing and feared dead: Francis X. Clines, "NATO Refocuses Targets to Halt Serbian Attacks on Albanians in Kosovo," *New York Times*, March 30, 1999,   http://partners.nytimes.com/library/world/europe/033099kosovo-rdp .html.

195   "justice over genocide": Tom Doggett, "Cohen Fears 100,000 Kosovo Men Killed by Serbs," *Washington Post*, May 16, 1999, www.washingtonpost.com/ wp-srv/inatl/longterm/balkans/stories/cohen051699.htm.

195   President Clinton compared: Charles Babington and R. Jeffrey Smith, "Kosovo Albanians Greet Clinton with Cheers, Tears," *Washington Post*, June 23, 1999, www.washingtonpost.com/wp-srv/inatl/longterm/balkans/stories/ clinton062399.htm.

196   "a semantic pirouette": "There Is as Yet No Evidence That Genocide Took Place in Kosovo. But That Fact Is Nigh Impossible to Find in the Press," John Pilger, *New Statesman*, November 15, 1999, http://www.newstatesman.com/ node/136124.

196   "genocide against ethnic Albanians": "Kosovo Assault 'Was Not Genocide,'" BBC News, September 7, 2001, http://news.bbc.co.uk/2/hi/europe/1530781.stm.

196   "The best evidence that Khadafy": Alan Kuperman, "False Pretense for War in Libya?" *Boston Globe*, April 14, 2011, www.boston.com/bostonglobe/ editorial_opinion/oped/articles/2011/04/14/false_pretense_for_war_in_libya/.

197   "of his barbaric behavior": David Kirkpatrick, "Hopes for a Qaddafi Exit, and Worries of What Comes Next," *New York Times*, March 22, 2011, www .nytimes.com/2011/03/22/world/africa/22tripoli.html.

197   "Benghazi has been prevented": "Libya Letter by Obama, Cameron and Sarkozy: Full Text," BBC News, April 15, 2011, www.bbc.co.uk/news/world -africa-13090646.

197   "repeat as fact over and over": David Kirkpatrick and Rod Norland, "Waves of Disinformation and Confusion Swamp the Truth in Libya," *New York Times*, August 24, 2011, www.nytimes.com/2011/08/24/world/africa/ 24fog.html.

198   "Any Libyan with a black skin": Patrick Cockburn, "Rebels Wreak Revenge on Dictator's Men," *The Independent*, August 28, 2011, www.independent .co.uk/news/world/africa/rebels-wreak-revenge-on-dictators-men-2345261 .html.

198   killed Qaddafi in a cross fire: "Muammar Gaddafi: How He Died," BBC News, October 31, 2011, www.bbc.co.uk/news/world-africa-15390980.

198   "The dark shadow": Ewan MacAskill, "Obama Hails Death of Muammar Gaddafi as Foreign Policy Success: President Warns Other Middle Eastern Dictators, Particularly Syrian President Bashar al-Assad, That They Could Be Next," *The Guardian*, October 20, 2011, www.theguardian.com/world/2011/ oct/20/obama-hails-death-gaddafi.

199   "Libya and its neighbors": Alan Kuperman, "Lessons from Libya: How Not to Intervene," *International Security*, September 2013, http://belfercenter .ksg.harvard.edu/publication/23387/lessons_from_libya.html.

199   vast northern stretches of the country: Ibid.

199   came from a "chaotic Libya": Lori Hinnant and Sylvie Corbet, "Summit Combats Boko Haram Funds, Arms, Training," ABC News, May 17, 2014, http://abcnews.go.com/International/wireStory/african-leaders-work-counter -boko-haram-23761350.

200   "the fall of the Qaddafi government": James Risen et al., "U.S.-Approved Arms for Libya Fell into Jihadis' Hands," *New York Times*, December 5, 2012, www.nytimes.com/2012/12/06/world/africa/weapons-sent-to-libyan-rebels -with-us-approval-fell-into-islamist-hands.html.

200   history of the Obama presidency: Peter Baker, "How Afghanistan Decision Was Made," *New York Times*, December 6, 2009, http://articles .sun-sentinel.com/2009-12-06/news/0912050080_1_national-security-team -bell-curve-afghanistan-review.

200   "finish the fight": "2008 Barack Obama Convention Speech Transcript," Zimbio.com, August 28, 2008, www.zimbio.com/Democratic+National+Con- vention+Speech+Transcripts/articles/17/2008+Barack+Obama+Convention +Speech+Transcript.

201   "in Pakistan and Afghanistan": "A New Strategy for Afghanistan and

Pakistan," whitehouse.gov, March 27, 2009, http://www.whitehouse.gov/blog/09/03/27/A-New-Strategy-for-Afghanistan-and-Pakistan.

201 "Obama clearly didn't know": Michael Hastings, "The Runaway General," *Rolling Stone*, June 22, 2010, www.rollingstone.com/politics/news/the-runaway-general-20100622.

202 "will begin to come home": "Remarks by the President in Address to the Nation on the Way Forward in Afghanistan and Pakistan," The White House, Office of the Press Secretary, December 1, 2009, www.whitehouse.gov/the-press-office/remarks-president-address-nation-way-forward-afghanistan-and-pakistan.

202 "itself create governance reform": Hastings, "The Runaway General."

202 "a MacArthur moment": Helene Cooper and David Sanger, "Obama Says Afghan Policy Won't Change after Dismissal," *New York Times*, June 23, 2010, www.nytimes.com/2010/06/24/us/politics/24mcchrystal.html.

203 "all about getting out": Gates, *Duty*, 299.

203 there were 1,671: "Operation Enduring Freedom," *icasualties*, http://icasualties.org/oef/.

203 "I have, and I will": "Transcript: President Obama's Convention Speech," NPR.org, September 6, 2012, www.npr.org/2012/09/06/160713941/transcript-president-obamas-convention-speech.

203 "He never said that all the troops": Reid Epstein and Josh Gerstein, "Carney [Clarifies] Obama Words on Afghanistan," *Politico*, September 2, 2012, www.politico.com/politico44/2012/09/carney-clarifies-afghanistan-drawdown-timetable-134156.html.

204 "end of 2024 and beyond": "Security and Defense Cooperation Agreement between the United States of America and the Islamic Republic of Afghanistan," MSNBC, http://msnbcmedia.msn.com/i/MSNBC/Sections/NEWS/BSAdocument.pdf.

204 "finally come to end": "Remarks by the President on Memorial Day—Arlington National Cemetery," The White House, Office of the Press Secretary, May 26, 2014, www.whitehouse.gov/the-press-office/2014/05/26/remarks-president-memorial-day-arlington-national-cemetery-0.

205 "going to get into it": "Briefing by Press Secretary Robert Gibbs," The White House, Office of the Press Secretary, September 23, 2009, www.whitehouse.gov/the_press_office/Briefing-by-White-House-Press-Secretary-Robert-Gibbs-and-Obama-National-Security-Speechwriter-Ben-Rhodes-9/23/09.

205: "behind the curtain": Sal Gentile, "Robert Gibbs: I Was Told 'Not Even to Acknowledge the Drone Program,'" MSNBC.com, September 12, 2013, www.msnbc.com/up-with-steve-kornacki/robert-gibbs-i-was-told-not-even-acknowl.

205 "for the President to authorize": John Gerstein, "Holder: Obama Could Order Lethal Force in U.S.," *Politico*, March 5, 2013, www.politico.com/politico44/2013/03/holder-obama-could-order-lethal-force-in-us-158548.html.

205   "America's values": Obama for America, *Blueprint for Change*, undated, www.astrid-online.it/rassegna/Rassegna-26/28-10-2008/OBAMA_Blueprint ForChange.pdf.

206   "a catastrophic attack": Gerstein, "Holder: Obama Could Order."

206   "counter to the rule of law": "Obama's Speech on Drone Policy," *New York Times*, May 24, 2013, www.nytimes.com/2013/05/24/us/politics/transcript-of -obamas-speech-on-drone-policy.html.

207   "We were not—I repeat": Marc Thiessen, "Ex-CIA Counterterror Chief Says Pelosi 'Reinventing the Truth' about Waterboarding," *Washington Post*, April 30, 2012, www.washingtonpost.com/opinions/ex-cia-counterterror-chief -pelosi-lied-about-waterboarding/2012/04/30/gIQAQFGtrT_story.html.

207   "We held back nothing": Ibid.

208   "imminent threat to life": Kenneth Roth, "Absent a War, Law Enforce-ment Principles Apply," *Huffington Post*, August 26, 2013, www.huffingtonpost .com/kenneth-roth/absent-a-war-law-enforcem_b_3818815.html.

208   in the history of the presidency: "O'Reilly Interviews President Obama," FoxNews.com.

209   "I've got one television station": Peter Drivas, "Obama Hits Fox News: They're 'Entirely Devoted to Attacking My Administration'—Fox News Re-sponds," *Huffington Post*, June 16, 2009, www.huffingtonpost.com/2009/06/16/ obama-hits-fox-news-theyr_n_216574.html.

209   "competitive in the world": Jann S. Wenner, "Obama in Command: The Rolling Stone Interview," *Rolling Stone*, October 14, 2010, www.rollingstone.com/ politics/news/obama-in-command-br-the-rolling-stone-interview-20100928.

210   preparing to strike back: Unless specified otherwise, all the action se-quences on the ground in Benghazi that follow come from Jack Murphy and Brandon Webb, *Benghazi: The Definitive Report* (New York: William Morrow, 2013), Nook Edition. This reference, 25.

210   "mitigated the dangers there": US House of Representatvies, House Armed Services Committee, *Majority Interim Report: Benghazi Investigation Update*, February 2014, http://armedservices.house.gov/index.cfm/files/serve? File_id=C4E16543-8F99-430C-BEBA-0045A6433426.

210   "The inaction in Libya": Ibid., 9.

211   makeshift State Department compound: Murphy and Webb, *Benghazi*, 34.

211   themselves in the DSS villa: Ibid., 37.

211   "Mission in Benghazi under Attack": "Transcript: Testimony of Gregory Hicks on Benghazi," thetowntalk.com, May 8, 2013, http://www.thetowntalk .com/article/20130508/NEWS01/130508017/Transcript-Testimony-Gregory -Hicks-Benghazi.

211   Secretary of Defense Leon Panetta: Armed Services Committee, *Interim Report*, 14.

212   a half hour of the initial attack: Murphy and Webb, *Benghazi*, 41.

212   safe and accounted for: Ibid., 42–43.

212   with Secretary of State Hillary Clinton: House Armed Services Committee, *Interim Report*, 14.

212   to join the fray: Murphy and Webb, *Benghazi*, 46.

213   the attacks via Twitter: "State Department Names Groups behind Benghazi Strike," FoxNews.com, January 10, 2014, http://www.foxnews.com/politics/2014/01/10/state-department-names-groups-behind-benghazi-strike/.

213   what happened that night: "Gregory Hicks on Benghazi," thetowntalk.com.

213   at 9:18 that evening: Lynn Sweet, "Obama, Netanyahu: Hour Phone Call Tuesday Night; White House Denies Snub," *Chicago Sun-Times*, September 11, 2012, https://www.quibids.com/en/landing/index.php?c=us&mb=ss&lp=108&sub=523.

214   "violent acts of this kind": Donovan Slack, "Hillary Clinton Condemns Benghazi Attack," *Politico*, September 12, 2012, www.politico.com/politico44/2012/09/hillary-clinton-condemns-benghazi-attack-135265.html.

214   mortars killed them both: Murphy and Webb, *Benghazi*, 47.

214   out of Benghazi alive: Ibid, 48.

215   "values that we stand for": "Remarks by the President on the Deaths of U.S. Embassy Staff in Libya," The White House, Office of the Press Secretary, September 12, 2012, www.whitehouse.gov/the-press-office/2012/09/12/remarks-president-deaths-us-embassy-staff-libya.

215   "a response to a hateful": "Transcript, September 16, 2012," *Meet the Press*, NBCNews.com, http://www.nbcnews.com/id/49051097/ns/meet_the_press-transcripts/t/september-benjamin-netanyahu-susan-rice-keith-ellison-peter-king-bob-woodward-jeffrey-goldberg-andrea-mitchell/#.U0R7QJhh0aV.

215   "unfounded and preposterous": Eugene Kiely, "Benghazi Timeline," *FactCheck*, May 16, 2013, www.factcheck.org/2012/10/benghazi-timeline/.

215   interview with David Letterman went as follows: Tom Bevan, "What the President Said about Benghazi," *Real Clear Politics*, November 30, 2012, www.realclearpolitics.com/articles/2012/11/30/what_the_president_said_about_benghazi_116299.html.

216   "them for forty years": Ibid.

216   "be greeted as liberators": *Meet the Press*, March 16, 2003, http://www.informationclearinghouse.info/article5145.htm.

217   "directed at Westerners or Americans": Bevan, "What the President Said."

217   and even then he did so grudgingly: "Obama Won't Call Benghazi Terrorism," YouTube video, posted by "Tod Feinburg," September 25, 2012, www.youtube.com/watch?v=ZPGmN7Zw9Fk.

217   asked a disbelieving Graham: Stephen Dinan, "Obama Made no Phone Calls on Night of Benghazi Attack, White House Says," *Washington Times*, February 14, 2013, www.washingtontimes.com/news/2013/feb/14/white-house-no -phone-calls-benghazi/.

218   "an update on the situation": Fred Lucas, "WH: Obama Called Hillary on Night of Benghazi Attack—More Than Six Hours after It Started," Cnsnews .com, February 20, 2013, http://cnsnews.com/news/article/wh-obama-called -hillary-night-benghazi-attack-more-six-hours-after-it-started.

218   their 10:00 p.m. phone call: Ibid.

218   he told Congress: "Gregory Hicks on Benghazi," thetowntalk.com.

218   Bristol answered, "No": House Armed Services Committee, *Interim Report*, 15.

218   "as soon as possible": Edward Klein, *Blood Feud: The Clintons vs. the Obamas* (Washington: Regnery Publishing, 2014), Nook Edition, chapter 20.

219   "workplace violence": Ibid.

219   an act of terror: Manny Fernandez and Allen Blinder, "At Fort Hood, Wrestling with Label of Terrorism," *New York Times*, April 8, 2014, http://www .nytimes.com/2014/04/09/us/at-fort-hood-wrestling-with-label-of-terrorism .html?_r=0.

219   "that night to pursue Benghazi?": Daniel Greenfield, "It Doesn't Matter Where Obama Was While Benghazi Happened, Says Obama Aide," *FrontPage*, May 19, 2013, www.frontpagemag.com/2013/dgreenfield/it-doesnt-matter-where -obama-was-while-benghazi-happened-says-obama-aide/.

220   "night of September 11": Andy McCarthy, "The 10 P.M. Phone Call," *National Review Online*, May 18, 2013, www.nationalreview.com/ article/348677/10-pm-phone-call-andrew-c-mccarthy.

221   was allowed to squirm away: "ABC News' Jon Karl Hammers Jay Carney over New Bombshell Benghazi Emails," YouTube video, posted by "LSUDVM," April 30, 2014, www.youtube.com/watch?v=Y0G5QhrWXPA.

222   exchange began inauspiciously: "Second Presidential Debate: Libya," CBSNews.com, October 16, 2012, www.cbsnews.com/videos/second-presidential -debate-libya/.

224   "the resolve of this great nation": "President Obama Speaks on the Attack on Benghazi," The White House, Office of the Press Secretary, September 12, 2012, www.whitehouse.gov/photos-and-video/video/2012/09/12/president-obama -speaks-attack-benghazi#transcript.

225   "international terrorist groups": David Kirkpatrick, "Brazen Figure May Hold Key to Mysteries," *New York Times*, June 17, 2014, http://www.nytimes .com/2014/06/18/world/middleeast/apprehension-of-ahmed-abu-khattala-may -begin-to-answer-questions-on-assault.html.

225   labored to distinguish: Joseph Miller, "The Top 8 White House Bergdahl Lies," *Daily Caller*, June 9, 2014, http://dailycaller.com/2014/06/09/the-top-8 -white-house-bergdahl-lies/.

225 "deeply concerned about": "Press Conference Transcript: What Obama Said Thursday about Bergdahl Controversy," *Washington Wire*, June 5, 2014, http://blogs.wsj.com/washwire/2014/06/05/press-conference-transcript-what -obama-said-thursday-about-bergdahl-controversy/.

226 "to save his life": Julian Barnes, "Chuck Hagel Says Health Concerns Justified Bergdahl Swap," *Wall Street Journal*, June 1, 2014, http://online.wsj.com/ articles/chuck-hagel-says-health-concerns-justified-bergdahl-swap-1401615231.

226 American helicopter: Holly Yan, Masoud Popalzai, and Catherine E. Shoichet, "Taliban Video Shows Bowe Bergdahl's Release in Afghanistan," *CNN Politics*, June 5, 2014, http://www.cnn.com/2014/06/04/politics/bowe -bergdahl-release/index.html.

226 "that there was": Jonathan Topaz, "Dianne Feinstein: No Threat to Bergdahl," *Politico*, June 6, 2014, http://www.politico.com/story/2014/06/dianne-feinstein -bergdahl-no-threat-107526.html.

226 "anyone in Congress": Michele Kirk, "White House Says Up to 90 Staffers Knew about Bergdahl Swap, but Congress Couldn't Be Trusted," *BizPac Review*, June 10, 2014, http://www.bizpacreview.com/2014/06/10/white-house -says-up-to-90-staffers-knew-about-bergdahl-swap-but-congress-couldnt-be -trusted-124430.

226 the answer was "no": *CNN State of the Union with Candy Crowley*, June 1, 2014, https://archive.org/details/CNNW_20140601_130000_State_of_the_ Union_With_Candy_Crowley.

226 a terrorist group: Miller, "The Top 8."

227 "honor and distinction": "Susan Rice Cites 'Sacred Obligation' in Making Deal for Bergdahl's Freedom," ABC News, June 1, 2014, http://abcnews.go.com/ blogs/politics/2014/06/susan-rice-cites-sacred-obligation-to-deal-with-taliban -for-bergdahls-freedom/.

227 "wasn't the case": Noah Rothman, "Gen. Barry McCaffrey: Susan Rice Misled the Public on Sunday Shows . . . Again," *Mediaite*, June 3, 2014, http:// www.mediaite.com/tv/gen-barry-mccaffrey-susan-rice-misled-the-public-on -sunday-shows-again/.

227 "the American uniform behind": "Press Conference Transcript: What Obama Said Thursday about Bergdahl Controversy."

227 "sacred obligation": *ABC News*, June 1, 2014.

Chapter 12: The Transformer

229 "transforming the United States of America": Mary Daly, "Obama Revs Up MU," *The Maneater*, October 31, 2008, www.themaneater.com/stories/ 2008/10/31/obama-revs-mu/.

229 "you can get ahead": "O'Reilly Interviews President Obama," FoxNews .com.

230   by her medical team: Edie Littlefield Sundby, "You Also Can't Keep Your Doctor," *Wall Street Journal*, November 3, 2013, http://online.wsj.com/news/articles/SB10001424052702304527504579171710423780446.

230   "in the wilds of Alaska": Edie Littlefield Sundby, "Living Longer Than Predicted," *New York Times*, October 18, 2011, http://well.blogs.nytimes.com/2011/10/18/living-longer-than-predicted/.

230   "Perhaps that's the point": Sundby, "Can't Keep Your Doctor."

231   "fundamentally wrong about that": "Transcript of second McCain, Obama Debate," CNNPolitics.com, October 7, 2008, www.cnn.com/2008/POLITICS/10/07/presidential.debate.transcript/.

231   "the dangers of smoking": "Vice President Al Gore Speaks at the Democratic National Convention," *PBS NewsHour*, August 28, 1996, www.pbs.org/newshour/bb/politics-july-dec96-gore_08-28/.

232   on cigarette warning labels: Debra Saunders, "Al Gore's Convenient Fiction," *Real Clear Politics*, June 11, 2006, www.realclearpolitics.com/articles/2006/06/al_gores_convenient_fiction.html.

232   "dispute with her insurance company": Kevin Sack, "Book Challenges Obama on Mother's Deathbed Fight," *New York Times*, July 13, 2011, http://www.nytimes.com/2011/07/14/us/politics/14mother.html.

232   "several hundred dollars a month": *Janny Scott, A Singular Woman: The Untold Story of Barack Obama's Mother* (New York: Riverhead Books, 2011), 335-336.

232   "broader point remained salient": Sack, "Book Challenges Obama."

232   "health insurance issue": Ibid.

233   of Obama and his mom: Glenn Kessler, "'The Road We've Traveled': A Misleading Account of Obama's Mother and Her Insurance Dispute," *Washington Post*, Fact Checker, March 19, 2012, www.washingtonpost.com/blogs/fact-checker/post/the-road-weve-traveled-a-misleading-account-of-obamas-mother-and-her-insurance-dispute/2012/03/18/gIQAdDd4KS_blog.html.

234   "Mitt Romney is concerned": Olivier Knox, "Pro-Obama Ad Ties Romney to Woman's Death from Cancer," ABC News, August 7, 2012, http://abcnews.go.com/Politics/OTUS/pro-obama-ad-ties-romney-womans-death-cancer/story?id=16947016.

234   "sharing your experiences": "Obama Campaign Caught in Lie over Joe Soptic, Possible Violation of Law," Examiner.com, August 10, 2012, www.examiner.com/article/obama-campaign-caught-lie-over-joe-soptic-possible-violation-of-law.

235   "what we were told": "Colorado Woman Who Championed Obamacare Loses Insurance Plan," CBS Denver, November 8, 2013, http://denver.cbslocal.com/2013/11/08/colorado-woman-who-championed-obamacare-loses-insurance-plan/.

235   health coverage for adults: Mike Glover, "Obama Touts Health Care Plan," *Washington Post*, November 25, 2007, www.washingtonpost.com/wp dyn/content/article/2007/11/24/AR2007112400834.html.

235   "echoing right-wing talking points": Paul Krugman, "Mandates and Mud-slinging," *New York Times*, November 30, 2007, www.nytimes.com/2007/11/30/opinion/30krugman.html.

235   Obama dismissed that argument: Glover, "Obama Touts Health Care Plan."

236   people would merely be "required": "Health Care Speech to Congress," *New York Times*.

237   just a little bit testy: "Democratic Debate in Las Vegas," CNN.com, November 15, 2007, http://transcripts.cnn.com/TRANSCRIPTS/0711/15/se.02.html.

237   said to lack health insurance: Susan Monroe, "A Politics of Conscience," *Devotion Reader*, January 7, 2010, www.devotionreader.com/politics/a-politics-of-conscience.

238   "a moral commitment": Ibid.

238   through the year 2024: "Insurance Coverage Provisions of the Affordable Care Act—CBO's February 2014 Baseline," Congressional Budget Office, www.cbo.gov/sites/default/files/cbofiles/attachments/43900-2014-02-ACAtables.pdf.

238   costs along to the insured: Glenn Kessler, "President Obama's Claim That Insurance Premiums 'Will Go Down,'" *Washington Post*, Fact Checker, August 10, 2012, www.washingtonpost.com/blogs/fact-checker/post/president-obamas-claim-that-insurance-premiums-will-go-down/2012/08/09/424048f2-e245-11 e1-a25e-15067bb31849_blog.html.

238   at South Central College in Mankato: Ed Morissey, "Video: 'I Thought the Affordable Care Act Would Save $2500 per Family?'" *Hot Air* (blog), February 20, 2014, http://hotair.com/archives/2014/02/20/video-i-thought-the-affordable-care-act-would-save-2500-per-family/.

239   up $2,581 a family: Ron Johnson, "Under Obamacare, Health Insurance Premiums Haven't Gone Down, They've Gone Up, Ron Johnson Says," *PolitiFact Wisconsin*, December 5, 2013, www.politifact.com/wisconsin/statements/2013/dec/15/ron-johnson/obamacare-health-insurance-premiums-havent-gone-do/.

239   "still glad we tried": Hillary Clinton, *Living History* (New York: Simon & Schuster, 2003), 249.

239   "conducting secret meetings": Ibid., 153.

240   public policy cable channel C-SPAN: Clemente Lisi, "Obama Promised 8 Times during Campaign to Televise Health Care Debate," *New York Post*, January 6, 2010, http://nypost.com/2010/01/06/obama-promised-8-times-during-campaign-to-televise-health-care-debate/.

240   subject of health care transparency: Angie Holan, "Obama Said He'd Televise Health Reform Negotiations on C-SPAN," *PolitiFact*, July 10, 2009,

www.politifact.com/truth-o-meter/promises/obameter/promise/517/health
-care-reform-public-sessions-C-SPAN/.

240   "Debate on Health Care Fading": David Lightman and Margaret Talev,
"Obama Campaign Vow of Public Debate on Health Care Fading," McClatchy
Newspapers, July 9, 2009, available at www.mcclatchydc.com/2009/07/09/71584/
obama-campaign-vow-of-public-debate.html.

241   "behind-the-scenes committee negotiations": Ibid.

241   "fifty-plus-one strategy": Noel Sheppard, "Obama 2007: Healthcare
Won't Pass with 50-Plus-One Strategy," *NewsBusters*, October 27, 2009, http://
newsbusters.org/blogs/noel-sheppard/2009/10/27/obama-2007-healthcare
-wont-pass-50-plus-one-strategy.

242   reminded them, "I won": Jonathan Martin and Carol Lee, "Obama to
GOP: 'I Won,'" *Politico*, January 23, 2009, www.politico.com/news/stories/
0109/17862.html.

242   "long-term challenge": "Remarks by the President to a Joint Sesssion of
Congress," whitehouse.gov, September 9, 2009, ON HEALTH CARE, http://
www.whitehouse.gov/the_press_office/Remarks-by-the-President-to-a-Joint
-Session-of-Congress-on-Health-Care.

243   "It's compromise": Chris Frates, "Payoffs for States Get Harry Reid to 60
Votes," *Politico*, December 19, 2009, www.politico.com/news/stories/1209/30815
.html.

244   and they bit as well: Lori Montgomery and Shailagh Murray, "In Deal
with Stupak, White House Announces Executive Order on Abortion," *Washington Post*, March 21, 2010, http://voices.washingtonpost.com/44/2010/03/
white-house-announces-executiv.html.

244   "signing statement on steroids": Terrence Jeffrey, "Kagan to Tribe on Day
Obamacare Passed: 'I Hear They Have the Votes, Larry!! Simply Amazing,'"
Cnsnews.com, November 10, 2011, http://cnsnews.com/news/article/kagan
-tribe-day-obamacare-passed-i-hear-they-have-votes-larry-simply-amazing.

245   "violates statutory law": Tabitha Hale, "Stupak: HHS Mandate Violates My
Obamacare Compromise," *Big Government* (blog), Breitbart.com, September 4,
2012, www.breitbart.com/Big-Government/2012/09/04/Stupak-President-Played
-Me-with-Obamacare-Deal.

245   staff in the Washington, DC, area: Jeff Sagnip, "Another Obama Promise
Broken: Affordable Care Act Massively Funds Abortion, Violates Hyde Amendment," chrissmith.house.gov, January 28, 2014, http://chrissmith.house.gov/
news/documentsingle.aspx?DocumentID=367957.

245   "life in health care reform": Hale, "Stupak: HHS Mandate."

246   the president knew it: Tommy Christopher, "Here's How the White House
Reacted to the Hobby Lobby Ruling," *Daily Banter*, June 30, 2014, http://the
dailybanter.com/2014/06/watch-white-house-reacts-hobby-lobby-ruling/.

246   mentioning the word "abortion": "President Obama Addresses Planned

Parenthood," C-SPAN, April 26, 2013, www.c-span.org/video/?312395-1/
president-obama-addresses-planned-parenthood.

246 performed 149 abortions: Drew Belsky, "Planned Parenthood's Annual
Report Shows Abortion Pays," *Daily Caller*, January 9, 2014, http://dailycaller
.com/2014/01/09/planned-parenthoods-annual-report-shows-abortion-pays/.

247 "provide women with mammograms": Lori Robertson, "Planned Parenthood and Mammograms," *FactCheck*, October 18, 2012, www.factcheck
.org/2012/10/planned-parenthood-and-mammograms/.

247 do not "provide" mammograms: Ibid.

247 the website of a typical clinic: Planned Parenthood of Kansas and Mid-
Missouri, www.plannedparenthood.org/kansas-mid-missouri/.

248 "and need care the most": "2008 Barack Obama Convention Speech Transcript," Zimbio.com.

248 including the passage that follows: "Obama's Speech on Health Care
Reform," *New York Times*, June 15, 2009, www.nytimes.com/2009/06/15/
health/policy/15obama.text.html.

249 committees, were enacted: "Promises, Promises: Obama's Health
Plan Guarantee," Associated Press, June 19, 2009, available at www.wbur
.org/2009/06/19/obama-health-care-3.

249 just signed into law: "Remarks by the President on Health Insurance
Reform in Portland, Maine," The White House, Office of the Press Secretary,
April 1, 2010, www.whitehouse.gov/the-press-office/remarks-president-health
-insurance-reform-portland-maine.

250 Republicans had already proposed: Sally Pipes, "Seven Steps to Replace
Obamacare with Something That Works," *Washinton Examiner*, August 17,
2013, http://washingtonexaminer.com/article/2534366.

250 services, and pediatric services: Kessler, "President Obama's Claim."

251 cohorts to lack insurance: "Essential Health Benefits: Individual Market
Coverage," Department of Health and Human Services, Office of the Assistant
Secretary for Planning and Evaluation, December 16, 2011, http://aspe.hhs.gov/
health/reports/2011/IndividualMarket/ib.shtml.

251 much they liked them: Kessler, "President Obama's Claim."

251 quickly and in passing: "Transcript of First Presidential Debate," Fox
News.com, October 3, 2012, www.foxnews.com/politics/2012/10/03/transcript
-first-presidential-debate/.

252 tried to do just that: Stephanie Condon, "Obama Stands by Promise
That You Can Keep Your Plan,'" CBSNews.com, October 30, 2013, http://www
.cbsnews.com/news/obama-stands-by-promise-that-you-can-keep-your-plan/.

253 "particularly in the individual market": Kerstin Beronio et al., "Affordable Care Act Will Expand Mental Health and Substance Use Disorder Benefits
and Parity Protections for 62 Million Americans," Department of Health and

Human Servivces, Office of the Assistant Secretary for Planning and Evaluation, http://op.bna.com/dlrcases.nsf/id/kpin-955u7c/$File/rb_mental.pdf.

253 "because it's not true": "Cancer Survivor Edie Sundby Responds to 'Condescending' Attack by White House on 'Kelly File,'" *Real Clear Politics*, November 7, 2013, www.realclearpolitics.com/video/2013/11/07/cancer_survivor _edie_sundby_responds_to_condescending_attack_by_white_house_on_ kelly_file.html.

253 UnitedHealthcare for her problems: John Nolte, "White House Blames Stage IV Cancer Victim for Insurance Loss," *Big Government* (blog), Breitbart .com, November 4, 2013, www.breitbart.com/Big-Government/2013/11/04/ Obamacare-white-house-blames-cancer-victim-for-insurance-loss.

253 "felt that was necessary": "Cancer Survivor Edie Sundby Responds," *Real Clear Politics*.

Chapter 13: Consequences

255 "the next messiah": "Barbara Walters on Obama: 'We Thought He Was Going to Be the Next Messiah,'" *Real Clear Politics Video*, December 17, 2013, www.realclearpolitics.com/video/2013/12/17/barbara_walters_on_obama_ we_thought_he_was_going_to_be_the_next_messiah.html.

INDEX

ABOUT THE AUTHOR

Jack Cashill is an investigative journalist who has written for *Fortune*, the *Wall Street Journal*, the *Washington Post*, the *Weekly Standard*, AmericanThinker.com, and WorldNet-Daily. He is the author of *First Strike*, *Ron Brown's Body*, *Hood-winked*, *Sucker Punch*, *What's the Matter with California?*, *Popes and Bankers*, and *Deconstructing Obama*.